37120

PA
3013
.A8
1961
v.1

ATKINS
Literary
antiqui

PA
3013
.A8
1961
v.1

ATKINS
Literary criticism in
antiquity

37120

MAR 25 75
OCT 20 81

346465936
I 26404

WITHDRAWN

**Illinois Central College
Learning Resource Center**

LITERARY CRITICISM IN ANTIQUITY

VOLUME I

GREEK

By the same author

LITERARY CRITICISM IN ANTIQUITY, 2 vols:

    I GREEK

    II GRAECO-ROMAN

ENGLISH LITERARY CRITICISM, 3 vols:

    THE MEDIEVAL PHASE

    THE RENASCENCE

    17TH AND 18TH CENTURIES

LITERARY CRITICISM IN ANTIQUITY

A SKETCH OF ITS DEVELOPMENT

by

J. W. H. ATKINS, M.A., 1874 –

Formerly Fellow of St John's College, Cambridge; Late Rendel Professor
of English Language and Literature, University College
of Wales, Aberystwyth

VOLUME I

GREEK

GLOUCESTER, MASS.
PETER SMITH
1961

Originally published by the Cambridge University Press, 1934
Reprinted, 1961, by permission of the Cambridge University Press

PRINTED IN UNITED STATES OF AMERICA

Haec neque indoctissimis nec
doctissimis sed viris bonis et
non inlitteratis.
        (Cf. Cic. *de Or.* ii, 6, 25.)

And now...will be the time to read with them those organic arts, which inable men to discourse and write perspicuously, elegantly, and according to the fitted stile of lofty, mean, or lowly. Logic, therefore, so much as is usefull,...untill it be time to open her contracted palm into a gracefull and ornate Rhetorick, taught out of the rule of *Plato, Aristotle, Phalereus, Cicero, Hermogenes, Longinus.* To which Poetry would be made subsequent, or indeed rather precedent, as being lesse suttle and fine, but more simple, sensuous, and passionate. I mean not here the prosody of a verse, which they could not but have hit on before among the rudiments of grammar; but that sublime art which in *Aristotles poetics,* in *Horace,* and the *Italian* commentaries,...teaches what the laws are of a true *Epic* poem, what of a *Dramatic,* what of a *Lyric,* what decorum is, which is the grand master peece to observe. This would make them soon perceive what despicable creatures our common rimers and play writes be, and shew them what Religious, what glorious and magnificent use might be made of Poetry, both in divine and humane things.

Milton, *Tractate of Education,* 1644

PREFACE

THIS attempt at recalling the views on literature current in ancient Greece and Rome is intended not so much for classical specialists as for that larger body of readers, students of English literature among them, who, interested primarily in the critical activities of more modern times, may yet find a discussion of origins not without its value. This at least is the aim that animates this present work; and it accounts for certain features with which a severer scholarship would doubtless have dispensed, the lists of translations, for instance, the frequent references to modern literature, or again, the efforts made to supply some sort of intellectual background to the narrative. At the same time it is hoped that the treatment has not suffered greatly in consequence. At any rate no pains have been spared to embody the best of what has been thought and said by established authorities on the subject, as well as the findings of more recent workers in the field of classical scholarship. So that this much at least may be said, that the endeavour throughout has been to render the survey as complete as possible within the prescribed limits.

With regard to the plan adopted, which is to some extent an innovation, a word of explanation is perhaps needed; for an attempt has here been made to approach the critical activities of antiquity from a purely historical standpoint, to view them, that is, as one continuous and unbroken movement, and not, as they are generally regarded, as two separate contributions—"Greek criticism" and "Latin criticism"—grouped in accordance with the language employed. That the linguistic classification has disadvantages is clear when the works of such writers as Dionysius of Halicarnassus and "Longinus" are considered. With them the choice of medium is comparatively unimportant, the key to their understanding lying mainly in the problems with which they deal, and which are obviously problems of the first century A.D or thereabouts. So that to detach these Greek critics from their Roman contemporaries is to lose sight of much of their real significance. On the other hand an historical approach has not a little to recommend it, apart from the fact that it enables one to interpret each critic in the light of his environment. For one thing, it throws into a clearer light the perspective of the whole movement; it also brings out more effectively the relations existing between the criticism at Rome and that which preceded it. And indeed, nowadays, it would seem that such a treatment was essential, especially in view of the misunderstandings that have arisen in the past from the study of the subject in isolation. Hence the nature of the present venture with its resultant grouping: first, Greek criticism (down to the end of the second century B.C.), and secondly, Graeco-Roman criticism (comprising, roughly, the work of the first century B.C. and the first century A.D.), to each of which a separate volume is devoted.

In the pages that follow, the first stage of the critical development is treated. And the main interests here are, briefly, the formulation by the classical Greeks of a number of important basic theories, the subsequent modification of those theories during the Hellenistic period, and the persistent efforts from the first at forming literary judgments. To some extent, no doubt, the ground covered will be familiar to many readers; for there has been no lack of previous observers in the field. Nevertheless it is hoped that the survey is something more than the re-telling of an old story, and that it will be found to direct attention to certain aspects of the subject which have not received hitherto the notice they deserve. Among such details must be included Plato's sporadic but far-reaching remarks on literary theory, Aristotle's pronouncements as a judicial critic, as well as the working-out of a new poetics by post-classical Greeks. All features alike are of fundamental importance, and they form a vital part of the achievement in criticism at this stage.

In conclusion, it is with gratitude that I acknowledge my indebtedness to that distinguished company of scholars, who, by their labours in a generation now past, have made this first volume possible. Chief among the great names are those of Butcher, Bywater, Jebb, Jowett, and Saintsbury, to whose

memory in the first place grateful homage is due; though with
them I would also include in my tribute of thanks Mr E. E.
Sikes and Dr C. Jensen, upon whose more recent writings
I have also freely drawn. To these and to others I am under
obligations which cannot be expressed in footnotes; and where
such recognition may be wanting, I take this opportunity of
making a yet fuller acknowledgment, recalling that "having
walked in the sun, I must needs be sunburnt". Of what I owe
to friends and former colleagues I am also deeply conscious;
and to Professor H. J. Rose and Professor J. F. Mountford in
particular I am indebted for assistance of an invaluable kind.
With unfailing generosity they have placed at my disposal their
wide learning and fine scholarship; they have been untiring
in response to my many queries; and at all stages of the work,
from preliminary sketch to proof-reading, they have furnished
very real guidance and inspiration. Debts of this kind are
pleasant to recall, though difficult to discharge. Then, too, I am
grateful to Professor H. B. Charlton for his kindness in reading
the book in proof and for his helpful comments. Special
acknowledgment is also due to Professor E. J. Wood and Mr
E. D. T. Jenkins who have been good enough to discuss with
me various points of detail. To the Librarian of the National
Library of Wales I am indebted for help in the matter of books,
while to the Librarian (and his staff) of the University College
of Wales, Aberystwyth, my best thanks are due for their consistent courtesy in supplying my various needs. And finally
I have to thank the Syndics of the Cambridge University Press
for undertaking the publication of the work, as well as the
staff of the Press in general for their skilled workmanship and
for consideration shown in making corrections.

J. W. H. A.

ISLWYN
ABERYSTWYTH

June 1934

CONTENTS

differences between the two forms and their relative values—Comedy—the
essence of the "ridiculous"—remarks on the sister arts—the irrational and
the impossible in poetry—the principle of development in literature—
Aristotle's judicial criticism—comments on contemporary literary judgments
—preoccupation of critics with irrelevancies—his own judgments of an
aesthetic kind—on Homer, Sophocles, Euripides, and Agathon—his conception of the ideal critic—summary of his achievement in the *Poetics*—its
shortcomings and its positive contribution to poetic theory—Aristotle's place
in critical history

CHAPTER V

The Development of Rhetorical Theory: Isocrates, Aristotle, and Theophrastus *page* 120

Conditions which led to a renewal of rhetorical theory—Isocrates and his
writings—his new conception of rhetoric—attacks on earlier rhetoricians—
the value of eloquence—the proper methods of teaching rhetoric—his conception of style—remarks on poets and poetry—Isocrates's main achievement
—Aristotle's *Rhetoric*—the genesis of the work—its form and treatment—
Aristotle's definition of rhetoric, its province, and its three kinds—main
principles of his rhetorical theory—literary style—historical comment on
earlier conceptions of style—the fundamental virtues of all good writing—the
diction best calculated to attain these effects—further effects due to words in
combination—the larger harmonies of sentence-form—the loose and the
periodic styles—further methods of giving vivacity to expression—the styles
characteristic of the three branches of rhetoric—*obiter dicta* concerning
literature generally—practical hints on writing—references to literary theory
—occasional literary judgments—Aristotle's achievement in his *Rhetoric*—
limitations due to contemporary factors—his influence on later ages—
Theophrastus—his critical writings—his treatise *On Style*—traces of Aristotelian theory and developments of that theory—definitions of tragedy and
comedy—further critical works—*Rhetorica ad Alexandrum*—the contribution
of Heraclides of Pontus—Zoilus's *Homeromastix*—decline in critical activity
at the close of the fourth century B.C.

CHAPTER VI

The New Poetics: Neoptolemus of Parium, Calli-machus, and Aristarchus *page* 164

The post-classical age—changes in the intellectual conditions—literary
developments—main factors underlying the new critical activity—sources
of information concerning contemporary criticism—the new poetics—
changes of method and form—the problems discussed—Art *versus* Nature—
the essential element of poetry—the function of the poet—the feud between
Callimachus and Apollonius of Rhodes—its significance—Simylus—historico-
critical writings—philological and grammatical studies—the *Grammar* of
Dionysius Thrax—the study of rhetoric—Analogy and Anomaly—Polybius's
History—judicial criticism—the contribution of Eratosthenes—Aristarchus,
his critical principles and defects—the Greek *Anthology*—the main characteristics of Hellenistic criticism

CHAPTER I

INTRODUCTION

ONE of the outstanding features of the literary studies of recent times is the growing interest that has been shown in those works of the ancients which are concerned with literary criticism. Writing not so long ago, in the year 1900, a distinguished historian complained with justice of the absence of works dealing with that particular subject. Since then, however, the gap has in some measure been filled; and now it may be said that a truer sense of the value of these critical writings in general prevails: while interest in them, so far from being confined to professed students of the classics, is shared by others whose main concern is with one or other of the modern literatures. Nor are the reasons for this far to seek; for ancient criticism has much of interest to offer to all students of literature. There is, for one thing, a definite historical value attached to the works. Coming first as they did in order of time, they represent the earliest application of the critical spirit to literary matters; and what is more, they constitute the first inquiry into that Graeco-Roman tradition in art upon which most of the modern literatures are ultimately based. In those literatures are embodied forms and principles originated by Greece and Rome; and since by the ancients the tradition was investigated in process of forming, while by the moderns it was examined anew at a later stage of its development, it is therefore not strange to find that many of our present-day problems are anticipated by the ancients, or that their theories have a bearing on modern thought. In addition, these critical works of the ancients possess considerable value of an intrinsic kind. In their pages were first brought to light certain literary principles of enduring value. They were, for instance, the first to set forth certain profound views as to the nature and art of poetry, as well as some of the laws that govern good writing in prose, while they also led the way in the discussion of literary values, and in the formation of aesthetic judgments.

These then briefly are some of the things that commend these works to readers of all the ages; yet this does not exhaust their claims to the notice of posterity. Equally significant is the fact, at least from the modern standpoint, that this critical work of antiquity formed the inspiration and starting-point of much of the criticism that followed. For two centuries or more after the Renascence, classical influence gave direction to critical effort throughout Western Europe and led to the establishment of a creed which, formulated by Scaliger and others, was everywhere regarded as the orthodox literary doctrine, until a new order of ideas was ushered in by the nineteenth century. What criticism there was consisted mainly of an exposition of the doctrines of Aristotle and Horace, together with reminiscences of Plato, Cicero, "Longinus", Quintilian and others. And to this critical output English writers made their contribution. In the pages of all critics from Sidney to Johnson we meet with ideas that are obviously borrowed and can be understood only in the light of an earlier mode of thinking; so that to embark on a study of modern criticism without some acquaintance with these sources is a task that is likely to be both perplexing and futile. It would be like beginning a narrative at a point where the story is already half told.

And this is not all. It is not merely that modern critics borrowed freely from the works of antiquity. Such borrowings all too frequently were imperfectly and incorrectly made; so that some knowledge of ancient criticism becomes an indispensable preliminary to an intelligent reading of the later work. For one thing, the ancient texts themselves were by no means free from difficulty, and thus lent themselves readily to serious misinterpretation. Then, too, ancient theories were often adopted without any regard to historical considerations; and, detached from their context and the conditions which produced them, such theories became misleading, if not wholly devoid of meaning. Or again, undue authority might be attached to this or that author or pronouncement, so that mere *obiter dicta*, or statements as to common practice, were viewed in the light of dogmas, and as such were held to be binding on later ages. The general result was therefore an altogether mistaken conception of the work of antiquity, and the adoption of a system that was disastrous in its effects. Throughout the seventeenth and eighteenth centuries the history of criticism in England was little more than one long attempt to escape from a false position, by correcting theories which, based on misunderstandings, had in consequence been found to be hopelessly unsound. Hence for a true appreciation of Renascence criticism and of the course subsequently taken by modern critics, the first thing necessary is a clear conception of ancient critical work. The key to modern criticism, in short, lies in antiquity; and this is why we must go back beyond the Italians to ancient Greece and Rome, if we are to read with understanding the critical works of later ages.

Before entering on our main task, however, which is an attempt at tracing the development of literary criticism in antiquity, something must first be said as to what is meant by "literary criticism", or at least the sense in which it is to be understood in the pages that follow. And it may at once be said that it is taken to mean something more than the formation of judgments, or the assessment of the value of this or that piece of literature from the artistic point of view. To say, for instance, that criticism has to do solely with evaluation of this kind would be to limit unduly the range of its activities; though etymologically, of course, such a statement might perhaps be justified. In so doing, however, we should be ignoring the way words have of extending their meaning; as well as the important fact that modern criticism in particular is animated by widely divergent aims which differ materially from those of earlier ages. On the other hand, the nature of anything, according to the Aristotelian canon, is its completed development; and any statement as to what is meant by "literary criticism" must therefore of necessity be based on its completed development, that is, on the whole body of extant critical writings and those various activities for which "criticism" has nowadays become recognised as the only convenient term. And taking this as our basis, we shall find that the critical treatment of literature has assumed different functions in different ages; that those functions have varied in accordance with the demands of the age and the angle from which literature was in consequence approached; and that criticism in general may not unfairly be described as the play of mind on the aesthetic qualities of literature, having for its object an interpretation of literary values. Thus there is a criticism that deals with literature in the mass, that seeks to explain not only its nature and functions, but also the secrets of the literary craft, the principles that underlie its creative processes. Then, too, there is a criticism that deals not so much with abstract questions of literature in general as with literature in the concrete, with specific literary works; and then it aims at discussing particular qualities, or at estimating the value of a given artistic performance. And again, criticism may aim at a yet more subtle treatment when it seeks to realise the manifold appeal of a work of art and to interpret it imaginatively, so that all who read may read with understanding. Criticism is therefore an activity of a many-sided kind; it may consist of theorising or judging, legislating or appreciating; and with this conception in mind we shall attempt our present inquiry. Not all aspects of criticism, it is true, will be found equally represented in antiquity. Of an aesthetic appreciation of this or that piece of art, for instance, we shall find comparatively few traces, and fewer still of that imaginative interpretation characteristic of the best modern work. It is, in short, with "the preliminaries of criticism" that we shall be for the most part concerned, with inquiries into the nature and art of poetry and into matters of prose style; but within those limits the work done will be found to be lacking neither in historical nor in permanent value.

With this, then, as our conception of literary criticism we turn to consider in some of its more general aspects the contribution of the ancients; and for the main body of that work we must look to a number of writings which appeared between the great age of Pericles in Greece and the close of the Silver Age at Rome—during the time, that is, when the Greek and Roman geniuses were engaged in the aesthetic civilisation of the world. The works may thus be said to constitute a record of the reflexions of antiquity on literature; and they fall roughly into three main periods. First comes the contribution of Athens during the fifth and fourth centuries B.C.; then the somewhat different activities at Alexandria and other Hellenistic centres during the third and second centuries B.C.; and lastly, the Graeco-Roman criticism associated with Rome during the two centuries that followed. Each of the three periods has its own peculiar interest; and the performance at no one stage can be safely neglected, if we are to form a just estimate of the significance of the whole. The most remarkable of the periods was doubtless the great age of Greece, for it supplied many basic doctrines of lasting value, while its influence may be traced, directly or indirectly, in much of the speculation that followed. But Graeco-Roman criticism, too, has an importance of its own. If less original in kind, its intrinsic and historical values are great, while its influence on later ages is hardly inferior to that of the Greeks. Nor is the Hellenistic stage without its interest, for it is the link between Greek and Graeco-Roman activities; while it also forms the background against which the later criticism is best interpreted. The problems discussed at Rome, for instance, were partly of Hellenistic origin, as was also the form of many of the works produced; thus Horace in particular is best understood in the light of that earlier culture.

Of the writings which thus appeared, many without a doubt have completely perished. From the days of Pericles onwards, there would seem to have been a constant output of works bearing on literary problems, of which only a comparatively small section has actually come down. In many cases, indeed, the titles or the merest fragments are all that remain, their authors being little more than forgotten names, preserved from oblivion by the chance reference of some later scholiast, or by the cataloguing zeal of Diogenes Laertius (third century A.D.); so that we are left to surmise the range of the actual output, as well as the value of that section which has since been lost. At the same time, what has come down forms no inconsiderable body, and in that work we have a miscellaneous collection, consisting of rhetorics and treatises, Socratic dialogues and commentaries, satires, comedies, essays and letters, both in prose and verse—altogether a strange variety of forms, though not without their significance. For the fact is that literary criticism in antiquity never really attained the dignity of a recognised art; it had not as yet distinguished itself from other forms of intellectual activity, from philosophy, rhetoric, grammar, and the like. It was a sort of by-product of these kindred studies; and was primarily due, not to attempts at training rational lovers of literature, but rather to the need for dealing with certain important practical problems—what place to assign to poetry in the life of the state, or how to improve the practice of oratory. While therefore the earliest criticism took the form of philosophy concerning itself with certain aspects of literature, after this, it has been well said, "the main current of ancient criticism flowed in the channel of rhetorical theory". Most of the critical works were devoted probably to oratory or rhetoric, though a host of writings on poets and poetry has doubtless been lost; and in the later treatment of poetry the influence of rhetorical studies is clearly seen. From rhetoric, for instance, are possibly drawn the methods and terminology of later poetic studies; the very form of the poetic τέχνη or *Ars Poetica* is rhetorical in origin; while most of the critical judgments are from the same standpoint, having as their object, not the assessment of literary values but the provision of suitable reading for orators in training.

Such then were the lines along which ancient criticism travelled. It arose primarily out of no conscious effort to discuss literature as such. It was rather the result of attempts to grapple with problems political and social, while its form was largely determined by certain existing studies of which it originally formed part. But the movement was conditioned by yet other factors which were connected with the geniuses and the circumstances of the peoples concerned. And first there were the Greeks—the Greeks of Athens—with whom the critical instinct was one of the primary endowments. With them, it has been said, "criticism was an instinct before it was a science, a practice before it was a theory"; and filled as they were with a disinterested desire for knowledge, an eager impulse to arrive at a rational explanation of things, it was inevitable that their curiosity should extend to those matters of art which played so important a part in the life of the state.

And for such inquiries they were unusually well fitted, by reason of their philosophical bent, their unsparing logic, their powers of keen analysis and illuminating reflexion. Moreover, the sense of art was present with them in an unrivalled degree; it was indeed this artistic sense which distinguished them above all other races. And the results are seen in the abundance and perfection of their literary work, as well as in their creation of literary forms which were destined to be permanent. That there were defects in their equipment is also of course true. For one thing, Greek literature up to Aristotle's day, in spite of its magnificence, had not as yet developed through all its phases, and therefore offered inadequate material on which to theorise. Nor were the Greeks acquainted with any literature but their own; and they were thus deprived of that larger outlook needed for a comprehension of those varieties and forms which were subsequently to be included under the head of literature. Then, too, there were certain directions in which the Greek genius was undoubtedly biased—a fact which militated against the formation of sound aesthetic judgments. The early world in general assumed that literature had a didactic purpose; and indeed, so intimately was art bound up with the religious life of the Greeks that the ethical and aesthetic spheres were never clearly distinguished, while aesthetic values were with difficulty realised. Nor must we forget the marked political bias at Athens. The Attic spirit was notably self-centred in kind; it conceived of life as essentially life in the state; and its treatment of art questions was at all times coloured by its predominant interest in social morality.

With the Greeks of the Hellenistic period, however, things were different. Scattered as they were in their new intellectual centres—at Alexandria, Pergamum, Rhodes, and the like—critical activities with them underwent a complete change as the outcome of new conditions which tended to modify their whole nature and outlook. With the decay of the national life, which at Athens had produced so glorious an art, there set in a decline in both the intellectual and the artistic spheres; thus philosophy for the most part had ceased to concern itself with ultimate issues, while increasing rationalism tended rapidly to destroy the artistic instinct. Not that there was an entire absence of developments in the sphere of literature; on the contrary, new artistic experiences seemed to be preparing the way for a profounder treatment of art, while a new oratory was already challenging the earlier Attic tradition. Yet the chief intellectual interest lay in none of these things; it lay rather in the attempt at preserving the artistic legacy of the past, in the collecting, cataloguing, and editing of texts which had come down. It was in short an age of scholastic discussion and learned studies, of scholiasts, grammarians, and rhetoricians, all of whom were concerned with assimilating and systematising the earlier culture.

Then in the two centuries that followed, criticism took yet another turn when the main object became that of adapting this ancient culture and of bringing it into the service of the literary activities at Rome. For the larger philosophical inquiries of the early Greeks the Roman mind was by nature but ill fitted; it was lacking in speculative ardour, interested rather in affairs, and characterised by certain practical and legal tendencies, the effects of which are seen in the literature of the time. Nor was the artistic endowment of the Romans comparable with that of the Greeks. Inferior both in initiative and range, they strove, not without success, to emulate the earlier masters, so that the all-absorbing task was the creation of a national literature which should have as its basis the Greek models of the past. Hence the main business became that of expounding sound methods of writing both in verse and prose; and criticism in general became a sort of "modified rhetoric" which aimed at laying down rules for the guidance of the artist. At the same time, it should be added, there were other things that counted, and influenced in one way or another the critical activity at this date. Rome, for instance, had inherited from Alexandria more than one unfinished controversy, and there were also certain special problems bound up with the age—all of which called urgently for treatment at the hands of the critics. Nor, again, is it without its significance that the critical activity at this time was by no means confined to Roman writers. Some of the most valuable contributions, in fact, came from Greek scholars who had associations with Rome and whose work showed signs of the earlier originality and insight. Apart from this there were further considerations which seemed to hold out the promise of more fruitful critical methods. Most of the men of letters, for instance, were acquainted with both Greek and Latin literatures, and they were therefore at least competent to make use of the comparative method in criticism. Moreover the formation of a new conception of history and of the relations existing between literature and life opened up further possibilities in the treatment of literary questions; while the vogue of letter-writing and the development of satire—both characteristic products of the Roman genius—incidentally provided fresh media for critical work.

These, then, were some of the factors that went to determine the nature and range of ancient criticism. And of the work in general this further may be said, that in spite of its casual and heterogeneous character, in spite, too, of obvious defects and limitations, it represents work of substantial and far-reaching value, in which were posed some of the fundamental questions. Now, for the first time, literary art was being regarded as a form of activity with its own history and its own laws. And efforts were accordingly made to explain poetry, its nature and function, to lay bare the inner mechanism of literature as a craft; and at the same time a beginning was made with literary judgment. Not that finality was reached in any one branch of these activities; there was much that was defective in their methods and processes alike. For one thing, the thinking was largely of an *a priori* kind. Observational activity, with but few exceptions, practically began and ended with Aristotle, at least where poetry was concerned; and for the rest, much of the theorising was merely imitative in character, consisting of the repetition of ideas and commonplaces drawn from earlier authorities. Apart from this, critical discussion suffered also from a vagueness of terminology, as well as from a fondness for all sorts of technicalities which led critics astray from the greater issues. In matters of judgment, too, wrong standards were used, the tests generally applied being reality, utility, or morality. There was in fact as yet but little of "criticism for criticism's sake"; while equally rare were the attempts at aesthetic appreciation, at reasoned inquiries into the sources of literary charm. Yet to this criticism contributed some of the master-minds of the ancient world; Plato the most daring and subtle of thinkers, Aristotle the greatest of investigators in all fields of thought, Cicero unrivalled among Roman orators, Horace unique as a poetic artist, and "Longinus" the unknown with his theories, enthusiastic, suggestive and compelling. And the results were in keeping with the minds at work. By each in turn some fresh revelation was made, while there were others, less gifted, who shared in the work. It may be that in the simpler atmosphere of ancient culture, what was essential in art stood out more clearly and vividly than in the more complex civilisation of later days. There was certainly less variety, less eccentricity, in the literature produced; and the effects in consequence would be more easily analysed, the underlying laws more clearly discerned. Moreover much of the critical theorising was firmly based on philosophy; it was but the application of earlier philosophical generalisation to the special province of poetry. But whatever the causes, the results are undeniable. These ancient critics grasped firmly some of the main problems of art; they set forth for the first time many of the basic principles which underlie literary excellence. And many of the things said were said in final fashion; they could never again be put so simply and convincingly.

CHAPTER II

THE BEGINNINGS: ARISTOPHANES[1]

IN the history of criticism, it has been said, there are no
absolute beginnings. However successfully we may seem to
have traced the origin of a particular idea or doctrine, we
shall still, as a rule, be able to find some anticipation of that
idea, some earlier statement leading up to the actual doctrine.
Thus many of the critical ideas that run throughout antiquity
appear first in Plato's pages. But if anything is certain, it is
that not a few of those ideas had their root in earlier thinking,
being either the development of earlier suggestions, or replies
to questions that had previously been raised. This being so, it
is evident that the real origin of things lies in yet earlier phases
of thought, in those centuries which had witnessed the gradual
unfolding of Greek literature; and it is therefore to those
earlier ages that we must turn first for an explanation of much
that is characteristic of ancient criticism, and for some idea of
the conditions out of which that criticism grew. Of material
that is capable of throwing light upon those earlier critical
activities, however, but little has come down. From the period
most remote little can be gathered beyond stray hints thrown
out by Homer and Hesiod; while all that the sixth century B.C.
has to offer are a few extant fragments of the works of philosophers such as Xenophanes, Heraclitus, and the like. Pindar
and the comic poets of the fifth century, it is true, have a
further contribution to make, as have also later sophists and
philosophers, such as Gorgias and Democritus; but this is
practically all, and much of it is fragmentary. Together with
later statements made by Plutarch and Diogenes Laertius,

---

[1] *Text and translation:* F.W. Hall and W. M. Geldart, *Aristophanis Comoediae*,
2 vols., Oxford, 1900; B. B. Rogers, *Aristophanes' Comedies*, 3 vols. (Loeb
Cl. Lib.), 1924; T. Bergk, *Aristophanis Comoediae*, 2 vols. (Teubner), Leipsic,
1892, 1895; *The Acharnians*, ed. with trans. W. J. M. Starkie, London,
1909; *The Clouds*, ed. with trans. W. J. M. Starkie, London, 1911.
Translations: by J. H. Frere, 2nd ed. New York, 1874; by J. P. Maine and
J. H. Frere, 2 vols. (Everyman's Lib.), London, n.d.; by W. J. Hickie, 2 vols.
(Bohn Lib.), London, 1896; *Frogs*, by G. Murray, London, 1912; extract (ll.
756–1533) in J. D. Denniston, *Greek Literary Criticism*, pp. 1–36, London, 1924.

these then are the main sources of our knowledge of this earliest phase; and however inadequate and vague their information may be, they afford some idea at least of the nature of those most distant speculations on literature and literary art. Then with Aristophanes critical activity may be said to have emerged from the obscurity of the past, and to have assumed for the first time tangible and definite form. In his comedies will be found judgments of a striking and suggestive kind; comments on not a few of the contemporary literary activities; and in particular, an interesting inquiry into the respective values of Aeschylus and Euripides as dramatists—the first attempt to deal with a decline of the poetic art.

For the earliest signs of speculation on literature we must turn first to Homer and Hesiod. And, to begin with, the very existence of a considerable body of epic poetry in those far-off ages seems to suggest that some body of artistic theory was already in being—a relic possibly of Aegean culture, though this, to be sure, is mere conjecture. More certain are the actual traces found in the poetry that has come down; early notions, for the most part, concerning the nature and function of poetry. That the theory of inspiration was already current in connexion with poetry is suggested in the first place by the opening lines of the Homeric poems. Both the *Iliad* and the *Odyssey* begin with an appeal to the Muse for inspiration to utter the truth of things; and this is confirmed by Hesiod, who, in his Preface to the *Theogony*, explains how the Muse breathed into him the art of divine music, while as yet he was tending his flock on Mount Helicon. Then, too, each poet pronounces indirectly on the function of poetry; but with some amount of difference. To Homer, on the one hand, the end of poetry was pleasure, produced by some sort of enchantment ($\theta \acute{\epsilon} \lambda \xi \iota s$); and this point he stresses in more than one place. To Hesiod, on the other hand, the poetic function was that of teaching or conveying a divine message; a survival of an earlier prophetic office. And in this difference between the Ionian and the Boeotian conceptions of the matter may be detected the first phase of a quarrel that persisted for ages to come.[1] Nor were these the only theories then current concerning the aim or mission of

[1] See E. E. Sikes, *Greek View of Poetry*, pp. 1–7, for a fuller treatment.

poetry. Traces of a civilising function attributed to poetry may probably be seen in those primitive myths, according to which Orpheus by his music tamed savage men and beasts, while Amphion with his poetry charmed stones and built the Theban walls. This doctrine, too, persisted in curious fashion; subsequently applied to poetry, oratory, and philosophy alike,[1] it was a notion that was still cherished by theorists centuries later at the Renascence of Western Europe.[2] Apart, however, from these foreshadowings of later theories, there are further details of interest associated with this period; and one is undoubtedly that passage in the *Iliad*[3] which represents the earliest extant judgment on the fine arts. There the poet comments on the workmanship of Hephaistos in depicting a freshly ploughed field on the shield of Achilles. He notes that the upturned soil seemed black, though the shield was made of gold; and this he describes as the "marvel" ($\theta a\hat{v}\mu a$) of the work. It was an implicit recognition of the illusion of art; a passing glimpse of an artistic truth which was to be developed later in more reasoned form. And lastly, there are the beginnings of literary judgment to be noted at this date; though the first criticism on poetry, it may safely be surmised, was pronounced when the reciter of the first epic lay had done reciting. At the same time criticism of a more formal type was being fostered by the singing match, which dated from pre-Homeric times; and again by the *agon*, which by Hesiod's day had become a recognised artistic device.[4] Both are of significance from the critical point of view; while the latter, it might be added, is of special interest on account of the part it was to play in Attic comedy of the fifth century, with its numerous contentions on literature and literary matters.

Such, then, are the earliest symptoms of critical activity in antiquity; and while they do not take us far, consisting as they do of hints and unformulated theories, at the same time their historical interest is obvious, for in them are marked out some at least of the paths which later criticism was to follow. Equally interesting, however, are the developments characteristic of

---

[1] See pp. 29, 127 *infra*; vol. II, 27.
[2] Cf. Sidney, *Apology for Poetry*, ed. Cook, p. 3.
[3] XVIII, 548–9.   [4] See Sikes, *op. cit.* pp. 8–10.

the sixth century B.C., when what Plato later on described as
"the quarrel of long standing between philosophy and poetry"[1]
first made its appearance. The quarrel had arisen out of the
speculations of Ionian philosophers, who, in their efforts to
explain the nature of the physical universe, were led to cast
doubt upon the Olympian mythology. Many theories had been
propounded by the Milesian physicists; but all alike were
agreed in this, that the universe was a cosmos, subject to law
and order, and not a blind product of ungoverned forces, or
a theatre for the arbitrary interference of immoral and jealous
gods. And the recognition of this theory brought the new
thought into conflict with Homer, whose epics, rooted in the
ancient mythology, were forthwith condemned on ethical and
metaphysical grounds. Of these attacks traces may still be
found in various places. Xenophanes, for instance, censured
Homer on moral grounds for attributing to the gods all the
vices of men; Pythagoras depicted Homer's punishment in the
underworld for his remarks about the gods; while Heraclitus,
for the same reason, was for expelling Homer entirely from the
public games. Of the censures on metaphysical grounds
Heraclitus provides the main places. He found in Homer, for
instance, a lack of true wisdom, which he illustrated from the
Homeric prayer for the abolition of strife; whereas, according
to his philosophy, Strife—or the balance of opposing forces—
was the governing principle of life.[2] Thus was the national poet
denounced for his impious and immoral fables, for the unprofitable teaching contained in his work; and in this way,
strange as it may seem, poetry at this stage met with a decided
hostility. At the same time there were those who tried to heal
the feud; and philosophy, which had led the attack, provided
also the main line of defence. Already among philosophers the
idea had obtained currency that the earlier poets in their
myths had concealed profound wisdom in enigmatic and
symbolic fashion; and that by means of an allegorical interpretation it was possible to arrive at the real significance of the
myths concerned.[3] Thus the literal meaning of Homer, it was

[1] *Rep.* 607b.   [2] See Sikes, *op. cit.* p. 17.
[3] See J. Tate in *Class. Rev.* XLI, 214.

argued, was not the only one; a deeper and truer sense lay beneath the surface, even in the case of the most offensive and immoral passages. And among those who thus explained the Homeric fables were first, Theagenes, and then, Anaxagoras, according to whose views Homer's stories were held to veil the mysteries of moral and scientific truths. Hence gods and heroes alike were said to stand for abstract qualities or the powers of Nature. Their combats might symbolise struggles between vices and virtues, or between the various elements of Nature; and while the arrows of Apollo might be taken to mean the rays of the sun, the web of Penelope, again, might be interpreted as the rules of dialectic. It was, in short, an allegorical line of defence, which made poetry out to be little more than a system of abstract truths; and as a method of literary inter-pretation it was destined to have a lengthy history, and to be a fruitful source of error for ages to come.

With the dawn of the fifth century B.C., however, we leave to some extent the region of conjecture, and enter upon an age in which literary criticism assumes a more tangible form, though there is still a dearth of texts. It was an age of unpre-cedented activities in the intellectual, artistic, and political spheres; for Athens in the course of that century was to become the scene of a great intellectual awakening, the first great revelation of the critical spirit in human affairs. With the earlier Ionian speculations had emerged a new rational faculty, and the intellectual power thus set free was applied at this time to social rather than to cosmological problems. Attempts were consequently made to establish a rational order in human life, first by testing at the bar of reason all existing institutions and traditions, and then by refashioning anew the various depart-ments of human thought; and in this way were ultimately transformed the religious, the political, and the ethical creeds. But Athenian society as a whole was also keenly interested in the free play of the mind; and in the intellectual ferment that resulted, literature too came in for some amount of notice, more especially on account of the great artistic triumphs of the age. For it was now that the glory of Greek literary art was consummated in the tragedy and comedy that crowned the earlier epic and lyric; while new ambitions were also forming in connexion with the art of rhetoric. Hence at this date poetry as an art was to be considered from various standpoints; a beginning was to be made with the study of oratory and prose style; and attempts were also made at pronouncing literary judgments, more particularly by the comic poets who flourished at the time.

Among the critical developments that call for notice during this fifth century B.C. none is of greater importance, in the first place, than the increasing attention that was being paid to matters of art in general. Much of the material doubtless consisted of ideas elaborated in the earlier poetic schools. Thus Pindar speaks of "the laws of art" and "the laws of hymns", as if alluding to rules and ideas already recognised as part of the poetic tradition; and the same poet is also aware of the charm ($\psi v \chi \alpha \gamma \omega \gamma i \alpha$) of poetry and its element of illusion.[1] Yet more definite were Pindar's pronouncements on the relative values of inspiration and art in poetry. His insistence on the supreme importance of inspiration (despite his own artistry) may well have been his reply to new claims that were being advanced on behalf of art. And at any rate he is clear in his own mind that the poet derives his virtue primarily from inspiration or natural genius ($\phi v \acute{a}$), whereas art ($\tau \acute{\epsilon} \chi \nu \eta$) by itself was useless.[2] To this matter he reverts again and again, contrasting "the man who knows by nature" and "the man who learns"; and it becomes evident that his conception of inspiration is something different from the primitive idea of ecstasy or madness. With him inspiration becomes a conscious effort of genius, the workings of natural gifts; and in these pronouncements may be traced the first (extant) signs of the controversy regarding "nature" and "art", which was to persist among critics for centuries to come. Then, too, of significance is his statement of the need for "brevity" in poetic expression. In fact, this he declares more than once to be the essential virtue of poetry. "To say much in few words", "to flit as a bee from flower to flower", "to know the paths that

---

[1] *Ol.* I, 28; *Nem.* VII, 20-3.
[2] *Ol.* II, 94-7, IX, 100; *Nem.* III, 40-2 (see Sikes, *op. cit.* p. 21).

shorten the road", these, according to his doctrine, belong to the art of the great poet;[1] and echoes of such statements may be found in later theorising. At the same time further pronouncements on art were being made by some of Pindar's contemporaries. And illuminating in this connexion is the dictum ascribed to Simonides of Ceos by Plutarch, in which the old poet defined "poetry as vocal painting, painting as silent poetry".[2] Or again, there is the well-known utterance attributed to Corinna, in her advice to the youthful Pindar concerning an ode which he had written, overloaded with fabulous matter. Her counsel was "to sow with the hand, and not with the whole sack";[3] and here in picturesque fashion was laid down one of the governing principles of all classical art. These, however, are but isolated comments—possibly fragments of an earlier body of doctrine of which no other traces survive—and evidence of a more definite kind is supplied by the activities of the later sophists, who set out to explore the working principles of language. Now, for instance, began a number of inquiries into the nature of words with a view to revealing the finer qualities of expression in prose and verse alike. New philological studies were inaugurated by Protagoras, Prodicus, and Hippias; and in this task Democritus subsequently joined, if we may judge from the titles of his works: *On the Beauty of Words*, *On Euphonious and Cacophonous Letters*. Apart from this, Protagoras is said to have lectured on the poets, Hippias on metre; while to Democritus were ascribed certain treatises on rhythm, harmony, and poetry. It may well have been from one of these works that Cicero and Horace later on borrowed, when they quoted his authority in the matter of poetic inspiration, and in particular his demand that sane poets should be excluded from the haunts of Helicon.[4]

Of these various treatises, however, no traces have come down; and for some idea of the current poetic theory we must turn to two extant speeches of Gorgias connected with the

---

[1] Cf. *Pyth.* x, 53, IV, 247–8; *Nem.* IV, 33–4, VII, 52, 104; *Ol.* XIII, 47–9; *Isthm.* I, 62, V, 59 (see A. Rostagni, *Arte Poetica di Orazio*, p. lxxvii note).
[2] Plutarch, *The Glory of the Athenians*, 346F (see vol. II, 312).
[3] *Ibid.* 348A.
[4] Cicero, *Divin.* I, 80; Horace, *A.P.* 295.

Trojan War, namely, *The Encomium of Helen* and *The Defence of Palamedes*.[1] There, to begin with, stress is laid on the power of speech (or the word) in general. It is described as "a mighty ruler...able to stop fear, remove sorrow, produce joy, and increase confidence";[2] and these effects, it is implied, are characteristic of both poetry and prose. Then poetry is defined as nothing more than metrical speech; though its psychological effects, on the other hand, are more happily dealt with. Thus it is said to produce in its hearers "a shuddering awe, a tearful pity, and a yearning for sorrow (sympathy)"; an anticipation, clearly, of the later Aristotelian doctrine. To this is added a further comment on the workings of poetry. "The inspired chants", it is said, "bring pleasure and remove pain; their power...charms ($\ddot{\epsilon}\theta\epsilon\lambda\xi\epsilon$) and persuades ($\ddot{\epsilon}\pi\epsilon\iota\sigma\epsilon$), and transforms (the soul) by its magic ($\gamma o\eta\tau\epsilon\dot{\iota}q$)."[3] And here will be noted the confusion still current as to the nature and function of poetry; while it was said to give delight, and to work by some magic or charm, it was also credited with the effect of persuasion, the intellectual process associated later on more especially with rhetoric. Such then are the extant pronouncements of Gorgias on poetry and the poetic art; and their existence renders more plausible the attribution to Gorgias of that later statement, in which the sophist commends the element of fiction or "illusion" in tragedy. It is where he is credited with the assertion that "tragedy deceives by myths and the display of various passions; and whereas the tragic poet who deceives is juster than he who does not, the deceived is also wiser than the one who is not deceived".[4] From such passages as these, all statements of a casual kind, it is but natural to infer the existence of a body of poetic theory at this date; and not without its interest is the attempt recently made to frame a definition of tragedy based on these fragments of Gorgias's doctrine. Thus tragedy (so the definition would run) is "a form of metrical composition, which aims at charming and persuading the audience, who willingly submit to the

---

[1] For a more complete account see Sikes, *op. cit.* pp. 29–33, to which source I am indebted for matter and translations.

[2] *Enc. of Helen*, 8. [3] *Ibid.* 10. [4] Plutarch, *op. cit.* 348 c.

magic of fiction, and feel awe and pity for the fortunes of others represented by the poet".[1] And however hazardous such a definition may be, it provides at least some illustration of the developments in poetic theory before Aristotle's day, as well as of the psychological treatment of art by one of his predecessors.

Evidence then is not wanting, amidst all the artistic glories of Athens of the fifth century B.C., that the critical impulse as applied to literature was becoming more and more articulate, and was finding expression in the working out of some amount of literary theory. And this is illustrated by yet another—and an important—phase of the critical activity, this time concerned with prose, the main inspiration of which was political in kind.[2] The establishment of a democracy at Athens in 510 B.C. had had far-reaching results. It had imposed on the citizens fresh demands in the shape of public service, for which some skill in oratory was above all things needed; and this led to efforts of certain sophists to make men better speakers by rules of art, thus setting up, however roughly, a system of rhetoric which was destined to play a great part in the life of antiquity. For the origin of this movement we must turn to Sicily, where the establishment of a democracy after the fall of the tyrant Hiero (472 B.C.) and the litigation that arose in the unrest that followed created a widespread demand for instruction in oratory; and to this demand one Corax and his pupil Tisias responded by compiling Arts or *technai* of rhetoric— apparently the first formal treatises in Greek on any branch of art. The main concern of these teachers had been with the subject-matter of oratory, with the finding of arguments and their most effective arrangement. When their influence spread to Athens through the visit of Gorgias of Leontini in 427 B.C. the study became characterised by new aims and methods, and took the form of an inquiry into the literary side of rhetoric and the rules which governed an artistic prose. To these new studies Gorgias and Thrasymachus were the chief contributors; though treatises on language came from other sophists, such as

---

[1] See Sikes, *op. cit.* pp. 32–3.

[2] See R. C. Jebb, *Attic Orators*, I, cviii–cxxxvii for an account of this development.

Protagoras, Prodicus, and Hippias already mentioned. Thrasymachus, however, is known to have compiled an *Art of Rhetoric*; whether Gorgias wrote one is not so certain. Yet both became famous as teachers and theorists; and both shared one aim in common, that of creating a prose which should rival poetry in its emotional appeal. Thus Gorgias, in the first place, taught the lesson of the beauty of language, inspired possibly in this matter by his master Empedocles of Agrigentum. The latter, according to Aristotle,[1] was the "inventor" of rhetoric, in the sense that he first employed poetic devices for the adornment of public speech, an artifice which was subsequently adopted by Gorgias.[2] By Gorgias, therefore, sentences were broken up into short symmetrical clauses, with the thought divided by means of antithesis, and united by the devices of alliteration, assonance, and rhyme. He was also the first to recommend the Figures of speech, to substitute metaphors for plain straightforward descriptions, and in general to introduce into prose the colour and variety of poetry.[3] Thrasymachus, on the other hand, stood for correctness of language. He was the first to point out that prose should be rhythmical, a discovery of the first importance; and for this rhythmical prose he advocated the use of the periodic style, as presenting thought in more ordered and rounded form. In this way were laid the foundations of later rhetorical study, though these beginnings were not free from serious defects. For one thing, the study as a whole was limited by the fact that it was primarily concerned with the prose of public speech. Then, too, the methods employed were mainly of an empirical kind; they rested upon no scientific basis; while the teaching, not infrequently, was marked by unreason and excess. Moreover, in theorising on style apart from subject-matter, there were manifest dangers of abuse; and indeed the formation of a cult of "Art for Art's sake" threatened to become the result of these activities. At the same time it is clear that new ground had been broken by this work of the sophists, and the way prepared for more competent investigators. Valuable attempts had

---

[1] See Diogenes Laertius, VIII, 57.
[2] See W. Rhys Roberts, *Greek Rhetoric and Literary Criticism*, p. 37.
[3] See Diodorus Siculus, *A Library of History*, XII, 53.

been made to reveal the inner mechanism of one side of the
literary craft; the idea of a *techne* or *Art* as applied to prose was
already familiar; and above all it had been shown that an
artistic prose was possible, and that form and style were as
essential in prose as they were in poetry.

While, however, the most significant of the critical developments at this date were perhaps of the nature of theorising,
considerable interest is also attached to the increasing frequency
with which judgments were pronounced on literature, and
more especially on the drama which loomed so large in the life
of the time. To begin with, it has been suggested that in the
latter half of the *Odyssey* occasional mock-heroic lines are to be
found, while more certainly the heroic epic was satirised in the
Margites and *The War of the Frogs and the Mice*, both of which
were obvious parodies—the earliest form of judicial criticism.
Then, too, in the fifth century B.C. appeared Homeric criticism
of a more serious type; as, for example, in the works ascribed
to Anaximander, Stesimbrotus, and Ion the rhapsode, each of
whom in his interpretations carried on the allegorical tradition.
Moreover, from Democritus came one of the earliest treatises
on Homer, a work not without its interest, if we may judge
from Dio Chrysostom's remarks[1] some centuries later, as to that
writer's comments on Homer's genius, the varied beauty of his
verse, and the elements of order and variety in his treatment. Of
greater interest, however, is the dramatic criticism contained
in the contemporary plays themselves; and in the first place
traces of such critical matter may sometimes be found even in
the tragedies. Thus Sophocles, for one, is occasionally found
parodying the style of Aeschylus; a fact which gave rise to
charges of "frigidity" and "unevenness" by later Graeco-
Roman critics.[2] Euripides, again, was not above criticising
some of the earlier dramatic devices; as when he ridicules the
way in which Aeschylus (in his *Choephori*) brings about the
recognition of Orestes by his sister.[3] Or again, certain fragments of Agathon contain passages that may apply to the poetic
art; as for instance the striking saying quoted by Aristotle in

[1] *Or.* 53. [2] See vol. II, 245 (n.).
[3] Eur. *Electra*, 526–44; cf. also Aristophanes, *Clouds*, 534.

his *Rhetoric* "that some things we have to effect by art; others come to us by necessity or chance".[1] It is in the comedies, however, that the main body of judicial criticism is found; and this was only to be expected, seeing that the Old Comedy concerned itself with everything of contemporary interest. Of such works, apart from the plays of Aristophanes, all that have come down are fragments and play titles. But these are sufficiently illuminating for our present purpose; they give a shrewd idea of the nature of the works and of the objects ridiculed.[2] Thus, in the first place, earlier as well as contemporary poetry was frequently attacked; in the *Cheiron* of Pherecrates, for instance, Hesiod was quoted and parodied, while in the *Hesiodi* of Teleclides there are references to contemporary poets, as well as possibly a passage relating to the indebtedness of Euripides to certain sources.[3] Elsewhere, again, may be detected anticipations or repetitions of Aristophanic *motifs*. In the *Muses* of Phrynichus, for instance, the Muses in full assembly consider the merits of the tragic poets and award the palm to Sophocles; while in the *Crapatalli* of Pherecrates there is a scene in Hades in which Aeschylus is the speaker. Interest of another kind is attached to the *Demoi* of Eupolis, in which famous men of the past are summoned from Hades; and among them Pericles, who is eulogised for his eloquence. He is praised above all for his keenness and force. "Persuasion", it is said, "sat upon his lips, he so charmed all hearers, and alone of all orators he thrilled the souls of those who listened"; a judgment which later became a commonplace, being quoted by Quintilian[4] and the younger Pliny.[5] Then, in addition, there is the *Poetry* of Antiphanes, with its humorous explanation that it was easier to write tragedy than comedy, because the plots of the former were already familiar and called for no invention; the *Phileuripides*, again, in which the admirers of Euripides were satirised; the *Poets* of the comic Plato, and

---

[1] *Rhet.* II, 19, 13 (Agath. fr. 8 Nauck²), though here, it is true, the pronouncement may be merely one of a general kind.

[2] See Sandys, *Hist. of Class. Schol.* I, 52–6.

[3] Meineke, *Fr. Com. Gr.* I, 88; II, 371. Baker, *De Comicis Graecis literarum iudicibus* (Harv. St. xv, 156).

[4] *Inst. Orat.* XII, 10, 65.   [5] *Letters*, I, 20, 17.

such plays as *Sappho* and the *Rehearsal*, all of which illustrate the extent to which literature and literary matters at this date fell under the lash of comedy.

Such then in summary form are the vague beginnings of critical activity up to the end of the fifth century B.C. Based as the statements are on mere fragments and hints, they yet go to show that by this time the foundations had really been laid, and direction given to future critical effort. Already, it is clear, important questions had been raised in connexion with poetry, its nature and function; a start had also been made in theorising on the arts of both poetry and rhetoric; while at the same time sporadic judgments on literature gave evidence of further critical interests. Imperfect and inadequate as our knowledge of the details must necessarily be, some acquaintance with the earlier achievement is not without its value; for it enables us to understand better the main tendencies of later criticism, and more particularly the work done by those who immediately followed. Of these the first to claim attention is Aristophanes (*c.* 450–380 B.C.), with whom may be said to culminate the judicial criticism of the fifth century B.C.; while in him also we see the first, and, in his own sphere, one of the greatest, of all the critics of antiquity. His literary criticism, for the most part, is embodied in some four of his comedies; and there it forms part of a larger criticism of contemporary life, a fact which is not without its bearing on his treatment of literature. Thus it is that his literary judgments are based primarily, not on aesthetic standards, but on those to which he submits contemporary social and political developments, the standards of usefulness to the state and to citizen life in general. And this it is important to realise from the first; for the key to Aristophanes's criticism lies, if anywhere, in the conditions of his time. Born during the greatest period of Athenian history, he was a life-long witness of the political decline of Athens, and of the slow fading of her artistic glories which accompanied that decline; and of these things he cannot but have been conscious. Along with these there also went changes in the intellectual and moral life of the time, innovations in education, a growing scepticism in religion, the rise of sophistry and of the arts of demagogy; all of which, it was suggested, contained elements of danger to the community, and were likely to lead to a weakening of the national fibre. Of these changing ideals, moreover, Euripides was to Aristophanes the living embodiment, as well as the most ardent and effective advocate; and indeed, during the latter half of the fifth century the many-sided genius of Euripides had gone far in determining the literary taste of Athens. Hence the general nature of Aristophanes's critical work, and the attention he gives to Euripides throughout. He deals incidentally with various aspects of contemporary literary activities; but it is upon Euripides that he concentrates, and that with increasing intensity and force.

Before however discussing the details of Aristophanes's criticism, something must first be said about the comedies in which that criticism appeared. And in the first place it might be noted that while three of the comedies deal more or less with literary topics, all four belong to those years that marked the culmination of sophistic activity, that is, to the last quarter of the century. First came the *Acharnians* (425 B.C.) which treats of a political theme, though it contains also some casual allusions to literature. Euripides, for instance, is already being caricatured in good-humoured fashion; while certain references, of interest historically, are also made to oratory and poetry. Then came the *Clouds* (423 B.C.) in which were satirised the sophists and the new education. In this play Strepsiades, a peasant, is represented as seeking to acquire the new rhetoric, in order to be able to deceive the judges and thus escape from his creditors. The task of learning, however, proves too much for him; whereupon his son, Phidippides, is substituted in his stead. Two allegorical personages, the Just Cause and the Unjust Cause, then contend for the new pupil; and the Unjust Cause emerges victor of the *agon*. Phidippides is therefore handed over to Socrates and the sophists, he becomes expert in the new thought, and in the end turns on his father with insult and violence—a lively commentary on the value of the training thus acquired. Of yet greater interest is the *Thesmophoriazusae* (411 B.C.), an amusing comedy with an ingenious plot which is devoted wholly to the ridicule of Euripides. The story runs that

Euripides was to be condemned at the festival of the Thesmo-phoria—to which only women were admitted—on account of his scandalous treatment of women in his tragedies. At first the poet Agathon is approached by Euripides for assistance; and on his refusal Euripides's father-in-law, Mnesilochus, under-takes to help by pleading the poet's cause in the assembly of women. He ventures thither in disguise, is discovered, then threatened with death; and the situation is only saved by the personal intervention of Euripides, who after resorting in vain to sensational devices (parodying situations in his tragedies) succeeds in outwitting the guard and in obtaining the release of Mnesilochus. The greatest of the comedies bearing on literary criticism, however, is undoubtedly the *Frogs* (405 B.C.), in which Aristophanes's artistry as a comic poet is fairly rivalled by his insight and sagacity as a critic. The comedy was written immediately after the death of Euripides; and in it Dionysus, patron of the theatre, is depicted as being greatly concerned about the future of tragedy. He therefore resolves to seek out Euripides and bring him back from the dead; and thus, guided by Heracles, he descends to the lower regions, rows across the Acherusian lake accompanied by the croaking of the frogs, and arrives finally in the infernal world before the palace of Pluto. There he learns that a contest is about to take place between Aeschylus and Euripides for the throne of tragedy; and to their discussion he listens, not without perplexity, being swayed this way and that by their charges and counter-charges. To Dionysus himself is allotted the task of making a decision. Scales are brought, the verses are weighed; and Aeschylus succeeds in turning the balance. Yet Dionysus remains still uncertain; he sees much to admire in both. But finally he awards the victory to Aeschylus, with whom he returns rejoicing to the light of day. Such in bare outline is the story of the *Frogs*. Its main theme is the relative values of Aeschylus and Euripides as writers of tragedy; and this is presented, along with much Aristophanic humour, in the *agon* of which the play affords an excellent example.

When we turn to consider the nature of Aristophanes's criticism it is surprising, in the first place, to find how wide is his survey of the literary art. In a sense it extends over the whole field of existing literature; and although his main interests are bound up with poetry—epic, lyric, comedy, and tragedy above all—references to other forms of literary activity are by no means wanting. Of poetry in general he has in essence one comment to make, that in his own day its glory was slowly but surely departing. It is the complaint he makes, for instance, in his *Gerytades*[1] (407 B.C.), and again in the *Frogs*, where Dionysus laments that "good poets are dead; only the false live on".[2] But the theme is one on which he enlarges more than once.[3] His younger contemporaries Iophon, Xenocles, and Pythangelus he dismisses with a word; as well as other "pretty fellows" who were innovating in tragedy. In Agathon alone he finds something to praise; and for the rest, they are "leaves without fruit; trills in the empty air, and starling chatter mutilating art".[4] In short, it was impossible to find anywhere a poet with power to soar. Nor are his remarks merely of a general kind. He has an eye for some of the defects of contemporary comedy; its hackneyed themes, such as the gluttony of Heracles or the demagogy of Cleon, its stale devices, such as the throwing of nuts among the audience, or again its comic *clichés* and catchwords, foolish jokes to raise a laugh, originated by Phrynichus.[5] Then, too, he has something to say about the dithyrambic poet-impostors of his day; the new and florid style of Kinesias, for instance, whose manner he parodies in more than one place.[6] Or again, it may be contemporary affectations that he satirises; as, for instance, in his references to Agathon, who is represented as something of an aesthete, effeminate in appearance, and precious and conceited in his utterance. In an amusing parody, in which his style is caricatured, Agathon is made to explain his reasons for his eccentric conduct, and the inspiration he derived in composing "female dramas" from his adoption of feminine attire, which he stated enabled him to enter more intimately into feminine thought and feelings.[7] Thus Phrynichus, he adds, was an

---

[1] Frs. 149, 150; Kock, *ap.* Athenaios, 551 *a*.
[2] l. 72 (tr. Murray).   [3] See ll. 73 ff., 1494 ff.   [4] ll. 92 f. (tr. Murray).
[5] *Wasps*, 57 ff.; *Frogs*, 1–20.   [6] *Birds*, 904–58; *Frogs*, 153.   [7] *Thesmo.* 150 ff.

exquisite, exquisitely dressed; and his tragedies in consequence partook in some measure of that quality. Or again, Theognis, being frigid (ψυχρός) by nature, is said to have composed in frigid fashion (ψυχρῶς);[1] as it is put elsewhere, "Zeus covered all Thrace with frost when Theognis produced his tragedy".[2]

Apart from these comments on the state of contemporary literature, however, Aristophanes has also something to say on other aspects of the literary activities of his time. And, to begin with, his attitude to the new rhetoric cannot possibly be mistaken. To him it was none other than an art of deception, designed to make the worse appear the better cause; and in the *Clouds*, as has been stated, he covers with ridicule the whole movement. In addition, he views with sceptical eye the new theorisings on literature inaugurated by Prodicus, Protagoras, Hippias and others. Hence his scathing satire of those studies of grammar, rhythm, and the like, which bewildered Strepsiades;[3] the scornful references in the *Frogs* to the measuring rods (κανόνες), the foot-rules (πήχεις), and the scales, for estimating the value of poetry;[4] or again, the hair-splitting quibbles on obscurities and synonyms in the contest between Aeschylus and Euripides.[5] But against the new learning Aristophanes has yet a further ground of complaint. To him it stood for mere charlatanry, with Socrates as its high priest;[6] a movement that marked the end of the old discipline and virtue. More than this, it was also a source of infection where literature was concerned; and therefore one of the factors that accounted for the contemporary literary decline. Thus in the new craze for novelty and cleverness, as illustrated in the person of Phidippides, old standards were being flouted and old poets condemned. Simonides, for one, was already regarded as antiquated and of no great merit; Aeschylus was derided for his bombastic and rugged utterance; while Euripides was being hailed as the new master, capable of the smartest things, in short, "the wisest of poets".[7]

And this brings us to the vital part of Aristophanes's criticism,

---

[1] *Thesmo.* 170.   [2] *Achar.* 140.   [3] *Clouds,* 635 ff.
[4] *Frogs,* 799 ff.   [5] *Ibid.* 1134 ff.
[6] Cf. the "thinking-shop" (φροντιστήριον) of Socrates (*Clouds,* 95 ff.).
[7] *Clouds,* 1360 ff.

the judgment he passes in the *Frogs* on the comparative values of Aeschylus and Euripides as poets. Previous to this, he had satirised Euripides in three separate places. In the *Acharnians*, for instance, he raises a laugh by an allusion to Euripides's sentimental realism—his fondness for lame beggars as heroes, seen in his *Bellerophon, Philoctetes*, and *Telephus*. In his *Clouds*, again, he had associated with Euripides all the vices of the sophists. And in the *Thesmophoriazusae* he had ridiculed his weakness for incestuous heroines, as well as his use of sensational situations—the latter being burlesqued when Euripides, in assisting the hapless Mnesilochus tied to a plank, is described as playing the part, first of Menelaus rescuing Helen from Egypt, then of Echo comforting the chained Andromeda, and lastly of Perseus releasing Andromeda from the rock.[1] In the *Frogs*, however, these earlier remarks are brought to a head; when parody and burlesque give way to a more reasoned treatment, in which use is made of analysis and comparison. The criticism takes the form of an inquiry into the question as to which of the two poets was really the greater; and it is important to note that standards for forming judgment are submitted in the course of the discussion. Thus the accepted tests are, first, skill in art (δεινότης), and secondly, wise counsel (νουθεσία) for the making of better citizens;[2] and in accordance with these two tests the discussion proceeds.

In the first place the art of Aeschylus is adversely criticised; as, for instance, the undramatic openings of many of his plays, in which veiled characters preserve a "blood-curdling" silence.[3] This, it was argued, was a mere trick to keep the audience in suspense; though (as Dionysus notes) somehow the trick proved effective. Then, too, the justice of the current complaint as to his magniloquence was also in general conceded. Attention was called to his wild and whirling words, words like mountain rocks, and expressions such as "hippalectors" and "tragelaphs",[4] unintelligible to the plain man; though here too it was pointed out that exalted thoughts and sentiments called necessarily for magnificence in expression.[5]

---

[1] *Thesmo.* 1015 ff.; the references are to the plays *Helena* and *Andromeda.*
[2] *Frogs*, 1009.   [3] *Ibid.* 833, 911 ff.   [4] *Ibid.* 834, 924 ff.   [5] *Ibid.* 1058.

At the same time the dramatic art of Euripides is dealt with in yet greater detail. The earlier charges are renewed; his fondness for unpleasant stories, his indulgence in affected and sophistical utterances, and his weakness for blind beggars—the "crutch-and-cripple" playwright, as he was called.[1] And now the objection to this last is further explained, as detracting from the majesty appropriate to gods and heroes.[2] On the other hand, some of the positive merits of Euripides are also recognised. For one thing, he is said to have clarified tragedy, notably by his formal prologues, in which all necessary details had been explained; or again, by his simpler expression which had purged tragedy of its earlier inflation and bombast.[3] Then, too, he had developed the use of dialogue in assigning speech to all his characters; while he could also claim to have brought tragedy nearer to men, by introducing a new realism based on the scenes and language of ordinary life.[4] All these are points of substance, significant developments in the dramatic art; and, judged solely by the evidence adduced, Aeschylus, it must be confessed, appears as the inferior craftsman.

There yet remains, however, a further test, namely, the extent to which each dramatist gave wise counsel ($\nu o \nu \theta \epsilon \sigma i a$) for the betterment of social life. And forthwith we are reminded that, from the time of Orpheus and Musaeus onwards, great poets had ever been civilising and ennobling influences in human life.[5] "Just as young children", it is added, "have a master to advise them ($\pi a \iota \delta a \rho i o \iota \sigma \iota \nu \; \dot{\epsilon} \sigma \tau \dot{\iota} \; \delta \iota \delta \acute{a} \sigma \kappa a \lambda o s \; \ddot{o} \sigma \tau \iota s \; \phi \rho \acute{a} \zeta \epsilon \iota$), so for grown men there are the poets."[6] Judged by this standard, Aeschylus is said to have followed Homer in holding up the heroic ideal; and to have done so with unfailing consistency, scorning such themes as those of Stheneboea or Phaedra.[7] The ancient virtues which had made Athens great—valour, manliness, loyalty, and the like—these were the qualities inculcated by his works;[8] and this fact is emphasised towards the end of the play, where Aeschylus's proposed remedy for the evils of the time is said to have been the fostering of

---

[1] *Frogs*, 842ff. (tr. Murray).   [2] *Ibid.* 1061.   [3] *Ibid.* 941ff.
[4] *Ibid.* 954ff.   [5] *Ibid.* 1030ff.; see also p. 13 *supra*.
[6] *Ibid.* 1054-5.   [7] *Ibid.* 1043.   [8] *Ibid.* 1013ff.

brave and manly citizens.[1] As opposed to this, Euripides at his best is said to have helped men to think for themselves, to question all things, and to speak with freedom:[2] faculties without doubt of a valuable kind. At the same time along with this had gone influences of a less desirable sort. Men had learnt from him to scheme and to think evil, to value shrewdness and cleverness, to be for ever prating, arguing instead of obeying, debating instead of exercising, until the whole city had become filled with "clerks, demagogues, and buffoons".[3] So that if by Euripides dramatic technique had been improved, equally definite was the inference that the national *morale* had been weakened as the result of his literary practices.

Such then are the main details of Aristophanes's comparative analysis; though in the course of the argument other considerations emerge. Thus, for instance, the lyrical qualities of both poets are dramatically presented in choruses which reproduce in parody form the Titanic utterance of the one, the light music of the other. Or again, references are made to the "cleverness" of Euripides,[4] to his worship of new-fangled deities, Ether, Reason, and the like;[5] and if there is much abuse, there is also some excellent fooling, to which category is probably best assigned the mechanical interjection of the famous half-line—"and found his oil-flask gone" ($\lambda\eta\kappa\acute{\upsilon}\theta\iota o\nu$ $\grave{\alpha}\pi\acute{\omega}\lambda\epsilon\sigma\epsilon\nu$)[6]—a piece of ridicule reminiscent of Touchstone's "butterwomen's rank to market". The main interest, however, centres in the judgment finally given. The claims of the two poets so far are equally balanced; yet to Aeschylus is ultimately assigned the first place in tragedy, not because he was the better artist or the wiser of the two, but because he was the one "in whom the soul of Dionysus delighted" ($\H{o}\nu\pi\epsilon\rho$ $\grave{\eta}$ $\psi\upsilon\chi\grave{\eta}$ $\theta\acute{\epsilon}\lambda\epsilon\iota$),[7] a decision not without its significance. Hitherto Aristophanes had been considering points of artistic interest, as well as the social influences exercised by each—the development of healthy character on the part of Aeschylus, intellectual

---

[1] *Frogs*, 1464 ff.   [2] *Ibid.* 954 ff.   [3] *Ibid.* 1069 ff.
[4] *Ibid.* 775 ff., 828 ff.   [5] *Ibid.* 886 ff.; cf. also *Thesmo.* 411.
[6] *Ibid.* 1200 ff.; see also *Aristophanes on Tennyson* in A. W. Verrall, *Collected Literary Essays, Classical and Modern*, pp. 236–46.
[7] *Frogs*, 1468.

stimulus in the case of Euripides. Yet none of these factors seems to him conclusive; and his final judgment is instinctive rather than rational. It is based on neither moralistic, nor utilitarian, nor didactic grounds; but rather on the aesthetic appeal to his whole nature, and this after all is the ultimate criterion of all literary values.

Of Aristophanes's merits as a critic there can therefore be no doubt; even though his comments throughout are of a dramatic kind, and utterances spoken "in character" are normally no safe clues to a writer's opinions. Nevertheless his views in general are sufficiently clear; they cover a wide range, and in connexion with Aeschylus and Euripides in particular they give evidence of keen insight and literary taste, though far from being adequate appreciations of either of the two dramatists. Whether the main question he raised—the relative value of the two writers—was worth while is however not so certain; it was the first attempt at assigning order of merit in literature, a species of criticism which proved to be by no means the most fruitful. At the same time it will be found that many of his remarks have reference to artistic matters, and thus represent criticism of an aesthetic kind; while for his consideration of tragedy in its bearing on life there is also much that might be said. Moreover, it must be added, there are no vague generalities in his criticism. Not the least of his merits is his direct treatment of actual texts; and the points he makes are often rendered effective by the brilliance of his parodies, lit up as they are by ingenious and opulent fancy. That he was not free from prejudice is obvious from the first. His scurrilous treatment of Socrates and his "thinking-shop" is ample evidence of this; and he is also guilty of exaggeration in dealing with Euripides, though in both cases the exaggeration may perhaps be in part discounted, owing to the nature of his medium and the consequent necessity for raising a laugh. Altogether, however, he is not wholly unfair even to Euripides; he attaches due weight for instance to the improvements wrought in tragedy by that poet. Of Aeschylus he presents us with some of the main features; and he also affords glimpses of the happy temperament of Sophocles, to whom he awards

second place in the hierarchy. To look to Aristophanes for
any body of critical doctrine would obviously be useless. His
function is that of a judicial critic, who in a period of decline
sought to guide literature on to sounder lines; and as such he is
seen to be no mere reactionary, no moralist obsessed with the
didactic function of poetry. His criticism, on the contrary,
shows him to be alive to some at least of the essentials of art.
He makes war on all sorts of excesses and affectations; he
recognises the relations existing between literature and life;
and as his criterion of literary values he proposes, tacitly at
least, the aesthetic appeal to natural human instincts. So that
what he stands for is sanity and good sense in literature; and if
he holds up as the standard for future dramatists that of the
Aeschylean tradition, it is because he sees in the fashionable
tragedy of Euripides a source of danger to the state, an
influence that made for licence and mere "cleverness" in
character and thought, in spite of its stimulating intellectual
qualities. Of his influence on the critical development there
is not much to say. His distrust of Euripides was not shared by
later generations; though traces of his judgments are found in
curious places, as in the frequent use made by later Graeco-
Roman critics of the thunderbolt as illustrative of the power of
true eloquence.[1] Nevertheless his critical achievement is by
no means inconsiderable; as represented in Plato's *Symposium*, he
disguises under a comic manner a serious purpose. In one sense
indeed his work may be described as almost unique; for rarely
was critical analysis to enter into the sphere of comedy, though,
in the form of parody, literary criticism was to be represented
centuries later in such English plays as *The Knight of the Burning
Pestle* and Buckingham's *Rehearsal*. In Aristophanes must therefore be recognised one of the founders of ancient literary
criticism. He was neither a philosopher nor yet a mere jester;
but in the history of criticism he takes rank as the first judicial
critic, and as the first of the critics whose works were literature.

---

[1] The notion was based on a passage in the *Acharnians* (l. 530) where
Pericles in his wrath is said "to have lightened and thundered and to have
thrown all Greece into confusion". The passage is quoted at length by
Quintilian (*Inst. Orat.* XII, 10, 65), and the younger Pliny (*Letters*, I, 20, 19),
while the metaphor is also employed by Dionysius of Halicarnassus and
"Longinus". Cf. also vol. II, 244.

CHAPTER III

THE ATTACK ON POETRY: PLATO[1]

IN the fourth century which followed, literary criticism will be found to enter on a new phase, in which for the first time solid and lasting work was done. Plato (428–348 B.C.) came first and was succeeded by Isocrates, Aristotle, and Theophrastus; and in their works were set forth some of the most momentous pronouncements on literature, doctrines which were to exercise men's minds down to the present day. It was a time of political decline and dissolution, in which nevertheless the intellectual supremacy of Athens was finally established. By the beginning of the century the wonderful flowering-time of Greek art was over, and the creative impulse had practically ceased. An age of reflexion followed, in which philosophers and orators were the leading spirits; and with the discovery of the new dialectic which put an end to the earlier speculative thinking, with the perfecting also of an artistic prose, efforts were made to explore the whole realm of knowledge, and incidentally some of the outstanding problems of a literary kind. To the fostering of these activities had gone more than one consideration; chief among which was undoubtedly the example of Socrates, who had taught men to think and to seek for truth in disinterested fashion. Further impetus was also derived from the confusion which prevailed in all spheres of the national life, in matters political, moral, and educational; and of these things the obvious deterioration of the Athenian spirit was a constant and bitter reminder. Such then was the movement of which Plato was in a sense the pioneer; for during the first half of the century he practically monopolises the

[1] *Texts and Translations: Platonis opera*, ed. J. Burnet, 5 vols., Oxford (1899–1906); *Dialogues of Plato*, tr. B. Jowett, 5 vols., Oxford (1871, 1875, 1892); tr. H. Cary and H. Davies, 6 vols. (Bohn Lib.), London, 1900; *Republic*, tr. J. Ll. Davies and D. J. Vaughan (Golden Treas. Ser.), London, 1866; *Phaedrus, Lysis and Protagoras*, tr. J. Wright (Golden Treas. Ser.), London, 1909; *Ion, Symposium, Meno, Phaedo, Phaedrus*, tr. various, ed. A. D. Lindsay (Everyman's Lib.), London, n.d.; *Laws*, tr. A. E. Taylor, London, 1934; extracts (trans.) in J. D. Denniston, *Greek Lit. Crit.*, London, 1924, pp. 38–114.

scene. A follower of Socrates, with his master's preoccupation
with social morality, with something too of his master's skill in
the matter of dialectic, though richly endowed as well with
literary gifts of his own, he was well equipped for the part he
was destined to play, both in the opening up of philosophical
thought, and in the inauguration of a new phase in the critical
development.

For Plato's contribution to criticism we must turn to certain
of his *Dialogues*, written at different periods of his life. To an
earlier period, for instance—probably before the founding of
the Academy (*c.* 388 B.C.?)—belong *Ion*, *Cratylus*, *Protagoras*,
Gorgias, and the *Symposium*; to a slightly later date the *Republic*
and *Phaedrus*; while judged by the same criteria of vocabulary
and style, *Philebus* and the *Laws* are generally assigned to
Plato's closing years. No one of the dialogues is wholly devoted
to literary criticism. On the contrary, they all deal with a
variety of topics—with politics, ethics, metaphysics, and
education—and art-criticism is mostly a sort of side-issue, discussed incidentally in connexion with other themes. As to the
common motive of the dialogues, they all may be said to aim
primarily at preserving the memory of Socrates and his
teaching; and with this object in view Socrates appears as the
chief interlocutor in all but the latest dialogues, an idealised
figure, clearly and convincingly drawn. Along with him there
appear also not a few of his contemporaries, Gorgias, Thrasymachus, Prodicus, Hippias, Cratylus, Aristophanes, Agathon,
and others; and in the course of their discussions, among the
matters debated are rhetoric (in *Gorgias* and *Phaedrus*), the
origins of language (in *Cratylus*), the teaching of the sophists
(in *Protagoras*), and the current interpretations of poetry (in
Ion). But while the imaginary re-creation of Socrates was thus
the animating motive of the dialogues in general, influences of
a further kind may be seen at work in the *Republic* and the
Laws, both of which were attempts at sketching an ideal
commonwealth. During the unrest of the latter half of the
fifth century B.C. vague longings for a better state had haunted
the minds of Athenians, and had found satirical expression in
such works as Aristophanes' *Birds* (414 B.C.) and the *Assembly*

of Women (392 B.C.). And now Plato in the *Republic* submits his views in a vein of uncompromising idealism, discussing at the same time the part to be played by poetry in his imaginary state. At a later date the problem arose in a somewhat different form. By the middle of the fourth century B.C. the break-up of the old city-states was practically complete; and attempts were being made at founding new cities or reviving old ones. For these communities new constitutions and laws were urgently needed; and Plato's *Laws* was written in response to this demand. It was a sketch conceived in the spirit of the *Republic*, though on more practical lines; and here again some consideration was given to the value of poetry in the life of the community.

Such then were the chief works of Plato bearing on literary criticism; though further matters of interest may in places be found, as for instance in the *Symposium* and *Philebus*, to which reference will subsequently be made. Nor was the dialogue form, in which all alike were written, without its significance. If not the inventor of the Socratic dialogue, Plato was at least its earliest great exponent; and in his hands it becomes a powerful device for appealing to the educated at large and for interesting them in the new philosophy. In a sense indeed the dialogue was to Plato an inevitable and essential medium; it was the natural result of his adoption of the dialectic method which aimed at arriving at truth by means of question and answer. And, apart from this, as a literary form it offered distinct advantages for philosophical and critical inquiry. For one thing, it enabled the writer to approach truth from various angles, and thus to present more than one side of a given question; it also afforded scope for an informal and a picturesque treatment, and for the exercise of those literary gifts which Plato possessed in a rare degree. On the other hand there were disabilities involved in its use as well, the most serious being the difficulty experienced by the reader in grasping what Plato really thought on any particular subject. For he speaks to us but indirectly through his dialogues, by the voice of the Platonic Socrates—a dramatic figure curiously blended of Socrates and himself—so that all we have are dramatic, not personal, utterances. Then, too, his views are nowhere expressed in definite or systematic fashion; they have to be pieced together from statements scattered throughout his works, arising almost by chance out of the discussion of any and every subject, and involving in places apparent inconsistencies and contradictions. Even at the end of a discussion no general pronouncement is made. The dialogue as an instrument of inquiry did not aim at a final summing-up or conclusion; its whole object was attained in clearing the ground. Yet in spite of this dramatic, discursive, and piecemeal treatment not a little may be gathered concerning Plato's general ideas on many of the great questions affecting literature. It is true that his attitude to poetry presents difficulties of a special kind; though, viewed in their proper setting, his remarks are by no means as contradictory and puzzling as they are sometimes made out to be. On the other hand his enthusiasm for certain profound truths of art can scarcely be mistaken; and in both poetry and rhetoric he gave direction to later critical efforts. To his pages, in short, may ultimately be traced a surprising number of the literary doctrines of antiquity; and in the suggestive and stimulating quality of his writings he remains unsurpassed.

When we turn to consider the nature of Plato's achievement as a critic it is necessary from the first to view his work in its historical setting, and to arrive if possible at his animating purposes. It is significant in the first place that for the greater part of his life he had been a witness of the swift decay of literature. By the middle of the fourth century B.C. the status of poetry was being seriously threatened. Tragedy, which had previously eclipsed both epic and lyric, was now itself in process of decline; and in comedy alone were there signs of life, a New Comedy being evolved which stood nearer to the realities of life. For the rest it was an age of pale followers and rash innovators, of poets like Choerilus, Timotheus, and not a few undistinguished craftsmen; and with the loss of the creative faculty, original work in literature was no longer forthcoming. With these things as such, however, Plato was not primarily concerned. Wholly occupied, as Socrates had been, with problems of politics, morality, and knowledge, and vividly conscious as he was of the social and political corruptions of his age, all his efforts were devoted to staying the deterioration of character, and to the restoring of health in both the individual and the state. And with the literary decline he is therefore interested only in so far as it affected social welfare and morality. That he ascribed to the debased literature of his day evil influences where public morality was concerned is amply shown in the first place by casual references of his. He wrote, it is true, in dramatic fashion on philosophical topics; but that does not prevent an occasional personal note, nor does it preclude him from voicing something of the emotion of the time. And to the demoralising effects of the contemporary stage he returns more than once, bitterly condemning it as a purveyor of sensations to a morbid and undisciplined age. Thus he attacks, for instance, the rôles played by women in tragedy, women quarrelling or blaspheming, women love-sick or lamenting;[1] whereas in comedy he decries the craze for novelty, the rough horse-play and the crude effects obtained by noises of all kinds, from the imitation of thunder-claps to the bleating of sheep.[2] Elsewhere, again, he points out that tragedy had become a mere instrument of pleasure pandering to popular taste, and presenting tales of men's pleasant vices, which rivalled in their guile and flattery the artful speeches of rhetoricians.[3] And this reign of lawless innovation, this widespread licence in theme and expression alike, he explains as being due to the ancient custom of Hellas, according to which judgment in dramatic matters was left to the many. This, he maintains, had led to the ruin of poets and of the drama as well; for poets had learnt to appeal to the baser instincts of an ignorant public, thus fostering by the way their insolence, lawlessness, and bad taste. In short the weight of ignorant opinion had become decisive in dramatic matters; a sort of evil theatrocracy (θεατροκρατία) had taken the place of the old aristocracy; and these things were disastrous to the national well-being.[4] At the same time it is important to note that it is not merely against the abuses of contemporary drama that

[1] *Rep.* 395 d.   [2] *Ibid.* 397 a.   [3] *Gorg.* 502–3.   [4] *Laws*, 659, 700–1.

Plato inveighs as dangerous to social morality. The insensate love of the sensational, the morbid, and the vulgar, all this obviously conduced to relaxed moral standards. But Plato's censure is yet wider in scope. It embraces practically the whole of existing Greek literature, that priceless contribution of the Greek genius to all the ages; and it is upon this literature with its proud traditions that Plato's attack, however strange it may seem, is mainly concentrated. His attitude in this matter was based on the conviction that in literature, as he knew it, there existed positive hindrances to the attainment of true knowledge, as well as influences unfavourable to the highest development of moral personality. In the first place he saw in Homer, Hesiod, and the rest, an unsuitable basis for an educational system. He recalls the current view of Homer as the educator of Greece; as one who, possessed of all knowledge both human and divine, was in himself a sufficient guide in all affairs of life.[1] And these extravagant claims Plato unequivocally rejects; it was a form of wisdom, he asserts, which the age had outgrown. Then, too, in tragedy and comedy at their best he discerned elements of danger to the state. To the Greeks, naturally imitative, with a tendency to pose, highly susceptible as well to words and the rhythm of words, the drama, so he held, came with a disturbing emotional appeal. It led in fact to a loss of simplicity, to the formation of a nation of actors devoid of genuine characters; and it is on these grounds that he challenges its existence. These then were the main motives which actuated Plato in the attitude he adopts towards poetry; and it is only in the light of such considerations that his position becomes intelligible and that the real meaning of his attack on poetry is seen.

For the main details of that attack we must look to remarks scattered throughout his works, which reveal fairly clearly the chief counts in his indictment. And in the first place Plato makes plain his view that the main avenue to knowledge or truth did not lie through the poets, and that poetry was no longer to be the ultimate authority in conduct and morals. A statement of the orthodox position is put into the mouth of

[1] *Rep.* 606e; *Laws,* 810e.

Protagoras, who maintained that poets from Homer onwards had been the recognised educators, and that, as the first sophists, they had consistently aimed at making good citizens.[1] And for the rest, as is well known, the use of poetry in moral discussion had become an established tradition by Plato's day, while its interpretation had long formed a recognised part of culture. To Plato, however, this indiscriminate reverence paid to poets was mere superstition, and nothing is more characteristic of his treatment than his frequent refutation of poetic pronouncements on matters of truth and conduct. Thus with ironical deference he turns to the poets for light in opening his discussions; but only to prove their shallowness and futility. Early in the *Republic*, for instance, the teaching of Simonides on "justice" is quoted. According to the poet—a wise and inspired man, as Socrates courteously concedes—justice is none other than "the payment of one's debts"; but on closer examination the definition is shown to be hopelessly inadequate.[2] Or again, in the *Laws*, Tyrtaeus is referred to as defining courage in war as the greatest of virtues; and here too the same deference is shown as to "a divine poet, wise and good". Yet a brief analysis shows also the weakness of his pronouncement; and courage in war is said to rank low in the order of virtues, coming after justice, temperance, and wisdom.[3] Then, too, it is with the same object in view that Plato reiterates his conception of the poet as being divinely "inspired". As opposed to the σοφοί, physicians and others, whose distinctive feature was their technique or craftsmanship, the poet, he declares, does not compose in virtue of σοφία, but rather by reason of natural endowment (φύσις) and inspiration of a non-rational kind (ἐνθουσιάζοντες);[4] and this inspiration he regards as an impulse from without, depriving the poet of the free play of his personality. Again and again Plato enlarges on this theme. Poets inspired are as Corybantian revellers or Bacchic maidens; they utter unconsciously only what the Muse impels them to say; they are not in their right minds when they sit on the

---

[1] *Protag.* 326a, 339a; cf. also *Lysis*, 213e, where poets are described as "the fathers and authors of wisdom".
[2] *Rep.* 331e ff.   [3] *Laws*, 629–30.   [4] *Apol.* 22c.

Muse's tripod; like fountains they allow to flow out freely whatever comes in.[1] Hence, argues Plato, the utter unreliability of all poetic pronouncements. That poets sometimes supply statements which contain elements of "right opinion" he is ready to allow; for he recognises that their utterances are divinely inspired, and as such are not due to the poets themselves. But, even so, imperfect truths of this kind have to be carefully scanned; and after all they are no substitutes for knowledge based on reason. And for the rest, the poets with their emotional frenzies and lack of moral restraint can afford no safe guidance to the sanc. They speak they know not what; and their utterances besides being untrustworthy are full of obscurities and contradictions.

At the same time Plato is aware of the current view that while a superficial reading of poetry might lead to no results, yet properly interpreted (for they spoke often in riddles) the poets were capable of yielding truths of the profoundest kind; and he is at some pains to expose what was fallacious in this view. From what has already been said it is clear that the poets were unable to explain themselves; and this point is emphasised by Plato in at least one place.[2] Nor were the rhapsodes any more successful with their attempts at interpretation. For infected by the poet's frenzy they too shared in his non-rational "inspiration"; and their comments were unreasoned and unconscious, utterly devoid of art or knowledge.[3] Concerning the method of allegorical interpretation then in vogue Plato has rather more to say; though here too he is doubtful of the results obtained. For one thing, such critics, he maintained, worked on no rational lines; they put forward differing interpretations which there was no sound method of testing, so that no finality was possible.[4] Then, too, he regards such interpretations as ingenious but unprofitable; and this he illustrates by his exegesis of the myth according to which Boreas stole Orithyia from the banks of Ilissus.[5] This fable he takes to mean that a maiden was swept away by the north wind. But such methods, he points out, involve much fruitless labour, for

---

[1] *Ion*, 534; *Laws*, 719 c.   [2] *Apol.* 22 b.   [3] *Ion*, 534.
[4] *Protag.* 347 e.   [5] *Phaedrus*, 229.

"the monsters of myth are many and formidable"; and for such "nice interpretations" he has no time. Moreover they result only in a crude sort of philosophy; and for his part, he would devote his efforts not to these ingenuities but rather to the study of man. As to the existence of underlying meanings in poetry generally, he makes, it should be noticed, no definite pronouncement. Nor can anything be inferred from his use of myths in his dialogues; for in most instances they are used as tentative explanations or illustrations only, not to be taken too seriously. One thing however is clear, and that is that allegory as a defence of poetry he dismisses as irrelevant and inadequate. If the subject-matter of a myth, he points out, is harmful in kind it matters not whether it was intended as allegory or not. Allegorical intention, in short, was no excuse for stories with a baneful influence.[1] There were however yet other methods of extracting hidden meanings from poetry, and with two at least of these methods Plato deals in trenchant fashion, showing up with the help of irony and caricature their utter futility. There was first the etymological method which was often resorted to by critics in search of allegory. It was a method based on the pseudo-science of etymology which professed to bring to light the original meaning of words. And since the original meaning of a word was said to supply its true sense, the etymological process was held to provide clues to the real meaning of obscure passages of poetry. All such attempts at elucidation, however, Plato shows to be sheer fancy, guesses without any scientific foundation.[2] As he points out, it was easy to obtain different results from the same data, such interpretations being, like Ion's, the mere result of "inspiration", and therefore productive solely of chance opinion. Moreover, even if such derivations could be arrived at by rational process, all that could be learnt would be the notion of the original name-giver—again, mere opinion. And so he dismisses not without some scorn all such attempts at poetic interpretation. Nor has Plato more to say for the methods pursued by such well-known

[1] *Rep.* 378d. See J. Tate, "Plato and Allegorical Interpretation" (*Class. Quar.* XXIII, 142–54), for an interesting treatment of the whole theme.
[2] *Crat.* 435 ff. *et passim*; see also J. Tate, *loc. cit.* pp. 152–3.

critics as Protagoras, Prodicus, and Hippias; in the *Protagoras*, indeed, he is found ridiculing their practices in delightful fashion.[1] There the matter in dispute is the correct interpretation of a passage in an ode of Simonides which appears to conflict with another passage in the same ode. And by way of clearing up the difficulty, Prodicus, the authority on the right use of words, proposes to distinguish between "being good" and "becoming good"; a piece of pedantry which succeeds only in darkening counsel. Hippias in his turn then suggests an arbitrary reading of his own, as if everything depended on the ingenuity of the critic. And he is followed by Socrates, who indulges in some first-rate quibbling which reduces the whole business to absurdity. In this way does Plato caricature the futile pedantries of those who professed to extract moral doctrines from poetry; the implication being that by such fantastic methods the critic could read anything or everything into a given text. The truth is that, in Plato's judgment, neither from poetry itself nor from interpretations of the critics could serious doctrines on the conduct of life be drawn, and that the time had gone by for relying on the aphoristic wisdom attributed to the poets. This in short is the sum and substance of his first indictment of poetry; and in a significant passage in the *Protagoras* he makes his position yet more plain. There the suggestion is made that the time had come when educated men should no longer be content with discussing poetry, but should venture more freely in their search for truth, "putting one another to the proof in conversation".[2] And here Plato was clearly advocating new methods of arriving at truth. The new instrument for the new age was to be philosophy; whereas in poetry he saw something less than the whole of wisdom, a wisdom moreover that was uttered vaguely and obscurely, and that rested as well on no sure foundation.

Such then in its main details was the first charge brought against poetry by Plato. And this he follows up with a second charge to the effect that in existing narrative poetry there were influences which militated against the highest development of

[1]   339–47.
[2]   *Protag.* 347 c–348 a; see also W. P. Ker, *Collected Essays*, II, ch. 33.

moral responsibility.[1] In the first place he attacks certain aspects of the subject-matter of such poetry; and, acutely conscious as he was of the influence of poetry on plastic human nature, he condemns outright all those narratives in which gods and heroes were represented in other than an ideal light. A right conception of the divine nature he held to be necessary for a healthy morality; and the gods, he maintained, were good and truthful and constant. Hence to represent them as fighting or quarrelling, guilty of disgraceful crimes, or responsible for the calamities that befell mankind, all this was dangerous to social well-being.[2] Nor was the danger less when "god-sprung" heroes were depicted in unworthy fashion, devoid of such qualities as fortitude, magnanimity, and self-control. To witness Achilles in his grief, for instance, ignominiously rolling on the ground, to hear of his avarice, or again of his arrogance in dragging Hector around Patroclus's tomb,[3] these things were not edifying but harmful in their effects; as were also scenes which depicted the horrors of the underworld, where flitting shades and gibbering phantoms brought terror to the souls of men.[4] It is however not only in the subject-matter of existing poetry that Plato finds danger to the community. There are also certain forms or styles of poetry which have in his opinion an undesirable influence; and the rest of his attack is directed against these particular forms. All narrative poetry, to begin with, he divides into three kinds in respect of form. There is first the purely narrative kind, represented by dithyrambs; there is, secondly, the "imitative" ($\mu\iota\mu\eta\tau\iota\kappa\dot{\eta}$) kind (i.e. poetry in which the poet conducts his narrative solely by means of impersonation, thus speaking in character), represented by tragedy and comedy; and thirdly, there is the "mixed" kind (in which the poet speaks partly in his own person, partly also through characters) represented by the epic.[5] And of these kinds both of those into which "imitation" (i.e. impersonation) enters, whether wholly or partially, he describes as pernicious

---

[1] For a full discussion of Plato's argument here, see R. L. Nettleship, *Lectures on the Republic of Plato*, ed. Lord Charnwood, 1929, pp. 84–123, 340–55.
[2] *Rep.* 379–83.   [3] *Ibid.* 390–1.   [4] *Ibid.* 386a–389b.   [5] *Ibid.* 394c.

in their influence on poet and hearer alike. The position he here takes up, though he does so with reservations, is therefore one of hostility to those epic and dramatic forms which had long been recognised as the glory of Greece. And his animating idea throughout is that in all such compositions the poet for the time being identifies himself with other characters, compels also the hearer (or reader) to share sympathetically in that identification; and such absorption in other personalities Plato conceives to be unhealthy and bad. Nor does he fail to give reasons for the attitude he thus adopts. For one thing, while recognising the imitative faculty as instinctive in man, he regarded it, in excess, as a sign of weakness, and as conducing further to the enfeeblement of character and personality. Moreover, the habit of impersonation, he maintained, was likely to impair the single-mindedness and integrity of the individual.[1] And this was especially true when the characters impersonated were those of cowards or ribald knaves, criminals or madmen. For, as he points out, by simulating a quality one soon forms a habit, and habits go to the making of a second nature; so that indiscriminate impersonation of this kind was inevitably attended with serious results. These, then, are so far his reasons for his denunciation of the dramatic and epic forms; though he also adds in passing that into the drama are introduced complex harmonies and rhythms which are likewise foreign to the expression of the single-minded man.[2] Elsewhere, however, he has other and more serious objections to make; and among the further inherent defects which he detects in the dramatic and epic forms is the fact that they abuse the understandings of those who do not possess "an antidote in a knowledge of the real nature of such poetry".[3] Up to this point Plato has used the term "imitation" in the sense of "impersonation", to describe the poet's methods of conducting his narrative, and his relation to the characters he depicts. From now on he employs the term mainly in its primary sense, to denote the relation in which poetry in general stands to things. And he proceeds to show that what both the dramatic and the epic forms give are representations of appearances and not the truth of things,

[1] *Rep.* 395c.   [2] *Ibid.* 397b.   [3] *Ibid.* 595b (tr. Jowett).

illusions instead of reality. Thus poetry, he states,[1] resembles painting in that both imitate things, the one in words, the other in colour, as they seem to be from this or that point of view. What the poet and the painter present are therefore not actual things—as things produced by craftsmen are actual—but merely copies or transcripts of those things: and in that sense both artists obviously fall short of reality. But even the work of the craftsman is shown to be none other than a copy, a defective copy of the original "form" or "idea" existing only in the mind of the Creator; so that he too fails to apprehend and reproduce reality. At the same time the craftsman is said to stand nearer to the truth of things; for he has some knowledge ("right opinion") of the things he makes, whereas the poet with his imperfect copy of the craftsman's imperfect copy stands two removes from the truth, and all that he attains to is mere conjecture (εἰκασία). In short, Plato's charge against poets on this score is that they produce only unsubstantial images, such as a man might make by "holding up a mirror to nature" (κάτοπτρον περιφέρειν πανταχῇ);[2] and in thus presenting the external and superficial for the whole, the unreal for the real, they themselves live in a world of illusion, into which they allure all those who read their works. Then finally, as the last item in his attack on dramatic and epic forms, Plato claims that such poetry had an unhealthy effect upon the emotional side of man.[3] And to begin with he adopts once again his analogy with painting. He points out that as the painter depends for his effects on achieving certain illusions of sight (by colour devices, for instance, making things appear concave or convex), so the poet takes advantage of certain illusions of feeling to produce a distorted view of life; and in each case it is necessary for the reason to be in abeyance and for full sway to be given to the emotions. Under such conditions, Plato goes on to explain, men allow themselves to give way to emotional disturbances of which otherwise they would be ashamed, and to sympathise with passionate and fitful temperaments which were for the most part the types of character favoured in such poetry. All this, contended Plato, had de-

[1] *Rep.* 595c–602c. [2] *Ibid.* 596d. [3] *Ibid.* 602c–605c.

bilitating effects; it led to loss of balance, with feelings un-
restrained by either reason or principle. Hence his condemnation of such forms of poetry on the grounds that "they
fed and watered the passions instead of drying them up, and let
them rule instead of ruling them as they ought to be ruled, with
a view to the happiness and virtue of mankind".[1]

These then are the main charges brought against poetry
by Plato. The old aphoristic poetry, as we have seen, he refuses
to regard as a repository of truth; the dramatic and epic forms
he censures for their baneful psychological effects. And this
attack he follows up with the well-known but sweeping pronouncement that into a state governed by ideal conditions "no
poetry should be admitted save hymns to the gods and panegyrics on famous men".[2] The statement, it would seem, is one
that could not well be mistaken. It follows naturally enough
from the previous argument; and indeed Plato's position had
already been anticipated in the ironical recommendation that
dramatists, wonderful fellows as they were, and worthy of
being anointed with myrrh and crowned with woollen fillets,
should nevertheless be expelled from the ideal community and
directed to another state.[3] Yet nothing is more remarkable
than the use made of this pronouncement by later ages. It
became perhaps the most frequently-quoted and the most
authoritative of all Plato's utterances; a fact that is probably
accounted for by the Puritanical bias of the early Fathers, to
whom such views on art were highly acceptable, and who
handed on the doctrine without Plato's reservations, and with
all the weight of a dogma. Hence, detached from its context,
it led to startling results. Plato, for instance, is said "to have
banished poets out of his Commonwealth";[4] more recently he
has been described as "the author of the only great negation of
art which appears in the history of ideas".[5] And thus the so-
called decree became the rallying-point of later Puritans and
Philistines, as well as a standing perplexity to others who saw
in it Plato's denial of the value of art.

---

[1] *Rep.* 606d (tr. Jowett).   [2] *Ibid.* 607a.   [3] *Ibid.* 398a.
[4] Sidney, *Apology for Poetry*, ed. Cook, p. 35.
[5] B. Croce, *Aesthetic*, tr. by D. Ainslie, p. 253.

It is therefore not strange to find that various attempts have been made to explain away this pronouncement of Plato. And representative in its way was the explanation put forward by Sidney, that Plato's attack was directed, not against poetry, but against the abuse of poetry. His hostility, so it was explained, was due to certain glaring defects in the literature of his time, and what he banishes is therefore poetry of an inferior kind. But the terms of Plato's indictment are sufficiently plain, and they definitely do not admit of this interpretation. What he rules out is epic and dramatic poetry as a whole; the works of Homer, Aeschylus, and Sophocles, as well as those of the "frigid" Theognis, and the affected Agathon, and the "starling chatter" of which Aristophanes speaks. Then there is the suggestion that Plato in the *Republic* is considering poetry under certain specific conditions and from a particular standpoint; and that his views are in consequence conditioned by the limitations thus imposed. Thus, it is argued, certain forms of poetry are condemned, not because they were lacking in aesthetic value, but because they failed to satisfy certain educational requirements, the requirements of a special type of citizen (statesman and soldier) in a special type of state. And, it is claimed, a statement concerning those forms of poetry, subject to such restrictions, based, too, on political and educational grounds, obviously could not be held to apply in general and under normal conditions. Such a suggestion, it must be allowed, is more plausible, and sound as far as it goes; but it fails to cover the whole meaning of Plato's statement. It is true that Plato is immediately concerned with the education of the guardians in his ideal state, for which he regards epic and dramatic poetry as unsuitable. But there is also the further implication that such poetry represented influences that were hostile to the highest development of man; and since it is on this ground, as the context plainly shows, that Plato ultimately bases his condemnation, the pronouncement is seemingly intended to be of general validity.

And yet, it may be urged, there are serious reasons for doubting such an estimate of Plato's intention, and for hesitating to accept his statement at its face value as final and absolute.

For one thing, dogmatic utterance of any kind was altogether foreign to his methods; and, it is not irrelevant to add, he was on his own showing an ardent admirer of Homer and the tragic poets.[1] What however is more relevant is the fact that he was prepared at a later date to recognise both tragedy and comedy provided they were properly censored;[2] as if conscious of the beneficent influence of a lofty and austere art in the state. And the modification thus introduced cannot wholly be ascribed to difference of mood. For although in the *Laws* he was discussing things on practical lines and legislating for something less than the ideal state, yet even in the less compromising mood of the *Republic* he gives evidence of his awareness of the possibilities of such literature, and the evidence is very definitely confirmed elsewhere. In the *Republic*, for instance, he is found commending both tragedy and the epic under certain conditions, that is, provided they dealt with themes that inculcated courage, purity, temperance, and the like.[3] For in such cases, he points out, impersonation would involve only a simulation of the best human qualities, and thus conduce to a development of what was best in human nature. Or again, he can conceive of comedy being justified on the score of amusement, even though it meant impersonating characters of the baser sort.[4] And if concessions of this kind are made in the *Republic*, what are the inferences to be drawn from his remarks elsewhere concerning the poetic process at its best and highest? The true nature of poetic inspiration he describes, not as a disturbing influence from without, but as a sort of divine madness that frees the poet from the yoke of ordinary conventions, an ecstatic power set working by the vision of the ideal, and enabling him to pass from the world of sense to the world of reality.[5] And it is surely incredible that Plato would have approved of poets thus gifted only on the understanding that they confined themselves to hymns and panegyrics.

It would therefore seem that unless Plato is to be charged with a lack of consistency (and this of course is a possibility) his famous pronouncement must be regarded as an inadequate

---

[1] *Rep.* 595c *et passim.*   [2] *Laws*, 817.   [3] *Rep.* 395c.
[4] *Ibid.* 396e.   [5] *Phaedrus*, 265a.

and even a misleading expression of his views on poetry as a
whole. But charges of inconsistency against so acute a thinker
as Plato are not to be lightly undertaken; and most readers
would agree, with Sir Philip Sidney, that it is wiser to attempt
"to construe him justly than unjustly to resist his authority".
It therefore remains to consider in what sense Plato's proscription might reasonably have been intended, and whether it
can be made intelligible in the light of all the facts. It is usual
to regard Plato's rejection of epic and dramatic poetry as the
outcome of pure reflexion, the result of a dispassionate inquiry
into literary values. Yet nothing seems more certain than that
Plato in the *Republic*, as in all his dialogues, was writing with
contemporary conditions in mind, with a keen desire for the
betterment of those conditions; and that these things determined for him the main aspects of poetry to be considered, as
well as the main lines of his thinking. Thus the chief influences
in the intellectual life of the time were the old aphoristic poetry
and poetry of the epic and dramatic kinds; and these, as we
have seen, were the matters with which Plato concerned himself. But the same factors, it would seem, were instrumental
also in determining the character of his thinking, which takes
the form, not of an inquiry based on first principles, but of a
sort of special pleading in support of a conviction already
arrived at; and significant in this connexion is his description
of the discussion in which he is engaged as one which continued the old quarrel between philosophy and poetry.[1] There
in the first place he suggests—as he does also in the *Protagoras*[2]—his deep-rooted conviction that the true remedy for
the prevailing corruption lay in accepting philosophy as the
guide to truth and conduct; and secondly he implies that his
method was that of attack as adopted by the earlier philosophers. It is as if he was conscious that the conviction at which
he had arrived was the outcome of his temperament and
training, and that it was therefore incumbent on him to give
rational grounds for the position thus adopted. And this is
borne out by the methods he adopts for convincing his readers
of the justice of his position; for throughout his work he calls

[1] *Rep.* 607 b.   [2] See p. 42 *supra.*

attention to whatever supported his instinctive conclusion, while
ignoring for the most part facts of an inconvenient kind. That
his main arguments go to disparage the prevailing forms of
poetry we have already seen; but equally significant are his
attempts to accommodate his reasoning to the matter in hand.
When, for instance, he denies to dramatic poets any true knowledge of the things they represent;[1] or when, again, he describes
the poetic process as nothing more than a holding up of a
mirror to nature,[2] a mere reflexion of sensible appearances; in
such places he is obviously employing the methods of an
advocate, utilising for his immediate purposes accepted theories
of the time, though he himself was aware, as he shows elsewhere, of the inadequacy of his descriptions. Then, too, he
does less than justice to the psychological results of impersonation and appeals to the emotions. Their evil effects he
consistently emphasises; whereas he ignores for the most part
their possibilities for good, their power of stimulating and
elevating human nature. It was not that he was blind to these
particular facts; but his task as an advocate compelled him to
minimise their importance. When therefore Plato's argument
is thus viewed as a piece of special pleading, a new light is
thrown upon his perplexing pronouncement, which renders it
intelligible and free from inconsistency. For here, it is suggested, he was passing no final judgment, the result of a
scrupulous weighing of all the evidence. He was rather
speaking to a brief, presenting, in modern parlance, a case for
the plaintiff (philosophy), without concern, for the time being,
for the rightful claims of the defendant (epic and dramatic
poetry). And in so doing he was but following the universal
procedure in argument. Nor as a consequence can he be
charged with casuistry or sophistry; for he was firmly convinced
of the profound truth underlying his main plea, which was for
the substitution of philosophy in place of poetry in the intellectual life of the time. His proposed suppression of epic and
dramatic poetry is therefore probably best regarded in the light
of a challenge; the first move in a bout of dialectics, to which,
it is important to note, he expected, and indeed hoped for, a

[1] *Rep.* 602 b.   [2] *Ibid.* 596 d.

reply.[1] And whereas he was on safe ground in his attack on poetry as the main avenue to truth, the same cannot be said of his wholesale proscription of epic and dramatic poetry. Indeed the latter is more notable for the questions it raises, than for any contribution made to either literary theory or heresy.

In considering Plato so far as a critic, it was inevitable that reference should be made to the peculiar difficulties connected with his work, and more especially to the puzzling position he takes up in relation to poetry generally. Equally interesting, however, and perhaps of greater importance, is the positive contribution he makes to the critical development in virtue of ideas scattered everywhere throughout his works. Not that he anywhere sets·out a coherent body of aesthetic theory. What he hands on are ideas suggestive and illuminating, hints more valuable than any formulated doctrine could ever have been; and it remained for later workers, Aristotle notably among their number, to realise their possibilities by modifying and applying them as occasion arose. Nothing, for example, is of greater interest than his remarks on the nature of art, and of poetry in particular. To begin with, in his works appears for the first time the conception of *mimesis* or imitation as the essential characteristic of all art; though the idea in all probability was familiar long before his day. That it was ultimately based on earlier philosophical speculation he explains in one place. He states that the greatest and most beautiful things—the primeval elements, the heavenly bodies, and the rest of creation—all came into being by nature (φύσις) and chance (τύχη); that art (τέχνη) came later, born of created things, producing as mere pastime (παιδιάς τινας) partial images of the truth, all related in essence, whether the products of painting, music, or the sister arts; and that there were also other arts with a serious (σπουδαῖος) purpose—medicine, agriculture, and the like—which were said to co-operate with nature.[2] Here then was apparently the first attempt at correlating the arts, with a further suggestion that, whereas all were intimately related, there existed also a distinction between the arts in accordance with

[1] *Rep.* 607 c, d.   [2] *Laws*, 889 b–d.

their purposes, which led to a differentiation between fine arts and useful arts. Moreover the statement helps to explain why "imitation" (and not "creation" or "expression") had been adopted as the process common to all the arts. To the Greeks before Plato, devoid of a mystical sense of an invisible order of realities, the plain and obvious fact was that the artist did not produce the objects of real life, but their appearances only; and it was therefore inevitable that the impression produced on their minds was rather that of imitative representation than of creation, interpretation, or the like.[1] Of this conception, as we have seen, Plato makes frequent use, maintaining that poets indulged in servile copying and in reproducing partial images of the truth.[2] Yet he also advances beyond this position; and indeed this is the position which he strives everywhere to refute, a fact that is not always fully realised. Alive as he was to an unseen reality existing behind the objects of sense, he conceived of an imitation of the ideal forms of that unseen world, ideas of justice, beauty, and truth, which were to be embodied in human character. And it is this kind of "imitation" that he associates with poetry in its highest form; a process which represented things as they ought to be, and not in their actuality.[3]

Closely bound up with this conception of "imitation" were Plato's views on "inspiration"; yet another factor that went to determine the nature of poetry. From Homer onwards, poets for their greater glory had claimed to write under the influence of the Muses or the gods, the suggestion being that they were thrown into a state of ecstasy or madness by some divine force from without. In a modified form the doctrine had been emphasised by Pindar; and Plato adopts it for the most part in his writings; though the current idea of the poetic process was rather that of a craft, in which, as in the rest of the arts, conscious attempts were made at producing artistic results, in the case of poetry, by a skilful use of words. Of the use made

[1] See Bosanquet, *History of Aesthetic*, p. 12.
[2] Cf. *Rep.* 600e.
[3] *Ibid.* 402b, c; *Laws*, 668b, *passim*; see J. Tate, "Imitation in Plato's Republic" (*Class. Quart.* 1928, pp. 16–23), also "Plato and Imitation" (*Class. Quart.* 1932, pp. 161–9).

by Plato of the traditional doctrine something has already been said. He has been shown to dwell mainly on the non-rational conception of the poet's inspiration, on the wild unreason and irresponsible utterance that were among its effects. In the *Phaedrus* however he gives to the term a deeper meaning, describing it as an influence productive of elevating results that could not have been attained in a state of sanity and normal self-control.[1] And he goes on to explain that there were two kinds of madness, one which was the result of human infirmity, the other "a divine release of the soul from the yoke of custom and convention".[2] As illustrations of the workings of the latter form of exaltation he mentions the activities of the prophetess, the poet, and the lover; and he describes in some detail the upward flight of the soul of the inspired lover towards those changeless realities to which it is by nature akin. It is beauty, he asserts, that sends the soul on its quest for the vision of the ideal; and the quest ends with a sudden apprehension of truth in all its beauty, with insight into reality. And like to this, he implies, is the working of poetic "inspiration". It is a sort of intuition, an awakening of latent powers in the poet to a vision of ideal truth; and beyond this as an explanation it is impossible to go far. A distant echo of the doctrine is heard in the familiar passage of Shakespeare where Theseus ascribes to the poet (the lunatic and lover as well) strange powers of vision.[3]

In addition to these theories concerning the nature of poetry Plato has also something to say with regard to its practice as an art; and here again he breaks new ground, setting forth certain basic principles which were to lie at the root of much of the later theorising. Essential to all art, in the first place, was said to be the need for taking thought. This it was that distinguished an art like medicine from a sham art like cookery, the latter being described as the outcome of mere experiment ($\dot{\epsilon}\mu\pi\epsilon\iota\rho\acute{\iota}\alpha$) or rule of thumb. No true artist, added Plato,[4] whether painter or builder or poet, selected or applied his material at random; his effort was always directed towards giving definite and effective form to his work; and with that end in view some

---

[1] *Phaedrus*, 245a.
[3] *Mid. N. Dream*, v, i, 5–6.
[2] *Ibid.* 265a (tr. Jowett).
[4] *Gorg.* 501–3.

knowledge of the technique of art was held to be necessary. Nor was Plato content with mere arbitrary statement in these matters. As the foundations of his theory he takes certain broad philosophical truths; and indeed his whole conception of art rests on these truths of a general kind. Just as, for instance, it was necessary to understand life in order to live properly, so, he implies, a knowledge of art was needed for the making of a successful artist. Then, too, he finds in philosophy sanctions for some of his governing artistic principles, notably the law of order, restraint, and the like. To him God, not man, was the measure of all things: and man, he added, was like God in so far as he followed the law of right measure.[1] Or again, there is the use he makes of "the reconciliation of opposites" as applied to a musical scale (ἁρμονία), which he regards as a blending of high notes and low notes, and to rhythms based on short and long syllables; the elements differ in kind but are reconciled by the art of music.[2] Nor must we forget the notions he puts forward with regard to methods of attaining skill in art; for they too are ideas carried over from the sphere of philosophy. Thus the Platonic Protagoras is obviously making use of an accepted ethical doctrine when he states that virtues are due to neither nature (φύσις) nor chance (τύχη), but that they may be taught and are to be acquired by study, exercise, and teaching (ἐπιμέλεια, ἄσκησις, διδαχή).[3] And this doctrine, adapted by Plato to artistic purposes,[4] became later on one of the most familiar commonplaces in ancient literary theory.

Among the outstanding principles of art revealed in his writings none is however more illuminating than that principle of organic unity which he regarded as one of the primary conditions of art. The most familiar of his pronouncements on this point occurs in the Phaedrus,[5] where he states that "every discourse (λόγος) ought to be constructed like a living creature, having a body of its own as well as a head and feet, and with a middle and extremities also in perfect keeping with one

---

[1] Laws, 716c, 732d.

[2] Symp. 187; this interpretation I owe to Professor J. F. Mountford. Cf. also Coleridge's conception of metre as a balance of antagonists, spontaneous impulse and voluntary purpose (Biog. Lit. ed. Shawcross, II, 49–50).

[3] Protag. 323d.　　　　[4] Phaedrus, 269d.　　　　[5] 264c.

another and the whole". And here, it will be noticed, he requires not only the unity or completeness that is provided by a suitable beginning, middle, and end,[1] but also a unity that was vital in kind, all the parts being related as the parts of a living organism, so that nothing could be changed or omitted without injury to the whole. It was, in brief, a revelation of the fact that artistic beauty resides in a unity of effect, in a single animating principle; and it was one of the most fruitful utterances handed down by the ancients. Nor is the doctrine limited by Plato to matters of discourse or oratory. In *Gorgias*, for instance, he is speaking of art in general when he states that the artist "disposes all things in order, and compels the one part to harmonise and accord with the other part, until he has constructed a regular and systematic whole";[2] and elsewhere, again, he insists that harmony and rhythm in poetry must be in keeping with the subject-matter.[3] There can thus be no doubt that the doctrine of artistic unity was regarded by Plato as of universal application. He was, in fact, the first to bring to light the logic of art, and what is still more important, those vital relations involved in organic unity.

Yet Plato's observations on art are not limited to principles of a general kind. Scattered throughout his works are occasional remarks on poetry, more detailed in character, and significant in the highest degree for the use made of them by later theorists. Thus with him originated the classification of poetry into forms or styles. The narrative poets, as we have seen,[4] he distinguished according to their methods of relating their stories; and his differentiation between the dithyramb (or lyric), the drama, and the epic was to form the basis of all later classification of poetry. On one at least of the three main forms, namely, the drama, he has also some interesting remarks to make, and his remarks bear on tragedy and comedy alike: while in one place he implies that tragedy was inferior to the epic.[5] In the first instance he puts forward as his conception of the ideal (ἀληθεστάτη) tragedy that which was an imitation of the best and noblest life; and tragic poets at their best he accordingly ranks

---

[1] Cf. *Parmenides*, 145a.   [2] *Gorg.* 503e (tr. Jowett).
[3] *Rep.* 398d.   [4] See p. 43 *supra*.   [5] *Laws*, 658d.

with law-givers, benefactors of the community, since the efforts of both were directed towards the same end.[1] Then, too, of tragedy on its psychological side he also has something to say; and incidentally he makes it plain that he had accepted the traditional "pity" and "fear" (already mentioned by Gorgias) as the characteristic two-fold emotion aroused by tragedy.[2] Of the theory of "catharsis", subsequently developed by Aristotle in connexion with those emotions, it is true he has no trace. Yet it is not without its significance that in more than one place he hints at the principle underlying that theory; as, for instance, when he notes that for restlessness in infants the best cure was movement, a process of rocking, and for the frenzy of Bacchic women a strain of impassioned music.[3] In each case, he points out, the unrest was due to fear, an unhealthy condition of the soul; and external agitation, subduing the agitation within, brought about finally a state of peace and calm in the soul.[4] Here then was expounded the homoeopathic principle, that of curing emotion by means of emotion; and it only remained for Aristotle in due course to extend its application to tragedy. On yet one other aspect of tragedy does Plato comment in suggestive fashion, when he attempts an explanation of the pleasure arising out of the tragic spectacle. He conceives of the existence of "mixed feelings" in human nature; a whole range of emotions—anger, fear, malice, and the like—which, though painful in character, were not devoid of pleasure when freely indulged.[5] Thus Homer, he points out, had spoken of the delight in giving free rein to anger; and it was possible, adds Plato, to revel in lamentation. To these facts, then, he ascribes the pleasure in tragedy; and the explanation, ingenious if not wholly satisfying, was at least as adequate as many that have since been made in connexion with this most puzzling of psychological questions.[6]

Equally valuable are his remarks on comedy, with which indeed may be said to begin the theory of the ludicrous as

---

[1] *Laws*, 817 b.
[2] Cf. "pity" (*Rep.* 605 d), "fear" (*ibid.* 387 b–d); see also *Phaedrus*, 268 c.
[3] *Laws*, 790 d–e.
[4] *Ibid.* 791 a; see Butcher, *Aristotle's Theory of Poetry and Fine Arts*, pp. 250–1.
[5] *Philebus*, 47 d–48 a.   [6] See W. M. Dixon, *Tragedy*, chs. 1–6.

formulated in antiquity. In view of the large element of satire in the old Attic comedy, Plato not unnaturally takes as the essence of the comic the malicious pleasure afforded by the discomfiture of another. Such mirth, he explains, is generally evoked by the sight of self-ignorance or self-conceit, as when a man fancies himself wiser, more handsome, or more virtuous than he really is; and this self-ignorance, he adds, must be present in one who is powerless to inflict hurt on others, otherwise he would cease to be a source of mirth and become a source of danger instead.[1] This then is the substance of Plato's conception of the comic; harmless self-conceit, the quality that provokes laughter, a sort of malicious joy, the resulting emotion. And here Plato in some measure anticipates Hobbes who was to define laughter as "a sudden glory arising from some sudden conception of some eminence in ourselves, by comparison with the infirmity of others, or with our own formerly".[2] But Plato's further comments are also of interest. He notes for instance that the emotion thus aroused is of a mixed kind (as in tragedy), being a blend of malice, which is painfully-toned, along with sensations of a more delightful kind. Then, too, he discusses the ludicrous as the outcome to some extent of defects in friends (τὴν τῶν φίλων ἕξιν...γελοίαν εἶναι), i.e. those with whom we are in sympathy;[3] and here he seems to be hinting at a profound truth. For true laughter is evoked only when we like the person exposed, a Falstaff for instance; whereas the ridicule of one disliked is productive of pure malice, not comedy. Hence, further, his injunctions as to the range and use of comedy. All personal satire and all serious, ill-natured ridicule he condemns outright; and what he commends is that comedy alone which is concerned with the production of innocent humour.[4] Apart from this he sees dangers in an unseasonable employment of comedy and in an excess of laughter. "Excessive laughter", he explains,[5] "always leads on to violent reactions"; "a man in the habit of laughing

---

[1] *Philebus*, 48 b–49 c.
[2] Hobbes, *Human Nature*, ch. IX; quoted by Butcher, *op. cit.* p. 374. Cf. also Hobbes, *Leviathan*, ch. VI.
[3] *Phil.* 49 e.   [4] *Laws*, 935 e.   [5] *Rep.* 388 e.

at others", he adds,[1] "ceases to be serious, and misses greatness
for the most part"; and here he was probably following
Socrates who had held that "one should use laughter as one
uses salt".[2] At the same time he also suggests that comedy is
not without its uses, inasmuch as it enlarges our conceptions of
human nature and shows what actions are to be avoided as
ridiculous. "Serious things", he states,[3] "cannot be understood apart from laughable things"; and if these are not the
most cogent arguments from a modern point of view, they are
at least relevant from Plato's own standpoint.

There is yet one other important branch of literary theory in
which Plato does valuable pioneer work, that is, in connexion
with rhetoric. And here again he not only gives new direction
to earlier theorising; he also lays down certain broad principles
which from now on were to be fundamental, and characteristic
of all later study. In the first place, the new movement inaugurated by Gorgias and Thrasymachus for the improvement
of oratorical style he submits to a rigorous criticism. Not that
their devices for adding pomp and glitter to style were wholly
without merit. They embodied in a sense the earliest efforts
at raising expression above the level of colloquial and pedestrian
prose; and as such they might be regarded as representing the
first, and perhaps a necessary, stage in the development of style.
At the same time in their aims and methods alike Plato found
much that was radically wrong; and in the *Gorgias* he therefore
indicts the whole system in scathing terms. And this he supplements by his discussion in the *Phaedrus*, where he submits
principles of a more positive kind, and also extends his treatment beyond that of public speech, so as to include prose style
in general. First among Plato's complaints is the charge that
rhetoric as practised by his contemporaries had no regard for
either truth or justice.[4] Accepted by all as an art of persuasion,
its main object was said to be that of perverting facts and
producing false impressions, by the use of fine language,
spurious arguments, and all the possible tricks of pandering

[1] *Laws*, 935 b.
[2] See Stobaeus, *Florilegium* (3, 34, 18), ed. Wachsmuth u. Hense, 3, 686.
[3] *Laws*, 816 d.   [4] *Gorg.* 453 ff.

to the mob. And as such, Plato denounces it for a sham and a flattery:[1] a means, solely, of tickling the palate with words and phrases, and of giving to the ignorant a sort of ignoble pleasure. Then, too, he fails to detect in the current rhetoric the necessary qualities of an art. To him it was nothing more than the workings of shrewd and forceful minds skilled in handling men; a mere knack picked up by experience (ἐμπειρία καὶ τριβή),[2] but without any sound or rational basis. And he further derides the methods of contemporary rhetoricians, who were content to teach in mechanical fashion the recognised divisions of a speech—the exordium, the statement of facts, proofs, probabilities, confirmation, and the rest[3]—along with further divisions and sub-divisions, and an abundance of technical jargon, to which ingenuities each new teacher contributed in turn. Such efforts, declared Plato, did but scratch the surface; they dealt with non-essentials, with details that constituted merely the preliminaries of the art. And what was therefore needed was a more searching analysis, a more rational treatment, with attention directed to the things that really mattered. And this treatment Plato forthwith supplies, calling attention to four main principles that constitute the essence of the rhetorical art. To begin with, he notes as the first essential in all good speaking (or writing) a sound knowledge of the subject treated;[4] and here he had primarily in mind those contemporary orators who in their appeal to the prejudices of their hearers were content to deal with "opinion" rather than truth. Yet in his insistence on the need for sound subject-matter Plato was enunciating a truth of the first importance and of universal application. In order to write well it is necessary to have something to say; and sound thinking as the root of all good writing was not the least of the injunctions handed down from antiquity. At the same time he is aware that something more is required for artistic expression in prose. True rhetoric he defined as a sort of enchantment of the soul (ψυχαγωγία),[5] the result of verbal sorcery; and for that, above all, a knowledge of art was needed. Not that an acquaintance

---

[1] *Gorg.* 462c.   [2] *Ibid.* 463b; cf. also ἄτεχνος τριβή (*Phaedrus*, 260e).
[3] *Phaedrus*, 266e ff.   [4] *Ibid.* 260.   [5] *Ibid.* 261a.

with artistic principles was all-sufficing; for perfection in achievement, he held, was subject to universal law, whatever the field of activity might be. First was needed a natural gift for the particular task, then a knowledge of the principles governing that sort of work, and lastly, practice in the work itself. And these requirements held good in the matter of rhetoric. Natural endowment (φύσις) came first, then a knowledge of art (ἐπιστήμη), and finally, constant practice (μελέτη);[1] and the recognition of these three requisites constituted the second of Plato's great principles. This brings him then to the nature of that art; and, working as before from general principles, he points out that in all expression there is a natural or necessary sequence of thought, which determines the form of a particular composition and gives to it a sort of organic unity.[2] Of this characteristic of art in general something has already been said;[3] and Plato emphasises its importance in connexion with expression in prose. For good speaking (or writing), he maintains, a clear view of the subject as a whole must be attained; there must be a coherent plan, due articulation of the parts, and vital relations governing the whole structure. And in this insistence on the need for order and arrangement in prose lay the third of Plato's main principles. Nor was his fourth and last principle any less fundamental in character; for recognising that success in speaking (or writing) depended largely on the effects produced on hearers (or readers), Plato urges the necessity for applying psychology to the task of expression.[4] Just as the physician, he points out, considers the nature of men's bodies, so the true orator (or writer), he adds, must take into account the nature of men's souls. He must be aware of their various temperaments and moods, the different ways in which they are affected, and the times and seasons for making his appeal; and it was only by such means that he could speak (or write) well knowingly. A scientific knowledge of the workings of men's minds, in short, was essential for all good speaking and writing.

These then are among the more fundamental and far-reaching of the literary doctrines originated by Plato; and

[1] *Phaedrus*, 269d.   [2] *Ibid.* 264c.   [3] See pp. 54–5 *supra*.   [4] *Phaedrus*, 270ff.

embracing as they do basic ideas concerning the nature and
art of poetry, some of the governing principles as well of
tragedy, comedy, and prose style, it is not too much to claim
for this aspect of his work a unique and lasting value, sufficient
to warrant his inclusion among the great pathfinders in the
field of criticism. Yet this by no means completes the tale of
his contributions to the critical development. In his pages will
be found an abundance of further material, views casually
expressed on this or that aspect of the literary art, passing
references to current doctrines, or again passages that bear on
the business of literary judgment; and all alike have their
interest, if not of an intrinsic, yet most certainly of an historical,
kind. To begin with, there are the views he expresses as to
the function of poetry; and it is everywhere clear that to him
its main purpose is something more than the mere giving of
pleasure. In the *Philebus*, for instance, pleasure of the highest
kind ranks but fifth in the scale of goods; and poetry as merely
a pleasure-giving instrument he would class with the art of the
sophist or pastrycook.[1] That there is an innate charm in poetry
he is prepared to admit;[2] but that the communication of this
charm was the main business of the poet he stoutly denies. To
him the real and ultimate end of poetry was none other than
the influencing and the moulding of human character; the
bringing out of the best that was latent in the soul; thus
enabling men to better their lives and to rebuild the world
"nearer to the heart's desire". And this being so it followed
that the poetic art he advocated was one characterised by a
certain austerity and severe restriction—the first expression, as
it were, of the classical ideal in art, with its primary demand for
a simplicity based on order and restraint. Nor was this pronouncement merely a reaction from the relaxed and formless
complexity of the art of his own day. It was due rather to the
positive conviction that simpler methods and standards were
essential in the interests of character and taste. And the idea
runs throughout all his teaching: in his basic demands for an
organic unity and for order in general, and in what he says on
the matter of *decorum*, that claim for fitness and propriety which

---

[1] *Gorg.* 462 e ff.; *Rep.* 373 b–c.   [2] Cf. *Laws*, 667.

was to characterise most of the later critics. Thus he frequently condemns incongruities of style, melody, and rhythm;[1] he attacks also the ridiculous mixtures of effects that were a feature of the contemporary drama.[2] And whereas in more positive vein he demands, as we have seen, that all utterance should be suited to the hearer (or reader),[3] in one place he commends Prodicus's statement as to the governing principle of all artistic expression, namely, that of being neither long nor short, but of a moderate or convenient (μέτριος) length.[4] Furthermore, he discusses more than once the possibility of establishing permanent canons of aesthetic taste.[5] That such laws were possible he shows by a reference to the fixed forms of Egyptian sculpture and music, which had existed from time immemorial. And his suggestion seems to be that provided an art could be evolved having a natural truth and correctness, all innovations would represent departures from literature of the highest kind. It is true that he does not actually recommend such a stereotyping of art—the conception which was to prevail centuries later at the Renascence. Yet it cannot be denied that he plays with the idea, without regard to the possibilities of future literary development. Elsewhere he shows himself to be possessed of the historical sense, as when for instance he traces the development of society in both the *Republic* and the *Laws*; but this consideration does not enter into his discussion of aesthetic and literary matters.

Of less importance, perhaps, though still not without their interest are those further passages in which he alludes to some current theory, or anticipates others that were to be familiar at a later date. In one place, for example, he divides all writers into two classes, those who write in metre as poets (ἐν μέτρῳ ὡς ποιητής), and those who write without metre as prose-writers (ἄνευ μέτρου ὡς ἰδιώτης).[6] And here he is making use of a popular conception of poetry, according to which verse was said to be its essential element; a conception which was subsequently to be modified by Aristotle. Then, too, in his

---

[1] Cf. *Rep.* 399.   [2] *Ibid.* 397.   [3] *Phaedrus*, 270.
[4] *Ibid.* 267b.   [5] *Laws*, 656d ff., 797ff.
[6] *Phaedrus*, 258d; cf. also *Ion*, 534c for a classification of poets based on differences of verse-forms.

pages we find the first reference to poetic justice;[1] that doctrine
which prescribed an ideal equity in the fates of the good and the
bad, and which was destined to survive long in critical thought.
With him also appears first the idea of the "eternising"
function of poetry,[2] a theme that was to be repeated by Horace
and more especially by poets at the Renascence. Elsewhere
again he makes use of what was possibly a commonplace at the
time, that love was a prime source and inspiration of poetry: and
in this connexion he quotes the dictum of Euripides that "at the
touch of love everyone becomes a poet, though incapable of
poetry before".[3] Nor must we forget the idea he throws out
concerning the fundamental unity of poetic gifts. To his contemporaries the geniuses of comedy and tragedy were essentially
different, being the results of the inspiration of different Muses.[4]
To Plato, however, the genius of poetry was one and undivided;
he who could compose a tragedy by art ($\tau\acute{\epsilon}\chi\nu\eta$) was capable
also of composing a comedy.[5] Then too on style and language
he has also some interesting remarks to make; and notable in
the first place is his conception of style as a reflexion of character
($\acute{o}$ $\tau\rho\acute{o}\pi os\ldots\tau\hat{\omega}$ $\tau\hat{\eta}s$ $\psi\upsilon\chi\hat{\eta}s$ $\mathring{\eta}\theta\epsilon\iota$ $\mathring{\epsilon}\pi\epsilon\tau\alpha\iota$).[6] In antiquity this idea
gave rise to the doctrine of the *vir bonus*, according to which
morality was inseparably bound up with skill in eloquence;
whereas to later ages it was an anticipation of the dictum that
"style is the man". Apart from this he was among the first to
speculate on grammar; and in *Cratylus* more especially he discusses the origin and nature of language in the light of current
theories. According to Heraclitus (who was followed by
Cratylus) words existed by nature, being the natural images of
visible things; whereas Hermogenes held language to be conventional, arbitrarily imposed, and therefore capable of being
modified at pleasure. Plato's theory was in the main a combination of both; he held that while language was originally
based on nature, it was subsequently modified by convention;

[1] *Rep.* 392a–b; *Laws*, 660e.
[2] *Symp.* 209c; Professor J. F. Mountford points out that the idea is implicit in
Pindar (*Nem.* VII, 12). See also H. C. Beeching, *Sonnets of Shakespeare*, p. xxviii.
[3] *Symp.* 196e; the fragment is from *Stheneboea*, and is quoted later by
Plutarch, see vol. II, 316–7.
[4] Cf. *Ion*, 536a–b.   [5] *Symp.* 223d.   [6] *Rep.* 400d.

and here were involved principles which at a later date were
to give rise to the dispute concerning Analogy and Anomaly.
Nor were Plato's further comments without their interest. He
notes for instance that in linguistic development chance plays
a part, that language is subject to foreign influences and to
influences of time. Moreover he analyses the sound-qualities
of the various letters, pointing out among other details the
harshness of ϕ, ψ, σ and ζ, the liquid quality of λ, and the
rounded effects of o;[1] so that here, as in the sphere of literary
theory, Plato figures as a pioneer who prepared the way for
those who were to follow.

It yet remains to deal with his activities as a judicial critic.
And whereas this aspect of his work will be found to be perhaps
the least considerable, it is by no means devoid of interest, in
view of his remarks on the standards and methods of forming
judgment, and his occasional comments on existing literature.
Significant in the first place is his refusal to accept pleasure as
the sole or even the main test of literary merit. He denies, as
we have seen, that pleasure is the true aim of the poet; and he
is therefore so far consistent in his contention that poetry must
be judged by some other standard. Moreover he points out its
inadequacy as a test, since pleasure means one thing to childhood, another to youth, and yet another to old age;[2] so that the
real criterion of literary value, he asserts, is truth, and not the
pleasure given.[3] At the same time he admits that all art has its
charm; and elsewhere he agrees that a test of excellence may
also be the delight afforded by a given piece of art. To this
however he adds the proviso that such a test must be applied
by those qualified to judge. It must not be the delight of chance
persons, but rather of "the best and best educated, and
especially of the one man who is pre-eminent in virtue and
education" ($\H{\epsilon}\nu\alpha$ $\tau\grave{o}\nu$ $\mathring{\alpha}\rho\epsilon\tau\mathring{\eta}$ $\tau\epsilon$ $\kappa\alpha\grave{\iota}$ $\pi\alpha\iota\delta\epsilon\acute{\iota}\alpha$ $\delta\iota\alpha\phi\acute{\epsilon}\rho\sigma\nu\tau\alpha$).[4] The
true critic must, in fact, have wisdom and courage; he must
lead the many and not be led by them. And here Plato was
protesting against the view that the tastes of the general public
are the standards of literary excellence: an assumption which

[1] *Crat.* 427.
[2] *Laws*, 658.
[3] *Ibid.* 667-9.
[4] *Ibid.* 658e (tr. Jowett).

in his view had led to disastrous consequences in his own day.[1]
He was also raising one of those fundamental questions in
which his works abound. On the methods of forming judgment
Plato has not much to say; though his occasional hints are not
unworthy of note. One significant pronouncement, for instance, is that where he states that for the interpretation of
poetry some knowledge of poetry as a whole, and of the principles of its art, is necessary.[2] Originally applied to the Homeric
criticism of the rhapsode Ion, the statement has also a wider
bearing that can scarcely have been without its influence on
later writers. Or again, there is his commentary on the mis-
guided methods of Protagoras and others in their efforts at estimating the value of an ode of Simonides. Their verbal quibbles,
characteristic of contemporary critics, he simply ridicules. But
at the same time he points to a better way, in calling attention to
the workmanship of the poem, and its abundance of charming
detail; and in suggesting further that the true interpretation of
the poem lay in its meaning as a whole, and not in isolated
phrases.[3] Of his actual judgments on literature something has
already been said; and in the first place he condemns in no uncertain fashion the vulgar and morbid sensations of the contemporary stage, its lack of decorum, and its lawless innovations.[4]
Nor is this the whole of his complaint. Among other abuses
to which he alludes is the weakness of tragic poets for resorting to
the *deus ex machina* in any perplexity;[5] and in the distinction he
draws, rather pointedly it would seem, between ethical mono-
logues and properly constituted tragedies,[6] he may also have had
in mind yet another weakness of contemporary dramatists—a
tendency to rely on rhetoric rather than on plot. Apart from this
he has occasional comments to make on the orators and prose-
writers of the time; and most familiar perhaps are his remarks
on Lysias whom he commends for his sentiments, the clearness
and finish of his style, while condemning his neglect of ordered
arrangement of thought, and his indulgence in repetitions.[7]
More generally, however, Plato uses for this purpose the

[1] See p. 37 *supra*.   [2] *Ion*, 532 c.   [3] *Protag.* 344 b.
[4] See p. 37 *supra*.   [5] *Crat.* 425 e.   [6] *Phaedrus*, 268 c–269 a.
[7] *Ibid.* 234 c–235 a, 264.

instrument of parody, which in his hands becomes something of a fine art; and instances of such indirect comment are found where he parodies the formal manner of Protagoras, or again, the sonorous pedantic style of Hippias.[1] For yet more effective treatments we must turn to the *Symposium*, where, in a speech of Pausanias, are travestied the unmeaning tricks of rhythm and the neglect of ordered thought then fashionable;[2] while of still greater interest is the parody of the mannered style of Agathon,[3] which constitutes a masterpiece of its kind. In it are ruthlessly reproduced in yet more artistic fashion the insincerity and extravagance, the verbal patterns and the studied rhythmical effects associated with Gorgias and his school; and in this "fanciful tissue of jewelled conceits" we have a lively commentary not only on an individual but on all the "fine" writers of Plato's and other ages.

These then are among the main details of Plato's work as a critic; and in any attempt to sum up his critical performance a leading place must assuredly be given to those theories already mentioned, to that positive and constructive side of his work in which the substance of his achievement really lies. Compared with this, his so-called attack on poetry is of but secondary interest; while in his occasional judicial criticism he has obviously not much to offer. It is in short as a pioneer in literary theory that he figures mainly in the critical development; with him begins that larger and more philosophical criticism which aimed at viewing literature in its relation to life, and at arriving if possible at the innermost laws of its being. And its fruits are seen in those theories he propounds concerning poetry, its nature, its art, and its function, as well as in the principles he lays down for a higher rhetoric. Of the value of his methods moreover there can be no question; though his mode of revealing truth by lights and shadows, and by opposing different points of view, is at times confusing and perplexing. Apart from this, however, he works everywhere from first principles, consistently applying the psychological method to literary problems, on the ground that, since all

[1] *Protag.* 337 ff.; cf. also the parody of Polus's style in *Gorg.* 448 c.
[2] *Symp.* 180 ff.   [3] *Ibid.* 194 e–197 e.

artists aimed at affecting men's hearts, a knowledge of human nature was necessary for the proper understanding of art. Then, too, his theories are the outcome of no cold intellectualism; they are the product of a happy combination of logic and feeling, of an imaginative reason which allowed him to indulge in daring speculation, and yet at all times was instrumental in controlling his flight. And such processes account for the sanity and suggestiveness of his doctrines, and for his profound insight into the essence of art. That much of his thought was inspired by others has already been stated; it was in some measure derived from Socrates and the pre-Socratic philosophers. Yet that thought he re-interprets and transforms into something new, handing it on with the impress of his own genius, clothed too in simple language, the grace and beauty of which have never been surpassed. What therefore he says, he commends by his way of saying it; his glowing fancy, his idealism, his irony and humour, all go to make him one of the most persuasive of theorists, a philosopher, "the very dust of whose writings is gold".

Yet a mere list of theories or an analysis of his methods by no means explains fully the value of Plato's performance; nor does it account for his enduring influence down to the present day. For that we must look to the supreme quality of his achievement which lay in the unerring certainty with which he grasped fundamentals, passing instinctively to the heart of an inquiry, and bringing to light truths of a profound and permanent kind. Of these some instances have already been given; his recognition of the need for a logic of art, and for that organic fusion which goes by the name of unity; or again, the emphasis laid on clear thinking as a necessary preliminary to artistic expression. But his work is full of these far-reaching and penetrating pronouncements, often implied or hinted at in some general discussion. Thus he is the first to recognise adequately the mysterious power of poetry, its inexhaustible vitality, and its faculty of communicating life. It is true that he chooses for his illustration the radiating influence of a magnet;[1] whereas to Milton the virtue was that of the "precious life-blood of a

[1] *Ion*, 533.

master-spirit".[1] Yet in the minds of both the same idea was present; and it constitutes one of the deepest truths concerning literature. Or again, there is his re-interpretation of the traditional "poetic madness". This he takes to mean the emotional element present in all great art, and capable at its best of visions beyond the ken of reason; yet another of those ideas that lie at the root of our modern aesthetics, and which are present in Wordsworth's familiar description of poetry as "the spontaneous overflow of powerful feelings".[2] Then, too, of the first importance is his advocacy of a poetry based on an imita-tion of the ideal world, and produced in the light of ideal know-ledge. Here he would seem to have had in mind a poetry of a philosophic kind, having for its subject-matter the ideal forms of justice, truth, and beauty. Yet in this demand were embodied yet other fundamental principles, namely, that poetry at its best should deal with what was great and noble in human nature, and that, further, it should embody truth of a permanent and universal kind. It remained for Aristotle to show that such universal truth could be, and was, attained through the parti-cular by the poet; but the demand for an apprehension of reality had first been made by Plato. Nor must we forget, above all, his illuminating remarks on the essential virtue of art, more particularly in its relation to human life. Indeed, nowhere is his vision more penetrating or convincing; and his estimate still remains perhaps the most adequate pronouncement on the subject. Thus to him art is first and foremost an influence, not a means of instruction; it is said to aim primarily at moulding character and not at imparting moral principles or doctrines. And upon this he enlarges in more than one place. The first business of art, he explains, is to open men's eyes to the beauty of things ($\dot{\iota}\chi\nu\epsilon\dot{\upsilon}\epsilon\iota\nu$ $\tau\dot{\eta}\nu$ $\tau o\hat{\upsilon}$ $\kappa\alpha\lambda o\hat{\upsilon}$ $\tau\epsilon$ $\kappa\alpha\dot{\iota}$ $\epsilon\dot{\upsilon}\sigma\chi\dot{\eta}\mu o\nu o\varsigma$ $\phi\dot{\upsilon}\sigma\iota\nu$),[3] to what is great and noble in human nature; and then with its gracious effluences it invades men's souls, and, like some health-giving breeze, it nurtures in them what is good and noble.[4] The same idea is present in his description of the pro-cess as a turning of the soul's eye to the light.[5] And here again

[1] *Areopagitica*, ed. Coterill, p. 5.   [2] *Preface to Lyrical Ballads.*
[3] *Rep.* 401 c.   [4] *Ibid.* 401 c–402 a.   [5] *Ibid.* 518 c.

there is no question of direct teaching, but rather of bringing out the best that was latent in the soul by directing it to right ends. Elsewhere, it is true, there is a suggestion of the imparting of knowledge, where an acquaintance with the reflected world of art is said to enable men to read more correctly the world around them, by helping them to discern qualities of excellence wherever they are found.[1] But even here what is claimed to be imparted is a right sense of values, not moral doctrine; and in point of fact, Plato is as far removed from later moralistic theorists, as he is from those who advocated an "Art for Art's sake".

It is therefore in such places as these that the real greatness of Plato as a critic is perhaps best seen. And viewing his work as a whole, it may fairly be said that with him literary theory really begins. What he did was to make later criticism possible; he set men thinking, he gave inspiration and direction to critical effort, and at the same time he supplied ideas for generations to come. Nor must we forget the challenging nature of many of his utterances; for this fact undoubtedly gave a further stimulus to criticism. It is true that he left not a few problems for later discussion; among others, the question of terminology, the meaning of "imitation" and the like. At the same time, as we have seen, he was something more than a mere pathfinder. He stands for something positive and constructive in the critical sphere. His findings and his methods alike are of great and permanent value; he placed criticism from the first on an exalted plane; and he has something to say to all the ages. After he had written, the beneficent character of art had been once for all revealed. Poetry ceased to be regarded as mere technique, and became instead one of the loftiest and most mysterious of human activities; and in the meantime, the foundations of a higher rhetoric had also been laid. Yet valuable as was his teaching, his influence proved to be more subtle and enduring still. Formerly described as "the father of the greatest of critical heresies", to-day he is more fairly regarded as "the fountain of that which is most living in the orthodoxy of later ages". Right down to recent times, his

[1] *Rep.* 402 b–c.

ideas of poetry have acted as an unfailing stimulus to men's minds, leading them from the formal, the pedantic, and the petty, turning their eyes to the things that really matter, and causing them to rebel against the tyranny of the rule. And his influence remains to the present day, that of one of the greatest of critics, in the truest sense a light-bringer, ever guiding men's steps to the spiritual side of art.

CHAPTER IV

THE DEVELOPMENT OF POETIC THEORY:
ARISTOTLE[1]

THE same period which had produced in Plato one of the great masters of criticism witnessed also the arrival of another outstanding genius in the person of Aristotle (384–322 B.C.), a pupil of the earlier philosopher, whose work he was to develop on lines of his own, thereby bringing to light in connexion with art leading principles of great and permanent value. The achievements of the two critics differed as the men themselves—in their objectives, their geniuses, and their methods of work. Plato had set out to reorganise human life; he was a transcendentalist, a poet, whose splendidly suggestive *a priori* theories were presented indirectly in dialogues of enduring charm, and who wrote with an eye to the social needs of the state. Aristotle's aim, on the other hand, was to reorganise human knowledge: he was a scientist, an experimentalist, one who arrived at his principles by observation and analysis, and who normally set forth his theories in direct dogmatic fashion, but without any of the charm of Plato's work. Yet while there are clear differences, there is also between the two critics a close connexion as well. Aristotle throughout his work is covertly criticising Plato; his mind is filled with Platonic ideas; and everywhere in his discussions he draws upon Plato's doctrines and terminology, reinterpreting or confuting, while engaged in developing new doctrines of his own.

Any attempt at surveying Aristotle's achievement as a critic must however begin with some notice of his actual works. And it may at once be said that, like Plato, he is concerned with poetry and rhetoric alike, and that he endeavours to expound

[1] *Texts and Translations:* Aristotle, *Poetics*, text and trans. in S. H. Butcher, *Aristotle's Theory of Poetry and Fine Art*, London, 1895, pp. 1–111; ed. with trans. I. Bywater, Oxford, 1909; ed. with trans. W. Hamilton Fyfe (Loeb Lib.), London and New York, 1927; ed. A. Gudeman, Berlin, 1934; trans. by E. S. Bouchier, Oxford, 1907; Lane Cooper, *Aristotle on the Art of Poetry*, Boston, 1913; Twining's trans. ed. by T. A. Moxon (Everyman's Lib.), London, 1934; extracts (trans.) in G. Saintsbury, *Loci Critici*, London, 1903 (pp. 1–21); in J. D. Denniston, *Greek Lit. Crit.* (pp. 115–36).

a coherent theory of each, as if in accordance with the Platonic doctrine that for judgment in literature a knowledge of art was required.[1] Those theories he develops in his *Poetics* and *Rhetoric*; works to which no definite date can be assigned, though they probably belong to the maturity of his genius, to that period at Athens, when as head of the Lyceum (335–322 B.C.) he was organising research in every field of inquiry, and producing his systematic works of philosophy and science. Other critical works, now lost, he had also written; and among them were some early dialogues intended for popular reading, and written in a style subsequently commended by Cicero. To this class belong the works *On Rhetoric* and *On Poets*, the latter of which has been claimed to be the source of certain definitions of tragedy and comedy which were destined to play a large part in later critical history.[2] Whether this claim is justified has been seriously questioned; but what seems certain is that in these dialogues Aristotle had attempted a popular treatment of literary topics in imitation of Plato, and that their loss has deprived us of some interesting side-lights on Aristotelian theory. Apart from these works, to Aristotle are also attributed the *Didascaliae*, a record of the dates of various plays, whereby were founded literary chronology and history, and, in addition, the *Homeric Problems*, excerpts from which in the scholia are all that have survived. It may safely be taken, however, that in the *Poetics* and the *Rhetoric* the essence of Aristotle's critical thought has been preserved; and with them we have reached one of the supreme moments of critical history. While the *Rhetoric* is a philosophical treatise of unrivalled freshness and interest, the *Poetics* is a more or less systematic exposition of the theory and practice of poetry, which has exercised men's minds as few works of any age have done. In them both it is clear that criticism is entering on a new phase; we are there introduced to an important body of doctrine, to new and fruitful methods of theorising, as well as to original and profound ideas of the utmost significance in the critical development. And with the *Poetics* it is proposed to deal in the present chapter, as representing Aristotle's contribution to poetic theory.

[1] See p. 65 *supra*.   [2] See p. 159 *infra*, and vol. II, p. 39, 140 ff.

Before entering upon an analysis of the *Poetics* itself it is necessary, at the outset, to recall the real character of the work, the place it occupies in Aristotle's philosophy, and the nature of the truth enshrined in its pages. And the explanation of these things is supplied by Aristotle himself. He was the first to realise the importance of ordered knowledge; and his contribution to criticism forms part of a larger and an original scheme which aimed at nothing less than a survey of all knowledge, and thus included many sciences differing in kind.[1] Among the various branches of his philosophy, the *Poetics*, as well as the *Rhetoric*, belongs to what are known as the productive sciences; and these, together with the practical sciences, which were Politics and Ethics, differed vitally in character from what were known as the theoretical sciences, namely, Mathematics, Physics, and Metaphysics. The immediate purpose of all sciences alike was "to know"; but between the ultimate purposes of the productive and practical sciences on the one hand, and of the theoretical sciences on the other, there were important differences. Whereas the theoretical sciences aimed merely at knowledge and the contemplation of knowledge, the final object of the productive and practical sciences was the application of knowledge to some definite end. Thus the practical sciences aimed at knowledge with a view to influencing conduct, the productive sciences at knowledge with a view to making useful and beautiful objects; and this broad difference had its counterpart in the different nature of the truth arrived at in the theoretical as opposed to the other sciences. Upon this fact Aristotle insists in more than one place. The theoretical sciences, he maintained, dealt with matters independent of human volition, and therefore aimed at truth of a universal kind. The productive and practical sciences, on the other hand, had to do with matters into which the human factor entered; and in consequence they could yield only general rules, rules which held good in the majority of cases, but which lacked the finality of the truths of the theoretical sciences. Hence the real nature of the *Poetics* and also of the *Rhetoric*. As representatives of the productive sciences in Aristotle's scheme of philosophy,

[1] See A. E. Taylor, *Aristotle*, pp. 15-19.

they are not concerned primarily with a knowledge of art for its own sake; nor are they intended to supply universal truths about things that are fixed and unalterable. Their intention was merely to help in the making of a good poet or orator, by formulating rules of a general kind, that is, rules with no claim to any sort of finality. And this fact has to be remembered in any attempt to understand the works and their teaching. It is especially important in view of later history, and the use made of the *Poetics* at the Renascence.

Turning now to the *Poetics*, something must first be said as to its general plan and contents. And in the first place the treatise will be found to be surprisingly short. It consists of but twenty-six chapters, comprised in forty-five small pages; though there are grounds for thinking that it is imperfect as it stands, and that a second Book has been lost,[1] which contained in all probability a theory of comedy, as well as Aristotle's explanation of the much-discussed term "catharsis". As it is, however, the work includes among its main items certain introductory remarks on the nature of poetry, some fragments of epic theory, a few notes on comedy, poetic diction, and critical problems, as well as a theory of tragedy constituting more than half of the work—to all appearances neither an exhaustive, nor yet a coherent, treatment of the subject with which it purports to deal. Nor is the general plan any more reassuring. The first five chapters (I–V) are introductory to the main subject of the treatise, which is a discussion of poetry and its various kinds. Thus Aristotle begins with some general remarks on art; he deals summarily with the various imitative arts, reveals their psychological motives, and then sketches rapidly the early history of poetry, and the evolution of the various forms, including tragedy and comedy. The next fourteen chapters (VI–XIX) are devoted to tragedy. A definition is given, and the several formative elements, namely, plot, character, and the rest, are specified; but the discussion is confined almost wholly to plot, with one chapter (XV) on character, and two (XVII–XVIII) on practical hints for the tragic poet. Then some consideration is given to poetic diction (XX–XXII), though gram-

---

[1] See *Poetics*, ed. Bywater, Intro. xxff.

matical details are discussed at somewhat inordinate length. And lastly the epic is treated (XXIII–XXVI) in brief though pregnant fashion, particularly with regard to its value as compared with that of tragedy; and by way of digression, reference is also made to current problems in criticism, and the principles underlying their solution (XXV).

Such then in rough outline is the subject-matter of the work; and as a systematic treatise on poetry and its kinds, it has certain obvious defects. No one for instance can fail to notice a marked disproportion in Aristotle's handling of his subject. Lyric poetry, for one thing, is practically ignored; comedy and the epic are but slightly treated; and while on the other hand the larger part of the discussion is devoted to tragedy, it is upon the nature of the plot and the effects of tragedy that interest is mainly concentrated. A procedure of this kind at first sight seems fatal to a scheme which professed to deal with the whole art of poetry; and the treatment at any rate is perplexing to modern readers. Yet to Aristotle's contemporaries most probably no serious difficulties would have presented themselves. Tragedy to them would stand as the form in which all earlier poetry culminated. It was serious poetry in its latest and highest development, and therefore the only kind that called for intensive study. As for lyrical poetry, it would be capable of adding nothing to the inquiry. An elementary form of art, representing an early stage in the evolution of tragedy, an ancillary form as well, constituting a mere ornament in the completed drama, the lyric would normally be classed with music rather than with poetry proper, and could therefore be neglected in an investigation which aimed at revealing the essence of poetry. In thus attaching to tragedy an importance not warranted by later history, Aristotle was therefore betraying some of the limitations of his age. In fact his work throughout is coloured by contemporary influences; and to such influences may perhaps be attributed the consideration he gives to the plot and function of tragedy, which he singles out, as we have seen, for special and intensive treatment.

Apart from this partial treatment of the subject proposed, some amount of difficulty is also presented by the style and form of the work. Belonging as it does to the "acroamatic" or advanced discourses of Aristotle, as distinguished from others of a popular kind, the *Poetics* is written in an esoteric style, in a style, that is, which was intended for the initiated, and for circles already familiar with the author's terminology and thought. The work thus demands from its readers a certain preliminary knowledge to enable them to supply what is left unsaid, or else to interpret what is said obscurely. As Lessing first pointed out, Aristotle must everywhere be interpreted by himself. His *Poetics* must be read in connexion with his *Politics*, his *Ethics*, and his *Metaphysics*; for if read in detachment, no work is more liable to be misinterpreted and misunderstood. And this initial difficulty is increased by the condition in which the work has come down. Apart from the missing second Book, the work is obviously not in a form intended for publication by its author, for there are irregularities and anomalies which suggest a lack of revision, while the material throughout is presented in a strangely unequal fashion.[1] Some passages, for instance, are written in a clear consecutive style, others, again, in a loose elliptical form; there are contradictions, digressions, omissions and other marks of haste; while there is also an occasional uncertainty in the use of terminology, technical terms like "imitation" being used in more senses than one, whereas other terms are employed without any sort of explanation. What these facts suggest is therefore a collection of Aristotle's MS. or lecture-notes posthumously edited by some of his pupils; and this is probably the genesis of the *Poetics*, a parallel for which would be found in the case of his *Ethics*.

In spite of all such difficulties, however, it is when we consider the methods employed and the lines along which Aristotle worked, that we begin to realise the true greatness of the *Poetics* and its epoch-making quality. Casting aside the "oracular" methods of earlier philosophers who had depended for their results on a sort of prophetic insight, Aristotle discards also Plato's intuitive and dialectic methods as being inadequate for the purpose in hand, which was a positive and coherent presentment of the truth in regard to poetry. For him to

[1] See *Poetics*, ed. Bywater, Intro. xivff.

know a thing was to perceive its essential qualities; and these qualities he seeks, where poetry was concerned, by a systematic analysis of the existing Greek poetry. Thus he starts from concrete facts, and his principles are generalisations based upon those facts. He analyses poetic compositions and the practice of the great masters, proceeding as in his *Politics*, which is based on inquiries into the constitutions of many city-states; so that his method is alike analytic, inductive, and scientific in the best senses of the terms. At the same time he is aware that the laws he seeks are not laws of an arbitrary kind, that they are, on the contrary, firmly rooted in human nature; and throughout his work he considers poetry in close relation to man. The origin of poetry, for example, he traces back to fundamental tendencies in human nature—to a faculty of imitation inborn in man, to the delight generally felt in the imitations of others, and also to the instinct for harmony and rhythm[1]—just as elsewhere he had ascribed philosophy to the human impulse of curiosity or wonder. Tragedy, again, he justifies by its emotional effects; and he also defines the tragic hero in terms of the qualities needed to bring about those effects, in this way making use of psychological methods in his theorising. Then, too, he occasionally approaches his subject from the historical point of view. Realising that to study things in their growth is often the best means of appreciating their essential qualities, he notes carefully the different phases in the evolution of Greek poetry; how the drama for instance arose out of lyric or choric poetry, or how, from certain tendencies present in the Homeric epic both tragedy and comedy were ultimately evolved.[2] Aristotle's treatment of these matters is far from complete; but what he says is suggestive in the highest degree, and has formed the starting-point of all later literary histories. A biologist and a historian, he was the first to apply these methods systematically to problems of literature; and he did it in such a way that later ages accepted blindly his doctrinal teaching, without realising at all adequately the basis of human study upon which those doctrines ultimately rested.

At the same time there is this further to be said, that sound

[1] 1448b, 5, 9, 20.   [2] 1448b, 34ff.

as Aristotle's methods undoubtedly were, his theories in the *Poetics* are not wholly the result of free reflexion. They were necessarily affected by contemporary influences and conditions; and while in part they were based on earlier theories and terminology, they were also conditioned by certain doctrines which he had to confute, partly also by certain urgent questions belonging to his own day. Thus there is little doubt whence Aristotle derived his theory of "imitation". Into the term, it is true, he read a new meaning; but the term itself was drawn from Plato and earlier authorities. Moreover the main trend of Aristotle's argument is determined by Plato's "attack" upon poetry. Plato, as we have seen, had challenged both tragedy and the epic on account of their nature and effects; he had demanded a poetry of a philosophic kind, produced in the light of ideal knowledge. And the nature of the attack determined the line of defence; Aristotle replies to both counts in Plato's indictment. Or again, there is Aristotle's treatment of such questions as the comparative value of tragedy and the epic, or the relative importance of plot and character in tragedy. Such questions as these do not necessarily arise out of a general exposition of poetry; and Aristotle probably considered them because they were subjects of controversy in his day, at a time, that is, when the claims of Homer and the great writers of tragedy were under debate,[1] and when the vitality of the drama was being threatened by anarchic tendencies, of which Aristophanes and Plato had already complained.

But it is after all as a storehouse of literary theory that the *Poetics* has won its place among the great world-books. What Aristotle had to teach in the way of critical method meant unfortunately but little to later ages; whereas his broad and comprehensive theories, his subtle and profound views on the nature of poetry, his suggestive and far-reaching hints as to literary technique constituted an achievement which none could mistake, though more adequately appreciated in some ages than others. His purpose was inevitably limited. From the very nature of the case, the *Poetics*, as a treatise on one of the "productive" sciences, did not aim at laws which were rigidly

[1] Cf. Plato's view, p. 55 *supra*.

universal. Nor indeed would this have been possible, seeing
that the material on which he worked was limited in kind; for
he dealt with Greek literature alone, with a literature, that is,
that had not as yet completed all its phases of development. It
is, moreover, significant that Aristotle's attitude throughout is
retrospective in kind; he is merely seeking the laws in the facts
that lie before him, and he makes no pronouncements as to the
literature of the future. In one place, indeed, he refrains from
making such pronouncement as being outside his purpose;[1] and
here he seems to be hinting at the possibility of relativity in
literary standards. Nevertheless, the miracle of the *Poetics* is
that it contains so much that is of permanent and universal
interest. And this is so because the literature upon which it
was based was no artificial product of a sophisticated society,
but the natural expression of a race guided solely by what was
elemental in human nature. And so the work is full of original
ideas that are as true to-day as when they were first formulated;
though with them are mingled others that are limited in their
application, and some again that are misleading or definitely
wrong. Yet all alike are historically interesting, owing to the use
made of them by later theorists; and part of Aristotle's achievement doubtless lay in having raised the essential problems, even
though he was not always successful in providing solutions.

In what he has to say, to begin with, about the nature of
poetry, there is much that is of first-rate importance. That
poetry had features in common with the rest of the fine arts;
was, moreover, like them, based on "imitation";[2] this much
at least he had learnt from Plato. But into the term "imitation"
he read a new and definite meaning, which made the poetic
process out to be not one of mere copying, but an act of creative
vision, by means of which the poet, while drawing for his
material on the phenomena of life, was enabled to make something new out of the real and actual. For his material the poet
could take "things as they were or are, things as they are said
or thought to be, or things as they ought to be";[3] in other
words, he could deal with facts past or present, with established
beliefs, or with ideals unrealised. But in each instance a trans-

---

[1] 1449a, 7.   [2] 1447a, 13–24.   [3] 1460b, 10–11.

forming process was implied; and for all practical purposes, "imitation" to Aristotle was none other than "re-creation".[1] But from this conception of "imitation" as a creative act Aristotle arrives at a new position, at what is perhaps his most valuable contribution to literary theory, namely, his conception of poetry as a revelation of the permanent and universal characteristics of human life and thought. For if poetry be no mere transcript of life, it is also something more than pure illusion. What the poet does is to construct out of the confused medley of everyday existence an intelligible picture, free from unreason, in which are revealed the permanent possibilities of human nature (τὰ δυνατὰ κατὰ τὸ εἰκὸς ἢ τὸ ἀναγκαῖον),[2] and therefore truth of an ideal or universal kind. Hence Aristotle's statement that "Poetry is a more philosophical or higher thing (φιλοσοφώτερον καὶ σπουδαιότερον) than History".[3] The historian, confining himself to particular happenings, to "what Alcibiades did or suffered", is everywhere subject to the tyranny of facts, whereas the poet, taking a larger and a generalised view of things, represents the universal in and through the particular, and so shares in the philosopher's quest for ultimate truth. Thus did Aristotle enunciate a doctrine which holds good for all the ages—the presence of a universal element in all great poetry, accounting for its permanent appeal—while at the same time he showed how a reconciliation might be effected between poetry and philosophy. Plato indeed had shown that an element of intuition was common to the processes of philosopher and poet alike: but it remained for Aristotle to complete the vindication of poetry, and to reconcile the claims of philosophy and poetry by showing that both were avenues to the highest truth. And hardly less important is the view that Aristotle takes of the function of poetry, namely, as the giving of a certain refined pleasure; a view in conflict with that which at the time prevailed, of the poet as being primarily an ethical teacher. In the *Poetics*, it is true, this hedonistic theory is nowhere explicitly stated; yet it may be

[1] See Butcher, *Aristotle's Theory of Poetry and Fine Art*, pp. 121–62, for a full discussion.

[2] 1451 a, 39.   [3] 1451 b, 5–6.

inferred from what is said about music in the *Politics* and *Metaphysics*,[1] while it is assumed throughout in the *Poetics*, as when, for instance, Aristotle demands from each kind of poetry its own appropriate pleasure.[2] At the same time, something more than pleasure is also aimed at. Aristotle holds that, for a normal and healthy public, the proper aesthetic pleasure is possible only when the requirements of morality are satisfied;[3] and so a certain moral effect he regards as inevitably bound up with the exercise of the poet's art. Yet this is not to say that the poet's aims are educational or didactic, or that moral improvement is the chief end of poetry. The fact is that Aristotle seems to distinguish between the aesthetic purpose and the moral effect; the former being to him essential, the latter incidental. It was one of his great discoveries which opened up an approach to poetry from an entirely new angle; and it was left for later ages to confuse the issues.

But while these are among Aristotle's basic theories concerning the nature of poetry, they are far from exhausting what he has to say on this aspect of his subject. From time to time he supplements them with remarks arising out of various contexts; and whereas he has no complete theory of poetry to offer, he nevertheless presents, somewhat irregularly it is true, material out of which a coherent theory may be formed. Thus he enlarges on his theory of "imitation" when he states that "Art imitates Nature" (ἡ τέχνη μιμεῖται τὴν φύσιν);[4] or again, that "the objects of imitation are men in action" (μιμοῦνται οἱ μιμούμενοι πράττοντας),[5] that is, human actions, thoughts, emotions, in fact, human life in general. Here at first sight he would seem to be contradicting himself; but the ambiguity arises out of a looseness of terminology. In the former of these statements—one which passed current later as Aristotle's complete definition of art—Aristotle is referring to the process, not to the object, of "imitation". The poet, according to his theory, imitated the creative processes of Nature; but his subject-matter was man, and the objects of poetic "imitation"

---

[1] See Butcher, *op. cit.* pp. 198, 212.
[2] 1453b, 10–11.   [3] See Butcher, *op. cit.* pp. 211–13.
[4] *Phys.* II, 2, 194a, 21; see Butcher, *op. cit.* p. 116.   [5] 1448a, 1.

human life in all its manifestations. Nor does Aristotle, again, lose sight of the element of "inspiration" in poetry, though he refers to it but incidentally in his *Poetics*. In his *Rhetoric* he categorically states that "poetry is a thing inspired";[1] whereas in the *Poetics* he attempts indirectly a sort of rational explanation, by suggesting the existence of more than one kind of "inspiration", the variation arising apparently out of differences of poetic temperament. There are, for instance, "great wits", and also others touched with a form of frenzy; and with both are associated a sensitiveness of soul, a capacity for strong feeling.[2] But while "great wit" works consciously and under the control of a higher reason, the "enthusiastic" poet is possessed by his subject and dominated by his emotions. Hence Aristotle's distinction of the two permanent types; the plastic poet (εὐφυής) on the one hand, highly gifted and versatile, who could assume different rôles as occasion required, and the "enthusiastic" poet (μανικός) on the other, a man of intense feeling, who wrote in a transport of frenzy. Of the other points made by Aristotle concerning the nature of poetry, none is more significant than his recognition of the value of its emotional appeal. Plato had condemned both epic and dramatic poetry because of their disturbing effects on human emotions and character. Aristotle now showed that such emotional disturbances might have beneficent effects, might in fact lead to a health-giving "catharsis",[3] which brought in its train a sense of relief. And by this pronouncement was met one count in Plato's indictment, while at the same time the way was prepared for a sounder aesthetic appreciation of poetry. More questionable, on the other hand, is the attitude adopted by Aristotle towards verse-forms, when he suggests them to be a mere accident and no essential part of poetry.[4] The inference plainly was that the term "poet" included all imaginative artists in words, whether working in prose or verse; and in this identification of poetry with imaginative literature generally, Aristotle was followed by more than one later theorist. Yet it may reasonably be doubted whether so definite a disavowal quite

---

[1] *Rhet.* III. 7, 11.   [2] 1455a, 31 ff.
[3] 1449b, 28.   [4] 1447b, 14.

represents the truth of the matter, and whether Aristotle was not here unduly disregarding the part played by verse-form in poetry. Elsewhere there are grounds for thinking that something was lacking in his appreciation of the aesthetic qualities of poetry, more especially on its musical and rhythmical sides; though, on the other hand, he is well aware of the value of melody and rhythm in the choral parts of tragedy, while he himself notes that the human instinct for harmony and rhythm is one of the causes from which poetry springs.[1] Moreover it is not without its significance that while theoretically he includes in his conception of poetry such prose forms as mimes and the Socratic dialogues, in actual practice he omits them from further consideration in his *Poetics*, and confines himself to the versified forms of imaginative literature. Without a doubt there is an element of uncertainty in the position assumed by Aristotle on this point. It would seem that he has overstated his case in a desire to discredit what he regarded as an undesirable practice of his day, that is, of classifying poetry on the basis of verse. To Aristotle, the distinction between the various "kinds" lay deeper than this; it lay in the different modes of imitating in words. And in emphasising this fact by denying verse to be *the* essential, Aristotle has gone further and has implied it to be no essential at all.

So far, then, we have been concerned with Aristotle's exposition of the essence of poetry, of "poetry in itself". He has discussed its origin, its nature, and its effects; and in replying incidentally to Plato's earlier strictures, he has established its essential truth, its value to the community, and has also prepared the way for aesthetic as distinct from moral judgment. At the same time, while his treatment hitherto has been in terms of subject-matter, not form—a point of some importance in connexion with later history—he is none the less alive to the technical side of his subject. If poetry is to him a σοφία or wisdom, it is also a τέχνη or art with its own laws and principles; and indeed, his main object in the *Poetics*, as opposed to that of Plato in his dialogues, is to show that poetry is as much an art as rhetoric or painting, and to indicate sound methods of

[1] See p. 77 *supra*.

poetical composition. Not that he is of opinion that a knowledge of art will do everything; his incidental reference to
"inspiration" goes to show that he is aware of the need for a
gifted nature. But like the rest of the Greeks, he conceives of
poetry as being largely the outcome of trained skill; and however much he may attribute to instinctive genius, he is even
more insistent on the existence of certain artistic laws which
serve to guide and regulate the poet's activity. Agathon, he
notes, had maintained with the sophists, that whereas "some
things were effected by art, others came by necessity or
chance";[1] whereas later on at Rome the question as to the
comparative importance of genius and art in the make-up of
the poet was to be generally discussed. To Aristotle, however,
such questions had not presented themselves with any urgency.
His emphasis is on art; his aim is to enable poets "to write well
knowingly". And while he recognises that there is an empirical
skill which is the outcome of mere exercise or practice (διὰ
συνηθείας) as well as a skill that comes from a knowledge of
artistic principle (διὰ τέχνης),[2] it is to the latter that he
attaches the prime importance. The very existence of the *Poetics*
gives proof of that fact.

It is therefore with this object in view that he proposes to
discuss the species or kinds of poetry, so as to bring out their
distinctive qualities and the laws underlying their creation.
He proceeds in scientific fashion by classification and definition.
Poetry, a species of "imitation", is itself divided into several
sub-species or "kinds"—epic, tragedy, comedy, dithyramb[3]—
and with the nature of the first three kinds, to which he confines his attention, he professes to deal, thus preparing the way
for that doctrine of the literary "kinds" which was to play so
important a part in later critical discussions. His classification,
it will be noted, is somewhat limited. He excludes, for instance,
didactic and historical poetry, and this he does in accordance
with his conception of poetry in general. Historical poetry
dealt with particular facts, not with universal truths, while
didactic poetry did not imitate life in its universal aspects; and
so, logically, they both fall outside his scheme.

[1] *Rhet.* II, 19, 13.   [2] 1447a, 20.   [3] 1447a, 13.

Of all the "kinds", tragedy, as we have seen, is Aristotle's first concern; and he begins with a definition based largely on his previous generalisations. Tragedy he defines as "the imitation of an action that is serious, complete in itself, and of a certain magnitude; in language made beautiful by different means in different parts of the work; in dramatic, not narrative, form; through scenes of pity and fear (δι' ἐλέου καὶ φόβου) bringing about its purgation (κάθαρσις) of such emotions".[1] And here, in the first place, Aristotle has set down the main features which mark off tragedy from all the other "kinds". Its action is "serious" (σπουδαῖος), as distinct from that of comedy; it is performed, not recited as is the case with the epic; and it is distinguished from nomic and dithyrambic poetry by its peculiar use of verse and song, verse only being employed in the dialogue, lyric or song only in the choral parts. But there are other differentiae as well, features that distinguish the ideal tragedy from those cruder forms belonging to its earlier history; and these consist of a certain limitation in its extent, a certain order in its structure. Its action, for example, must be long enough to permit of an orderly development and a catastrophe, yet short enough to be taken in as an artistic whole without taxing the memory. It must also have, as Aristotle explains, "a beginning, a middle, and an end";[2] that is, an intelligible beginning, a satisfying end, and a middle which besides being the outcome of what has gone before, also leads on naturally to the conclusion. And as its last distinguishing feature there is its final cause, its specific function. This, according to Aristotle, is the purgation of the emotions of pity and fear, unhealthy conditions of the soul,[3] by the exciting of those emotions; a medical metaphor, apparently, carried over into the sphere of art, though Aristotle himself supplies no explanation. Hence the term purgation or "catharsis" has since been variously interpreted; most often it has been taken to mean a moral effect brought about by a purification of the passions, an explanation subject to further modifications. The truth would seem to be that a pathological effect is at any rate implied, an effect

---

[1] 1449b, 24-8. [2] 1450b, 27; cf. Plato, see p. 55 *supra*.
[3] See Plato, *Laws*, 791 a.

on the soul, analogous to that of medicine on the body, productive of a condition of emotional balance, and ultimately of
the pleasure arising from a state of calm. This at least is what
is suggested by a passage in the *Politics*[1] relating to the cathartic
effects of music on certain morbid states of mind; and, moreover, the working-off of emotions which, repressed, would bring
on hysteria, is a process which to-day would be perfectly intelligible. Whether Aristotle has here hit upon the whole, or
even the essential, truth is however not so certain; for to
modern minds tragedy seems to aim at something more than
the elimination of repressions; nor are the emotions of pity and
fear alone concerned. There is for instance the nobler function
of enlarging men's experiences, of giving them a truer insight
into human life and destiny, and of enabling them to endure
great moods; and with these matters Aristotle does not deal.
Yet his account nevertheless has its element of truth; for there is
a sense in which all poetry is "cathartic" in relation to both
poet and reader alike, inasmuch as poetic expression in itself is
a sort of safety-valve for the poet, a means of bringing relief to
a mind over-burdened. It is, however, in the light of the circumstances that produced it that the doctrine of Aristotle is
perhaps best understood. Plato had complained of the disturbing, debilitating effects of the drama; Aristotle's defence is
that the effects are really hygienic, curative in kind. And herein
probably lies the true explanation of Aristotle's argument. He
had a case to answer, a defence to make; and his theory of
"catharsis", thus conditioned, is to some extent at least a piece
of special pleading.

Having thus defined tragedy, Aristotle proceeds in analytical
fashion to consider the elements out of which it is composed;
and these he describes as (1) Plot, Character, and Thought, all
of which are concerned with the object represented, (2) Diction
and Melody, which have to do with the means of representation,
and (3) Spectacle, relating to the manner of representation.[2]
Of these elements, some naturally call for more attention than
others; and Aristotle at once declares the plot to be of supreme
importance, more important than the mere revelation of

[1] v (VIII), 7, 1341 b, 32 ff.   [2] 1450a, 9.

personal qualities (Character), or the intellectual processes
(Thought) of the dramatic characters concerned. And this
point he is at some pains to establish, as if anxious to meet
current criticisms of his day. For one thing, he maintains,
tragedy being an imitation, not of men but of men in action, the
plot is obviously the essential element. Characterisation he
regards as merely subsidiary, since it only adds to the revelation of what is best revealed in action. Nor does a string of
speeches, however finely-wrought or expressive of character,
provide the same tragic effects as a well-constructed plot; for
the latter with its elements of movement and surprise possesses
features which add greatly to the emotional interest. Hence to
Aristotle "the plot is the first principle, the soul of tragedy"
(ἀρχὴ μὲν οὖν καὶ οἷον ψυχή);[1] and there is undoubtedly logic
in what he says, though later ages have attached increasing
value to the delineation of character. With Aristotle, however,
most play-goers of to-day would probably agree; a stirring plot
with commonplace characters will be found to succeed where a
lifeless plot with well-sketched characters fails. But whether the
question was worth raising is another matter; for among the
different parts of an organism there can be no real priority,
all alike being essential to the well-being of the whole.

Such then being Aristotle's views concerning the importance
of the plot, it is not strange to find that he inquires at great
length into this element of tragedy, bringing to light by the way
some fundamental laws of poetry. According to his definition
of tragedy, the tragic action must be complete and of a certain
magnitude; and these features, it necessarily follows, are also
characteristic of the plot. "A well-constructed plot", he asserts,
"must neither begin nor end haphazard";[2] there must be a
limit of length, a certain order in its incidents; and these requirements are in accord with an aesthetic law, since "beauty
depends on magnitude and order" (τὸ γὰρ καλὸν ἐν μεγέθει
καὶ τάξει ἐστίν).[3] Concerning the requisite length some statement has already been made. Aristotle now adds that the
length is determined, not by considerations of stage-production,
but by the nature of the drama itself; and provided there be no

[1] 1450a, 37.   [2] 1450b, 34.   [3] 1450b, 38.

confusion or obscurity, the longer the flight the greater the achievement.[1] It is, however, in what he says about the requisite order of the plot that Aristotle is most illuminating; and in his insistence on order, logic, and perspicuity, we see the essence of the classical spirit of all the ages, an echo of the doctrine laid down by Plato. Moreover, he is but following Plato when he prescribes for the plot a unity of action; this is to render it definite, intelligible, and therefore effective. But this unity is also to be of an organic kind, consisting not of an outward symmetry of form, but of an inward principle, capable of admitting the complexity of living things, while possessing also the vital relations of their parts. Thus there are to be no irrelevant incidents; "a thing, the presence or absence of which makes no visible difference, is not an organic part of the whole".[2] And further, there must be a rigorous connexion of the incidents employed; they must be bound together in "a probable or necessary sequence" (κατὰ τὸ εἰκὸς ἢ τὸ ἀναγκαῖον),[3] incident following incident as its inevitable and natural result, with a sort of artistic logic. In this way would be obtained a consecutive whole, not a series of incidents following one another in mere order of time. And, moreover, what is thus depicted is not what actually happened (i.e. history), but what would logically and inevitably happen, in other words, things which are permanently and universally true (i.e. poetry). This then is what is known as Aristotle's law of "probability"; a law relating primarily to structure, not to subject-matter, and one of Aristotle's most valuable contributions to literary theory. The hint for this doctrine of the unity of action came originally, as we have seen, from Plato; and Aristotle makes it the basis of his whole poetic theory. But in taking over the idea he developed it and explained it. Organic unity of form, according to his conception, necessarily involved universality of content; and he is the first to establish the connexion between the two.

Thus does Aristotle lay down as his first great principle of dramatic structure the unity of action, coupling with it the doctrine of "probability", the law requiring the cohesion of the parts. And to these pronouncements he adds certain riders.

[1] 1451a, 11.   [2] 1451a, 35.   [3] 1451a, 39.

He notes for one thing that unity of action does not consist in the unity of the hero;[1] that the story of Heracles, for instance, is wanting in unity because of many incidents in his life which cannot be brought into relation with the rest. Or again, he points out that of all plots the "episodic" are the worst.[2] They are plots in which, as in chronicles, the various episodes follow one another in mere order of time; though he is careful to add that historical subjects may also be chosen for tragedy, provided they conform with the law of "the probable and the necessary".[3] This unity of action, moreover, is the only law of the kind prescribed by Aristotle; though later ages read into his work other laws known as the unities of time and place. The so-called unity of time was based on a statement of Aristotle to the effect that "tragedy endeavours as far as possible to confine itself to a single revolution of the sun (i.e. 24 hours), or but slightly to exceed that limit" (μάλιστα πειρᾶται ὑπὸ μίαν περίοδον ἡλίου εἶναι ἢ μικρὸν ἐξαλλάττειν).[4] Here, however, no law was implied; it was merely a record of common practice, which was far from inviolable, as was shown by the *Eumenides* of Aeschylus, the *Trachiniae* of Sophocles and the *Supplices* of Euripides.[5] But, misinterpreted, the statement gave rise to the doctrine of the unity of time, from which in due course the doctrine of the unity of place was deduced by Castelvetro;[6] though of this latter rule there is nowhere any trace in the *Poetics*.

So far Aristotle has been concerned with the form of the tragic plot; and in the *Poetics* as we have it, there is yet a further comment on the formal aspect of the subject, where the several quantitative parts of the plot, or the divisions of its structure, are enumerated; namely, Prologue, Episode, Choric Song (= Parodos and Stasimon), and Exodos.[7] It is doubtful, however, whether this statement is Aristotle's own; for he has previously supplied his analysis of the elements of tragedy, and the passage as it stands has the air of an unnecessary digression, interrupting the main argument. So that possibly it is best

---

[1] 1451 a, 15. [2] 1451 b, 33. [3] 1451 b, 29.
[4] 1449 b, 12. [5] See Butcher, *op. cit.* p. 291.
[6] See H. B. Charlton, *Castelvetro's Theory of Poetry*, pp. 89 ff.
[7] 1452 b, 14–27.

described as a later interpolation, due to the influence of those post-Aristotelian rhetorical treatises, in which there is the same two-fold treatment: first, the elements of oratory, εὕρεσις (*inventio*), τάξις (*dispositio*), and the rest, and then a systematic treatment of the parts of a speech, προοίμιον (*exordium*), διήγησις (*narratio*), etc.[1] Apart from this, Aristotle's attention is now directed to the subject-matter of the plot; and he proceeds to discuss the themes best calculated to produce the necessary tragic effects of pity, and fear. It is significant that, throughout the *Poetics*, "pity and fear" are mentioned in one and the same order. Pity comes first, pity inspired by the sufferings of the tragic hero, with which the Greek audiences were already familiar. But while pity was thus natural and inevitable, the element of fear, that is, fear on behalf of the tragic hero, was evoked by the skill of the poet, so as to enhance our sympathy. It is therefore clear that the tragic theme in general must be one of human suffering; also that an unhappy ending is the right ending, as indeed Aristotle in one place points out.[2] To this, however, he adds that those themes are best which contain an element of surprise (ὅταν γένηται παρὰ τὴν δόξαν),[3] though the thrill of the unexpected must not be due to mere chance, but must follow on naturally from what has preceded. And, furthermore, the most piteous calamities, he suggests, are the calamities that are brought about by those who are near and dear to the victim. A catastrophe may for instance result from the action of one of three kinds of agent; it may be the work of a friend, or of an enemy, or again of an utter stranger. But it is when the blow comes from an unexpected quarter, from the hands of kinsman or friend, that the circumstances are piteous as well as terrible;[4] and it is then that we get the true tragic material, the story out of which the ideal tragedy is made.

With these then as his ruling ideas Aristotle proceeds to formulate one of his profound generalisations as to the nature of the tragic plot. As we have seen, it must be a story of suffering ending unhappily, in which the trouble comes about unexpectedly, and contrary to the intention of the agent con-

---

[1] See vol. ii, 17.

[2] 1453a, 26.

[3] 1452a, 4.

[4] 1453b, 19.

cerned; and all this is implied in Aristotle's statement that the ideal tragic story must consist of a "complex action", i.e. an action containing two features, a *peripeteia* and an *anagnorisis*.[1] As to the exact meaning of these terms, it is true, there has been some confusion. *Peripeteia* (περιπέτεια), for the most part, has been taken to mean "a reversal of situation", and *anagnorisis* (ἀναγνώρισις), "recognition". But if this be what is meant, then, to say the least, "simple" actions (i.e. actions without *peripeteia*) are excessively rare, since almost all plays comprise "a reversal of situation"; and the *Iliad*, which Aristotle describes as "simple", has many such changes. Happily, however, Aristotle has not left us without some clue as to his real meaning; and the clue is found more particularly in the illustrations he gives of, first, the messenger coming to cheer Oedipus but producing the opposite effect, and secondly, of Danaus in *Lynceus* intending to murder the hero, but being slain himself in the end.[2] In each case, it is clear, it is not the mere "reversal of situation" that produces the peculiarly poignant effect, but rather the frustrated purpose, the unexpected catastrophe resulting from a deed unwittingly done. As Aristotle elsewhere explains, in his analysis of pity, "it is piteous that an evil should befall from a quarter whence good fortune is due"[3] And this is amply borne out by the further illustrations supplied in the *Poetics*; so that Aristotle's meaning would seem evident, namely, that *peripeteia* stands for "a reversal of intention", a deed done in blindness defeating its own purpose, and *anagnorisis* for a realisation of the truth, an awakening to the real position. Hence the ideal plot of tragedy, according to Aristotle, consists of a story in which the calamity is due to a false move blindly taken by friend or kinsman. It is a tragedy brought about, not by the deliberate purpose of some evil agent, nor yet by mere chance, but by human error; and "there is nothing more brilliant in the *Poetics*", it has been well said, "than this recognition by Aristotle of the Tragedy of Error, of the *peripeteia*, as the deepest of all".[4] And this is so,

---

[1] 1452a, 22; 1452b, 31.   [2] 1452a, 24ff.   [3] Aristotle, *Rhet.* II, viii, 10.
[4] See F. L. Lucas, "The Reverse of Aristotle" (*Class. Rev.* XXXVII (1923), pp. 98–104) for a full discussion; also his *Tragedy*, pp. 91 ff.

because the theory, for one thing, is eminently in keeping with the facts of life. No calamity is indeed more heart-rending than the destruction by friendly hands of the thing beloved, or the relentless fate that waits on mere error; and life we know is full of such issues. Then, too, the theory brings to light an important element in tragedy to which, strangely enough, Aristotle makes no other allusion. The presence of irony always adds a peculiar poignancy to the tragic effect. It may be of a verbal kind, "when words are caught up by circumstances and charged with a fuller meaning than the speaker meant".[1] But it may also arise out of the action itself, when "deeds are caught up out of an agent's grasp and charged with a meaning the very opposite of what was intended".[1] And this is the particular effect of the Aristotelian *peripeteia*; it introduces into a play the irony of circumstances, and is thus to the action what verbal irony is to language.

Here then we have what is to Aristotle the root of the matter; and he explains in passing that this is why the best Greek tragedies were confined to the stories of a few houses—those of Oedipus, Atreus, Thyestes, Telephus, and the rest—since such stories alone provided the sort of plot he had in mind.[2] It is true that he is careful to add that the writer of tragedy was not limited to such stories, and that there were narratives of a fictitious or an historical kind that served the tragic purpose. Yet the usual subjects of tragedy were nevertheless the familiar legends;[3] and he adds elsewhere that in taking over the traditional subjects the tragic poet did not necessarily cease to be an original artist, since there was ample room for invention and skill in his handling of the stories.[4] For the rest, Aristotle's remarks concerning the nature of the plot are largely the outcome of principles previously laid down. Thus he has already insisted on the unhappy ending; and he now explains that there is no need for the observance of "poetic justice", which, though recognised by some as a concession to popular taste, was nevertheless more in keeping with comedy than tragedy.[5] Elsewhere he reiterates the need for obtaining the tragic effect naturally and without any sort of artificial aids. He mentions for instance

---

[1] See W. Lock, "Use of περιπέτεια in Aristotle's *Poetics*" (*Class. Rev.* ix, p. 250).   [2] 1453a, 19.   [3] 1451b, 20.   [4] 1453b, 25.   [5] 1453a, 36.

six methods of *anagnorisis*; but the most effective surprise, he explains, is obtained, not by means of "scars and necklaces", but when it grows naturally out of the incidents themselves.[1] And the same holds true of the abuse of that device known as the *deus ex machina*, to which Plato had already called attention. According to Aristotle, the unravelling of the plot should proceed in logical and rational fashion, without any resort to arbitrary devices. And therefore the gods should intervene only where it became necessary to explain the past, or to announce future events external to the action.[2]

As a result of his inquiry into various aspects of the tragic plot, Aristotle, we have seen, has revealed some important dramatic principles. Less penetrating and far-reaching, perhaps, though interesting historically, are his remarks on character—the second element of tragedy—concerning which he lays down certain general guiding ideas, as well as the features that distinguish the tragic hero in particular. With regard to character-drawing generally he has several things to say. The characters of tragedy, in the first place, must be "good", as distinguished from those of comedy; they must in fact be idealised and ennobled, as is the way with portrait-painters, who, while preserving the distinctive features of an original, produce a likeness that is even more beautiful than the actual.[3] In the second place, the characters must be consistently drawn. They must be true to themselves and self-consistent, without change or modification in the course of a play; an inconsistent character, for instance, must be consistently inconsistent (ὁμαλῶς ἀνώμαλον).[4] Then, too, in conception they must conform with tradition (i.e. be like (ὅμοιον) the traditional persons);[5] it would be futile, for instance, to represent Clytemnestra as gentle, or Odysseus as foolish. And with these injunctions most modern readers would most probably agree; as they would also with a further remark of Aristotle, namely, that in character-drawing, as in dramatic structure, the law of "probability" holds good, so that what a dramatic personage says or does should be the necessary outcome of his

---

[1] 1454b, 19ff.   [2] 1454b, 3.   [3] 1454a, 17; b, 8ff.
[4] 1454a, 26ff.   [5] 1454a, 24; see Bywater's ed. of *Poetics*, note, *loc. cit.*

character.[1] Less convincing, however, is Aristotle's last requirement of "propriety" (τὰ ἁρμόττοντα),[2] i.e. that characters
should be "true to type", and in keeping with the respective
classes to which they belong. The suggestion presumably
was that mankind as a species was divisible into certain sub-
species or types, each with its distinguishing qualities; and that
dramatic characters should, broadly speaking, be "true to life",
or possessed of the qualities inherent in their respective types.
Yet however plausible theoretically, such a precept was mani-
festly difficult in its actual working, and the dangers attending
its application were already seen in the illustration supplied by
Aristotle himself, when he held it to be unnatural for a woman
to be either brave or clever in argument. Later on the idea
developed into the theory of dramatic *decorum*, with its plain
demands for fixed and formal types based on accidents of age,
rank, sex, and the like.[3] If not actually implied in what Aristotle
wrote, the theory was at least a natural extension of his idea;
and it led to much futile theorising and many absurd judgments
at the Renascence and after.

In his pronouncement on the character of the ideal tragic
hero Aristotle is on safer ground; and indeed his conception,
which follows naturally from his idea of tragedy, has in it much
of interest. If tragedy, he argues, aims at exciting pity and
fear, then there are three kinds of situation that can be ruled
out at once, as incapable of providing the necessary results.[4]
A good man, for instance, hurled from happiness into misery,
arouses primarily neither pity nor fear; his story merely shocks
or revolts us. Nor does the bad man who wins to happiness out
of misery excite either of the tragic emotions; indeed he makes
no sort of appeal to human feelings (τὸ φιλάνθρωπον). Or
again there is the villain who comes deservedly to a bad end; his
story, it is true, may appeal to our humanity, but it has nothing
either piteous or fearful in it. For the truth is, so Aristotle
states, that pity can be felt only for one who, while not entirely
good, meets with sufferings beyond his deserts; whereas fear is

---

[1] 1454a, 33.   [2] 1454a, 22.
[3] See J. E. Spingarn, *Critical Essays of the Seventeenth Century*, I, lxviii–ix.
[4] 1452b, 34ff.

aroused only when the sufferer is like to ourselves in nature.
And these conditions necessarily determine the nature of the
tragic hero. He is a man not pre-eminently good, though of
average virtue, who is overtaken by misfortune brought on,
not by vice, but by some *hamartia* (ἁμαρτία),[1] some error of
judgment. Such then in the main is Aristotle's idea; and the
definition stands as one of his great pronouncements. It is true
that he adds one other requirement, i.e. that the tragic hero
should be a distinguished person of high estate (ἐν μεγάλῃ δόξῃ...
καὶ εὐτυχίᾳ),[2] and this with a view of adding to the impressive-
ness of the catastrophe. It is a clause historically interesting,
for, misinterpreted in later ages, it led to the exclusion from
tragedy of all but characters of the highest rank: but it forms
no essential part of the real definition, the gist of which lies in
the *hamartia* doctrine. At the same time there are difficulties
inherent in the theory as stated above; for according to its
terms, both villain and saint are excluded as tragic heroes, a
procedure not wholly warranted by later history. Nor is any
account taken of that ethical fault, that "taint of nature",
which lies at the root of so many modern tragedies. Attempts
have therefore been made to reconcile the positions by taking
hamartia to mean "a defect of character" as well as "an error
of judgment". Yet this almost certainly is not what Aristotle
meant; it is reading into him something that is simply not there,
interpreting him in the light of later experience. And for a
correct understanding of his doctrine certain facts have to be
borne in mind: first, that Aristotle's theorising was definitely
retrospective in kind; secondly, that he is dealing, not with the
only form, but with what he regards as the ideal form, of
tragedy; and lastly, that his tragic theory is all of a piece, so
that the clue to the tragic plot is also the clue to the tragic hero.
His ideal tragedy we have seen is the Tragedy of Error; and
it therefore follows that the *hamartia* stands for "an error of
judgment", the tragic hero for one whose sufferings are due to
a false step blindly taken.

Aristotle by now has dealt with what he regards as the two
main elements of tragedy, that is, plot and characterisation.

[1] 1453a, 7.   [2] 1453a, 10.

The remaining four elements he dismisses rather more summarily, and on diction alone has he anything substantial to say.
Thus the element of spectacle—by which he meant all that
had to do with staging, costume, and the like—he describes as
something that has but slight concern with the poetic craft.
By spectacular means, he admits, the tragic emotions may be
excited; but he urges that it is better to depend on an artistic
handling of the story.[1] And for the rest, so far from spectacle
being essential to tragedy, the proper effects he maintains can
be obtained from a mere hearing (or reading) without an
actual performance—a point not without its bearing on the
modern stage and novel. Concerning melody, or the musical
element in tragedy, he has still less to say; and in view of the
importance of choric songs in Greek drama, his silence here is
both surprising and significant. His chief point is that this
lyrical element is the most important of those accessories that
make tragedy pleasing; though he further insists that the Chorus
should be regarded as one of the actors and its songs as an
integral part of tragedy, in accordance with the practice of
Sophocles.[2] Such songs should not be mere interludes loosely
connected with the action of the piece, after the fashion set by
Agathon and continued by Euripides; for this was obviously a
breach of the law of organic unity. And again, with regard to the
element of thought in tragedy (i.e. effective speech as employed
by the various characters), for a treatment of this matter he
refers to his *Rhetoric*,[3] where he had dealt with the principles
underlying the expression of ideas, and notably with the proper
use of arguments and the ways of appealing to the emotions.

On the remaining element of diction he has, however, some
important statements to make; and working in his suggestive
fashion from first principles, he outlines what is really a theory
of poetic diction in general. From the first it is clear that he
has no doubts as to the existence of essential differences between
the language of verse and ordinary prose speech. "To realise
the difference", he writes, "one should take an epic line and
see how it reads when ordinary words are substituted."[4] He
moreover illustrates the subtle qualities introduced by poetic

[1] 1453b, 1–10.   [2] 1456a, 25.   [3] 1456a, 35.   [4] 1458b, 15.

words; the prosaic quality of "the sea-shore is shrieking" (κράζουσιν), as compared with the poetic colouring of "the sea-shore is roaring" (βοόωσιν).[1] And indeed the idea generally was the conclusion he drew from the practice of Greek poets. He therefore proceeds to describe briefly the nature of the poetic vocabulary and the principles underlying its use. He begins by specifying the various forms that the poet may use. First there are words in common everyday use; then there are foreign words, dialect words, and words newly-coined; others again are of a metaphorical kind, others merely ornamental (i.e. periphrastic); and lastly there are archaic words, old uncontracted forms handed down by earlier poets.[2] As to their use in poetry, his main contention is that poetic expression should be clear without being trite or commonplace (λέξεως δὲ ἀρετὴ σαφῆ καὶ μὴ ταπεινὴν εἶναι)[3]—a profound and penetrating utterance. Thus clearness on the one hand demanded the use of ordinary familiar words, while distinction on the other hand was obtained by unfamiliar forms, by those deviations from the normal idiom that brought with them an element of fine surprise; and it was therefore in a judicious fusion of all the elements of the poetic vocabulary—common words, strange words, metaphors, and the like—that he held the perfection of poetic style to consist. But to this general statement he has certain additions to make. The use of unfamiliar forms, for instance, was to be reasoned and calculated. Strange words unseasonably used, or too much metaphor, would inevitably turn a passage into mere jargon. In short, there was to be a moderation in their use. "It is a great matter", adds Aristotle, "to observe propriety (πρεπόντως χρῆσθαι) in expression";[4] and here again he is enunciating the principle of *decorum*, that principle which was to colour most of the critical theories of later antiquity. Apart from this, he throws out certain guiding ideas as to the employment of these various forms. Compound words, for example, he regards as best suited to the ornate lyric (dithyramb, hymn, etc.); rare words on the other hand are more in keeping with the epic; while in the drama with its iambic verse (which he describes elsewhere as "the most

[1] 1458b, 31.   [2] 1457b, 1 ff.   [3] 1458a, 18.   [4] 1459a, 4.

colloquial of all measures ")[1] metaphorical diction finds a place
as being closest to the vocabulary of ordinary life.[2] And of all
these elements metaphor is said to be the greatest. "The gift
for metaphor", adds Aristotle, "cannot be taught; it is a mark
of genius, for the making of good metaphors means an eye
for resemblances (τὸ ὅμοιον θεωρεῖν),"[3] i.e. a faculty for recognising the common universal elements underlying externally
dissimilar objects.[4]

With these remarks on poetic diction Aristotle has at length
arrived at the end of his disquisition on tragedy; and in pur-
suance of his plan he now turns to epic poetry, another of the
specified poetic "kinds". Compared with his treatment of
tragedy however his treatment of the epic is relatively slight.
There are a few general statements as to its nature and form;
attention is called to the main differences between tragedy and
the epic; and lastly, the comparative value of the two forms is
discussed in a sort of appendix to the work. In spite of incompleteness of treatment, however, this section is by no means
lacking in interest. As before, Aristotle contrives, in discussing
a particular poetic form, to throw light incidentally upon
poetry in general; while the very incompleteness is historically
significant, for it suggests in part the reason why epic theory
at the Renascence was mainly based, not on Aristotle, but on
Virgil and his practice. The gist of Aristotle's epic theory is
given where he describes the epic as an imitation of serious
subjects, essentially narrative in form, employing a single
metre, and with a plot constructed generally on dramatic lines.[5]
From the first he insists on the close affinity between tragedy
and the epic. He never loses sight of the fundamental difference
of their methods, the one imitating by action, the other by
narrative; yet, like Plato before him, he regards the epic as a
semi-dramatic poem, in which the narrative element is best
reduced to a minimum, the most artistic results being obtained
when the poet himself says little, but leaves as much as possible
to the characters concerned. From this it follows that much of

---

[1] 1449a, 24.   [2] 1459a, 9–10.   [3] 1459a, 6 ff.
[4] See note, loc. cit. Translation of Poetics by E. S. Bouchier.
[5] 1459a, 17.

what has been said with reference to tragedy applies also to the epic. And indeed Aristotle says as much when he states that "whoever knows what is good or bad tragedy knows also about epic poetry";[1] thus leaving us to infer for the epic the main structural features of tragedy, the same emotional effects, and the same cathartic justification. But while he takes thus much for granted, he also refers definitely to certain points of likeness. For one thing, the literary elements of the epic, he points out, are the same as those of tragedy, consisting of plot, character, thought, and diction, with melody (lyric) and spectacle omitted. Epic plots, again, like those of tragedy, are said to vary in kind; they are stories of suffering, either complex or simple, that is, with or without *peripeteia* and *anagnorisis*.[2] But it is on the necessity for unity of action in the plot that most stress is laid. It would not do to take merely a single hero or a single period with all the disconnected events bound up with that hero or period. This he states is the practice of most poets; whereas the supreme excellence of Homer was said to lie in his observance of that unity. "The *Iliad* and the *Odyssey*", he adds, "each furnishes the subject of one tragedy, or at the most, two."[3]

On the other hand, there are also points in which the epic differs from tragedy; and, in the first place, there is its length. The principle already laid down with reference to tragedy, that the work must be short enough to be grasped as an artistic whole, also holds good of the epic. Yet it is likewise true that the epic can run to greater length than tragedy; and this from the very nature of things. The epic poet, for instance, can relate a number of incidents occurring simultaneously to different persons in different places, whereas the tragic poet can represent only such part of a story as is connected with one place (the stage) and one set of persons[4]—a statement of fact concerning the usual practice of Greek tragedy which later ages regarded as establishing the unity of place. And the epic, as Aristotle points out, has here certain advantages. Its greater scope admits of a treatment of things on a grander and more impressive scale than tragedy; while it also renders possible the

[1] 1449b, 16. [2] 1459b, 8. [3] *Ibid.* [4] 1459 b, 24.

introduction of episodes which relieve the monotony and give variety to the story. Then, further, there is a difference of metre; and despite Aristotle's previous remarks on the non-essential character of verse-form in poetry, he has here some interesting comments to make on metre in general. For the epic, he states, the hexameter alone is essential; it is "the stateliest and most dignified (στασιμώτατον καὶ ὀγκωδέστατον) of measures",[1] and as such it admits more readily than any other of strange words and metaphors. In tragedy, on the other hand, measures of a more stirring kind were suitable, namely, the iambic and the trochaic tetrameter; and just as Nature or experience had evolved the proper verse-form for tragedy, so Nature had also established the heroic verse for epic purposes.[2] The third difference noted by Aristotle has reference to the subject-matter. The epic is said to admit more freely than tragedy tales of an improbable and a marvellous kind, thus supplying in a greater degree that element of wonder which Aristotle describes elsewhere as a legitimate source of artistic pleasure. This was because in the epic no attempt was made at a visible representation of the marvellous, all being left to the imagination of the reader. "The pursuit of Hector on the stage for instance would be ludicrous", adds Aristotle, "whereas in the epic the absurdity passes unnoticed";[3] and here he incidentally recognises the part played by the improbable and the irrational in poetry, as well as the artistic possibilities of tales of a strange and supernatural kind.

As for the relative values of the two poetic forms, Aristotle, in deciding in favour of tragedy, is apparently contradicting current opinion, according to which the epic was regarded as the higher form of art, on the grounds that it appealed to a more refined audience and was free from the vulgar pantomimic effects of the tragic stage.[4] To Aristotle, however, such reasons were beside the mark. Tragedy, he maintains, is richer in its effects, adding music and spectacle to epic resources; it presents its stories even when read no less vividly than the epic; it has a stricter unity; its methods are more concentrated; and it produces more effectively the requisite emotional result, i.e. the

[1] 1459b, 34.   [2] 1460a, 5.   [3] 1460a, 15.   [4] 1461b, 26ff.

pleasure arising from a catharsis of pity and fear.[1] In other words, the difference between the two is essentially one of method. Tragedy attains the same end as the epic, but in a more direct and concentrated fashion; and as such it has a claim to be recognised as the higher of the two kinds.

Concerning comedy, the third of the Aristotelian "kinds", but little is said in the *Poetics* as it has come down, though there are grounds for thinking that a substantial treatment of the subject formed part of the lost second Book. It is significant for instance that early in the *Poetics*[2] a discussion on comedy is definitely promised, whereas in the *Rhetoric*[3] Aristotle refers to the *Poetics* as containing an analysis of the various kinds of laughter; and apart from this there are later indications of an established theory of comedy (notably in the *Tractatus Cois-linianus*[4] and in Cicero's discussion[5] of the ridiculous), all of which goes to suggest that Aristotle somewhere or other had dealt with the theme. As it is, however, all that have come down are a few scattered hints in the *Poetics* suggesting the broad lines of distinction between tragedy and comedy. Thus comedy, according to Aristotle, is an imitation of the baser sort of action. It has to do with characters of a lower type than those of tragedy,[6] characters below rather than above the level of ordinary human nature. But while the personages of comedy are "worse" than the average man, they are "worse" only in a special sense; they embody, that is, a certain element of the ridiculous, which is defined as "a mistake or deformity not productive of pain or harm to others".[7] Hence, to Aristotle, an action is ridiculous when it is a harmless blunder or mistake (ἁμάρτημα ἀνώδυνον); and again, a person is ridiculous who is possessed of some moral or physical deformity of a harmless kind (αἶσχος ἀνώδυνον). And it is here that the essence of Aristotle's conception lies, in the harmlessness of the defects associated with the characters of comedy. According to Plato, the deformities bound up with the ludicrous were to be harmless in the sense that the object of laughter was not to be powerful

---

[1] 1462a, 14ff.　　　[2] 1449b, 22.　　　[3] III, 28.
[4] See vol. II, 138–43.　　　[5] *De Orat.* II, 58–9.
[6] 1448a, 16.　　　[7] 1449a, 32 (tr. Bywater).

enough to retaliate. Aristotle with truer insight sees that there
are some deformities too painful to laugh at, being painful to
those afflicted and to spectators alike; and these he rules out of
the province of the ludicrous. True comedy, he seems to say, is
the outcome of human infirmities and follies which lead to
blunders, absurdities, and cross-purposes, and thus give rise,
not to censure or pain or aversion on the part of the spectators,
but to laughter produced by a sense of the ridiculous; and it
cannot be doubted that Aristotle has here made a striking
contribution to the theory of comedy. At the same time he
also clears up some amount of ambiguity in Plato's position,
who had conceived the essence of comedy to be a sort of
malicious joy, though at the same time he had condemned all
serious ill-natured ridicule.[1]

It therefore follows that what Aristotle has in mind is not the
comedy of personal satire, but that form which deals with the
permanent flaws and imperfections of mankind. And this he
makes plain when he refers with approval to the contemporary
practice of giving typical or characteristic names to the personages of comedy.[2] The older satirical form he thus condemns,
not because of the scandal it created, but because it dealt with
the particular and not with the general, which according to his
conception was the true aim of art. Then, too, it might safely
be inferred that many of the dramatic principles enunciated in
connexion with tragedy apply with equal force in the field of
comedy. There is for example the same need for an observance
of organic unity and of the law of "probability" in building up
the comic plot; the general remarks on characterisation would
also hold true of the comic personages. And although we have
no clear traces of a theory of comic "catharsis", it is by no
means improbable that the idea was present with Aristotle, and
that a purgation of some sort was conceived of as the end of
comedy, a purgation either of troublesome emotions like envy
or anger (the two emotions associated with comedy by Plato),[3]
or else, it may be, of laughter itself.

This then is the substance of what Aristotle has to say on the
nature of poetry and its three "kinds"; and here undoubtedly

---

[1] See p. 57 *supra.*   [2] 1451 b, 13.   [3] Cf. *Philebus*, 48–50.

we have the main body of Aristotelian doctrine, those literary theories upon which later criticism was to be largely based. Of the rest of his achievement in the *Poetics* but little can here be added; though the work is full of suggestive remarks carelessly dropped by the way, and important in critical history as marking the starting-point of some process or idea; and to some of these at least a passing reference must be made. Interesting, in the first place, are some of his casual remarks on points of abstract theory. Thus from time to time he throws light on poetic problems by reference to. the sister arts—a practice in which he was followed by later writers—but at the outset he drops a hint that the parallel is not complete. The painter and the sculptor, he implies, have certain limitations; they can represent many things (πολλὰ μιμοῦνται),[1] not all things. And upon the imperfections of their representations of character and feeling, Lessing's *Laokoon* was later on to be based. Or again, there is his explanation of the pleasure arising out of the tragic spectacle. Plato had already attributed it to the indulgence in "mixed" feelings; whereas Aristotle now explains it as a pleasure of an intellectual kind. Accuracy of imitation, he maintains, even in connexion with a distasteful object, invariably gives delight; while in identifying an imitation further delight results.[2] "All learning", he significantly adds, "is a source of the liveliest pleasure" (μανθάνειν...ἥδιστον).[3] Elsewhere, it is perhaps worth noting, the earliest extant treatment of grammar is to be found.[4] It was a scientific examination of the parts of speech made with a view to the interpretation of poetry, and in a sense it marked the beginnings of certain aspects of critical work. Most interesting of all is, however, the further light he throws upon the subject-matter of poetry, representing as it does a side of his teaching that is often ignored. Poetry he had previously described as the representation of the universal characteristics of human life and thought. When however he returns to the subject later, he enlarges on the fact that poetry, so far from being a mere transcript of life, a copy of the actual, has the power of dealing with the irrational, the incredible, and

[1] 1447a, 19; see Bywater, *op. cit.* note.   [2] 1448b, 10ff.
[3] 1448 b, 13.   [4] 1456b, 19ff.

even the impossible, thus including within its scope "a world of fine fabling". Everything, he asserts, depends upon a proper artistic treatment; the poet must be a master of illusion, of "the art of telling lies skilfully" (ψευδῆ λέγειν).[1] And this consists, he explains, in making the incredible seem credible by the addition of true details; just as Odysseus had beguiled Penelope into believing his false story by means of those particulars which she knew to be true (*Od.* xix, 164–248). In this way the marvellous or the supernatural might be made to assume coherent and convincing form, while things irrational or impossible are made to seem probable and credible. In poetry, states Aristotle, "a likely impossibility is always preferable to an unconvincing possibility" (προαιρεῖσθαί τε δεῖ ἀδύνατα εἰκότα μᾶλλον ἢ δυνατὰ ἀπίθανα);[2] and here was his defence of the highest flights of fancy, a plea for the poetry which dealt with the realms of romance.

Apart from these occasional remarks on the nature of poetry, however, the *Poetics* contains further passages that claim attention, and for other reasons. Nothing for instance is more striking in Aristotle's treatment than his power of combining abstract speculation with a keen sense of the practical; and his treatise consequently embodies much studio wisdom, practical hints for the poet, which give to the work something of the quality of an *Art* or τέχνη. Thus it is urged in general that the poet should write with his eye on the object, that he should visualise the action or situation he is describing (ὅτι μάλιστα πρὸ ὀμμάτων τιθέμενον);[3] and further, that he should himself feel the emotions he tries to convey, for in this way alone would he be convincing in his treatment (πιθανώτατοι γὰρ ἀπὸ τῆς αὐτῆς φύσεως οἱ ἐν τοῖς πάθεσίν εἰσιν).[4] The latter injunction was subsequently adopted by Horace,[5] while both were to be revived by modern critics. Then again there are the recommendations he makes to dramatists more particularly, all of which betray a keen insight into the dramatic craft. That he laid particular stress on the matter of plotting has already been stated; and he emphasises this point in more than one way. Thus

---

[1] 1460a, 19.   [2] 1460, 2, 26–7 (tr. Bywater).   [3] 1455a, 23.
[4] 1455a, 30.   [5] *A.P.* 102.

he remarks, as Plato had remarked before him, that a string of speeches, however excellent, did not constitute a tragedy;[1] that the outline, as in painting, was more important than imperfect colouring;[2] and that, in actual practice, beginners attained to skill in expression and characterisation long before they were able to construct a plot.[3] And this he follows up with advice of a positive kind. First he recommends that the dramatic structure in general should assume the form of a complication (δέσις), a turning-point or crisis (μετάβασις), and a *dénouement* (λύσις);[4] that speeches moreover should always be in character, thus throwing light on the personalities concerned;[5] and that diction of an ornate kind, again, should be employed in·descriptive passages only, where it would obscure by its brilliance neither the action, nor the character-drawing, nor the thought.[6] These then are examples of Aristotle's practical teaching, and they illustrate the interest attached to this side of his work. They illustrate too his insight into the psychology of the dramatic art; and their underlying principles are in the main as true to-day as when they were first promulgated.

Nor must the views he puts forward with regard to literary development be passed over unnoticed; for here he makes a start with literary history, and upon his foundations later historians have largely built. That earlier attempts had been made at discussing literary origins is made clear by what he says of the Dorian claim to the invention of the drama.[7] That claim had rested on an appeal to language; the words "drama" and "comedy" were said to be of Dorian origin, being derived from δρᾶν (to act) and κώμη (village), whereas the corresponding Athenian equivalents, it was pointed out, were πράτ-τειν and δῆμος. To philological arguments of this kind, however, Aristotle would seem to have attached but little weight; and it is worth noting that he uses the form δρῶντας in his definition of tragedy.[8] Setting aside therefore such conjectures as unconvincing, he conceives of the progress of poetry as bound up with natural causes; and he proceeds to trace its development

---

[1] 1450a, 27 ff.   [2] 1450b, 1 ff.   [3] 1450a, 34 ff.
[4] 1455b, 24 ff.   [5] 1450b, 10.   [6] 1460b, 3 ff.
[7] 1448a, 30 ff.   [8] See Bywater, *op. cit.* p. 125.

in accordance with that idea. From the first he presupposes two main tendencies at work, arising out of differences in the poets themselves.[1] First, there was the graver sort who represented noble actions, and again, there were those who dealt with ignoble deeds of ignoble men; and these differences were reflected in the early hymns, the panegyrics, and the Homeric epics on the one hand, and in the poetry of invective on the other hand, of which Archilochus was the chief representative. Such then were the determining influences in the earliest poetry as Aristotle conceived it; and to him they remained decisive factors throughout the later development, giving rise in due course to both tragedy and comedy. Indeed already in Homer the elements of both kinds were said to be present; for if tragedy was anticipated in the dramatic quality of the *Iliad* and *Odyssey*, in the *Margites*, so it was claimed, the general form of the later comedy was outlined, a dramatic picture of the ridiculous being given therein. The actual beginnings of the drama however he traces to those authors of dithyrambs who first introduced into their choral poetry improvised speeches (ῥῆσις), thus giving rise to the two constituent elements of later tragedy, that is, dialogue and song.[2] And in like manner comedy was said to have developed out of the popular phallus-songs, the author in this case relating some ribald story in the intervals of the songs. After this Aristotle gives a brief sketch of the gradual improvement of tragedy under the influence of Aeschylus and Sophocles. Thus Aeschylus in the first place is said to have brought on the second actor, while at the same time diminishing the part of the chorus, and making the dialogue the most important element. Sophocles, again, it is stated, introduced a third actor, and brought scenery on to the stage. And in the meantime a general refining process had gone on. Tragedy, which in its primitive stage had been akin to the satyric drama, soon learnt to discard its earlier crudities. In place of a comic diction and a trochaic measure with its associations of dancing, tragic poets devised a more appropriate mode of expression: they adopted the iambic measure for instance as being more suited for dialogue, and by lengthening their stories and increasing

[1] 1448b, 24ff.   [2] 1449a, 9ff.

their episodes they gave to their work a new dignity and grandeur. Concerning the early stages of comedy, on the other hand, Aristotle has less to say.[1] For a long time, he states, it was a dramatic form that was not taken seriously; and who it was that originated the plurality of actors and the use of prologues was said to be unknown. At the same time he calls attention to perhaps its most significant development, to the discarding of that personal invective which was characteristic of the oldest comedies, and the invention in its place of stories of a general and impersonal character. As pioneers in this movement he mentions Epicharmus and Phormis of Sicily; whereas at Athens Crates was said to have been the first to generalise his themes. Such then is Aristotle's exposition of the growth of dramatic poetry in its earlier stages; and it represents the first attempt to deal with literature from the historical point of view. Most of what he says on this matter of origins has since become the commonplaces of literary history; but that is merely a proof of the soundness of his analysis, and of the skill with which he has selected the salient and essential points. In establishing the principle of development in literature, and in seeking for natural causes in such development, Aristotle without a doubt pointed the way to a more fruitful study of literature; and the significance of his teaching is perhaps best realised when compared with the antiquarian and philological speculations concerning literature which characterised his age.

It yet remains to estimate Aristotle's achievement as a judicial critic. And this side of his work, though incidental to his main purpose, nevertheless contains much that is of lasting interest, not only in the light it throws on the contemporary methods of forming literary judgment, but also in its bearing on the theory and practice of criticism in general. His main contribution of this kind is found in that section of his work (c. xxv) which he devotes to "problems and their solutions"; and here for all practical purposes he is discussing the critical performances of his day, those judgments passed on literature in the schools or in social gatherings, or else by those cavilling critics, of whom the elder Euclid, Ariphrades, and Zoilus were

[1] 1449 b, 1 ff.

in all probability representative. The matter was one which had previously attracted the attention of Plato, who had censured the pedantic and arbitrary findings of Protagoras, Hippias, and others, in their efforts at interpreting poetry.[1] And now Aristotle attempts a more comprehensive treatment, classifying with some show of system the customary grounds of censure, and then suggesting in each instance how such destructive criticism was best met. That much of the contemporary criticism, in the first place, was concerned with verbal matters would appear from the consideration given by Aristotle to remarks of the kind. And in each case he reveals the weakness of the critical methods and the false judgments which resulted. Thus Ariphrades is said to have ridiculed tragic poets for their use of unusual words,[2] while the elder Euclid had derided the practice of lengthening syllables *metri causa*.[3] And both, so Aristotle explains, were ignorant that these were poetic licences which gave distinction and variety by their departures from the normal idiom. Or again, there were those who made it their business to show up absurdities, inconsistencies, and contradictions in expression. Thus objection might be taken to Homer's description of Dolon as "deformed" (εἶδος...κακός) "yet swift of foot" (*Il.* x, 316);[4] or again, of the whole (πάντες) Grecian host as wrapped in sleep, though music and the noise of men were heard by Agamemnon (*Il.* x, 13, 14).[5] Such irregularities, however, according to Aristotle, were mostly of the critic's own making; for εἶδος...κακός might stand for "ugly of face", while πάντες in a metaphorical sense might be taken to mean "many", thus removing all inconsistencies. The truth was, as Aristotle proceeds to point out, that in the verbal criticism then current many hasty and arbitrary assumptions were made; and he recalls with approval the earlier comment of one Glaucon on the critical methods of his time. According to that writer "critics jumped at certain groundless conclusions, passed adverse judgment, then proceeded to reason on it, and assuming that the poet had said whatever they happened to think, found fault if a thing was inconsistent with their own

---

[1] See p. 42 *supra*.   [2] 1458b, 31 ff.   [3] 1458b, 7 ff.
[4] 1461 a, 12.   [5] 1461 a, 16.

fancy".[1] And in view of such facts Aristotle recommends methods of a more reasoned kind. The correctness or incorrectness of a word was to be determined by an appeal to the custom of language or the usage of the poet; the context was to be considered, metaphorical usage and punctuation taken into account; and in this way was outlined a new art of interpretation which was likely to arrive at sounder results.

Apart from this verbal criticism, however, much of the contemporary critical activity, it would seem, was devoted to judgments on subject-matter. Thus, Aristotle explains, critics were wont to censure elements in poetic themes that seemed to them impossible or irrational or morally hurtful or technically incorrect; and such judgments, he adds, were in general ill-founded, being based on an imperfect understanding of poetry and poetic truth. In the first place, there were the objections raised against impossibilities ($\dot{a}\delta\dot{v}\nu\alpha\tau\alpha$) in poetry, those incidents or characters which were described as unreal or untrue, corresponding to nothing in the actual life of man; and these alleged "impossibilities", Aristotle states, were in general of three kinds. First, there were those elements which were said to be too good to be true; the ideal characters and forms of Sophocles and Zeuxis, for instance, which were indeed unreal in the sense that they surpassed reality. Yet, as Aristotle points out in his statement with regard to "imitation",[2] poetry was not necessarily concerned with empirical fact; it dealt also with what transcended fact, with higher truths ($\tau\dot{o}\ \beta\dot{\epsilon}\lambda\tau\iota o\nu$) that could not be realised. And Sophocles's characters and Zeuxis's forms came under this heading.[3] They were true to nature and her ideal tendencies; they were unrealised ideals of men as they ought to be; and, as such, fitting matter for poetry. Then, in the second place, objection was sometimes taken to details, not that they were idealistic, but that they were simply at variance with recognised facts or existing customs; and of this Homer's statement that "upright on their butt-ends stood the spears" (*Il.* x, 152) was quoted as an example.[4] Here again, however, Aristotle appeals to his conception of "imitation",

---

[1] 1461 b, 1 ff. (tr. Bywater).
[3] 1460 b, 36; 1461 b, 12.
[2] See p. 79 *supra*.
[4] 1461 a, 1 ff.

according to which the poet might deal with things either past or present. Since this fashion of fixing spears, he points out, had existed at the time of writing (and incidentally was still current among the Illyrians), he maintains that there was present no "impossibility" here, but rather a normal treatment of recognised poetic material. And in this judgment, it might be added, was anticipated the later historical method of Aristarchus, who, regarding Homer as the product of an earlier era, interpreted his work in the light of those earlier conditions. Then, thirdly, objections were being raised to the familiar tales of the gods as representing stories at variance with the truth, and therefore "impossibilities" of yet another kind. These objections Aristotle also disposes of by referring as before to his principle of "imitation". He concedes that such stories represented neither things as they had been or were, nor things as they ought to be;[1] they were neither true in fact, nor did they express a higher reality. Yet he claims that they formed part of the traditional belief; they stood, in other words, for things as they were thought to be; and according to his basic doctrine they too constituted suitable material for poetic treatment.

Concerning the irrational (ἄλογα) elements in poetic subject-matter Aristotle has rather less to say; though here again he is evidently commenting on judicial methods then current, and more particularly on the tendency to condemn outright all such irrational material wherever found. By these irrational elements were meant, not material impossibilities, but rather those anomalous, abnormal, incidents which were illogical in their working and improbable in their effects; such an incident, for instance, as Achilles's pursuit of Hector round the walls of Troy, with the Greek army looking on (*Il.* XXII, 205). And Aristotle makes it plain from his theorising elsewhere that in general he regards such flagrant improbabilities as defects in poetry; despite Agathon's suggestion that it is often the unexpected that comes about, it being "probable that many things should happen contrary to probability" (εἰκὸς γὰρ γίνεσθαι πολλὰ καὶ παρὰ τὸ εἰκός).[2] At the same time, Aristotle points out, there was need for discretion in handling such incidents, since there

---

[1] 1460b, 36.   [2] 1456a, 24.

were circumstances in which they could conceivably be justified in virtue of some other artistic law.[1] Thus the "improbable" he regarded as the chief factor in the "marvellous",[2] and therefore capable of adding an element of wonder, which would heighten the poetic effect. Provided that such effects could not have been attained otherwise, then the use of the irrational or the improbable was in his opinion fully justified. For it not only by its wonder effaced the sense of incongruity; it also served a legitimate purpose of art. It brought to poetry an element of pleasing surprise, specially suitable to the epic; and thus contributed materially to the aesthetic end.

Then, further, there were the objections brought against this or that passage of poetry that it was morally harmful; and Aristotle comments briefly on this particular point. That he held, generally speaking, that the requirements of morality were to be satisfied in poetry, has already been stated. What he now objects to in the critical judgments of his time was the unfailing and unconsidered condemnation of evil characters and unedifying incidents. In passing judgment, he maintains, the attention was not to be confined to the particular action or saying in question. On the contrary, all the circumstances had first to be taken into account; since some consideration of the conditions and motives concerned might alter things, and lead to a modification of the initial judgment. An evil action for instance might conceivably have been designed to avert a yet greater evil.[3] Or again, elements of a morally offensive kind were frequently justified by poetic necessity, or the requirements of a plot.[4] Without evil agents of some sort, for example, a catastrophe was impossible; whereas evil characters contrasted with good made characterisation more effective. Needless depravity of character or deed would always demand censure; but, for the rest, there were many factors to be considered before passing moral judgment.

And lastly, there were the judgments based on technical inaccuracies in poetry, that is, inaccuracies in subject-matter relating to some other art ($\tau \acute{\epsilon} \chi \nu \eta$) or branch of study. These, too, Aristotle calls in question, pointing out that adverse judgments

[1] 1460b, 24.   [2] 1460a, 13.   [3] 1461a, 4.   [4] 1461b, 19ff.

in such cases were often undeserved. He allows, to begin with, that inaccuracies due to the poet's failure to give adequate expression to his ideas were without doubt artistic blemishes, and therefore worthy of censure.[1] Yet the same was not true of incorrectness of detail arising out of a lack of knowledge of politics or medicine or history and the like. Such details, handled properly, would often be found to leave the total artistic impression unimpaired; they did not touch the essence of the poetic art, and were of the nature of poetic licences. In short, to censure a picture for errors of anatomy or a piece of poetry for its use of unscientific or unhistorical facts, meant nothing less in Aristotle's opinion than a confusion of standards. Each art, he implied, was to be judged by its own laws and standards; and "the standard of correctness", he asserted, "is not the same in poetry and politics, any more than in poetry and any other art".[2]

Here then in these penetrating comments on the critical activities of his contemporaries lay what was perhaps Aristotle's main contribution to judicial criticism. From them we gather indirectly something of the nature of the critical judgments then current; the superficial and arbitrary methods of verbal interpretation, as well as the destructive and short-sighted criticism based on the mechanical tests of reality and morality. And in place of all this Aristotle puts forward methods of a more reasoned and fruitful kind, pointing out above all that aesthetic criteria were the only tests, and that the true basis of literary judgment lay in the requirements and standards of art. Of the value of such teaching there can be no doubt; indeed an observance of the principles thus laid down would have prevented the futilities of much of the later Homeric criticism which continued throughout the centuries following. As it was, however, the *Poetics* was destined to exercise but slight influence on later critics, owing to the disappearance of the text for a century or more; and critics of Homer, as a consequence, with but few exceptions, persisted in their use of the methods condemned by Aristotle, and in forming their judgments on a purely ethical or matter-of-fact basis.

[1] 1460b, 17.   [2] 1460b, 14 (tr. Butcher).

Yet, in addition to his criticism of critics, Aristotle has also a contribution of his own to make to judgments on literature itself; and what he has to show, though incidental in character and illustrative mostly of points of theory he happens to be discussing, has nevertheless certain merits which distinguish it from earlier attempts at literary appreciation. For one thing his judgments will be found to rest solely on aesthetic grounds. They are concerned with artistic points only; and the verbal quibbles, the irrelevant discussions on inaccuracies of fact, improbabilities, and moral questions, which he had condemned in others, he avoids throughout. Then, too, his remarks for the most part deal with literature in the concrete. They are no mere generalities, but reasoned comments on actual texts; and the result is a body of criticism, which though limited in scope, is yet of considerable intrinsic value. Most of his appreciations concern Homer and the great writers of tragedy; and of Homer, in particular, he has some interesting remarks to make. In one place, for example, Homer is praised as a master of poetic expression, unrivalled in thought and diction, the model of all epic excellences;[1] his characters moreover are said to be of an ideal kind;[2] while elsewhere his supreme merit is said to lie in his observance of the unity of action, in his selection of a group of incidents making up a single coherent story, from which all irrelevant details are omitted.[3] In addition, his objective treatment of his story is duly commended; he allowed his characters to speak for themselves, and spoke "but little in his own person".[4] Or again, his skill in the methods of fiction is pointed out. The fanciful parts of his story he is shown to have commended to his readers by infusing an element of obvious truth, which gave an air of veracity to the whole, thus illustrating his mastery of "the artistic lie".[5] Of the dramatists it is Sophocles who receives the most favourable attention; Aeschylus is but seldom referred to, whereas Aristotle's admiration for Sophocles is manifest throughout the work. Thus Sophocles's *Oedipus* he probably regarded as his representative tragedy; he refers to it more than once in terms of

[1] 1448b, 35. [2] 1448a, 11. [3] 1459a, 30.
[4] 1460a, 5. [5] 1460a, 21.

praise, commending in particular the convincing nature of its
"recognition" (ἀναγνώρισις), in which the element of surprise
arose naturally out of the incidents themselves, and not out of
artificial devices.[1] In addition, Sophocles is praised for his
handling of the Chorus, which with him was one of the actors
and an integral part of the play;[2] and again, he is commended
more than once for his ideal characterisation. His claim that
"he drew men as they ought to be, Euripides, as they were"[3]
is quoted with approval by Aristotle; and here the reference is
not to moral goodness but to dramatic requirements, to the
ideally human qualities of Sophocles's characters as contrasted
with the realistic, everyday personalities of Euripides. On the
other hand Euripides is dealt with in less flattering vein. He is
described, it is true, as the most tragic (τραγικώτατος) of poets,
unique in his power of arousing pity and fear;[4] and this in
virtue of his unhappy endings, which Aristotle declares to be
the right endings for tragedy. Then, too, Aristotle appears to
be making a concession to the practice of Euripides when he
approves of the employment of a god to deal with matters
outside the play. At any rate in this direction Euripides had
previously innovated, making use of a divine being in the
prologues and epilogues of some of his plays.[5] Apart from this,
however, Aristotle's remarks on Euripides are mainly censorious;
and it is no longer on account of the dramatist's immoral
influence. What he finds fault with is Euripides's workmanship,
his defective structural ability (μὴ εὖ οἰκονομεῖ),[6] and his
occasional lapses in matters of characterisation. The rhetorical
qualities of his style, for instance, are indicated when Aristotle
declares that the characters of the older poets discoursed like
statesmen (πολιτικῶς λέγειν), those of the later poets like
rhetoricians.[7] And here the reference is evidently to the artifice
and point which distinguished the dialogue of Euripides from
that of his predecessors. Then objection is taken to his choral
songs, on the ground that they were apt to be but loosely connected with the plot;[8] or again, the *dénouement* in the *Medea* is

[1] 1455a, 18.   [2] 1456a, 25.   [3] 1460b, 33.
[4] 1453a, 30.   [5] 1454b, 2; see Bywater, note, *loc. cit.*
[6] 1453a, 29.   [7] 1450b, 7.   [8] 1456a, 27.

condemned as artificial and unconvincing, being brought about by a *deus ex machina*;[1] while to defects in his characterisation Aristotle refers more than once. Thus fault is found with Menelaus in *Orestes* as being unnecessarily base for the part he plays in the action;[2] the character of Iphigenia (in *Iphigenia at Aulis*) is said to be inconsistently drawn, Iphigenia the suppliant being altogether different from her later self;[3] Aegeus in *Medea* is described as a redundant character, contributing nothing to the play;[4] and Melanippe, again, is charged with indecorum, giving evidence in her speech of cleverness unbecoming in a woman.[5] These then are the main literary judgments passed in the *Poetics*; though to them must be added some occasional comments on Agathon, who, it is worth noting, is mentioned throughout with the respect due to a successful playwright. Thus in one place reference is made to his skill in inventing successful plots for the stage; and his *Antheus* is quoted as an example of this.[6] On the other hand it is suggested that his pathos is not always of a legitimate kind, his tragic situations inspiring not so much the overwhelming pity and fear of the best tragedies as a sort of inferior sympathy (φιλάνθρωπον) with the sufferers.[7] And again, he is definitely charged with those innovations in the chorus, as a consequence of which the choral songs became mere interludes, detached entirely from the rest of the play.[8]

From these various comments of Aristotle on the great writers of the preceding age something of his merits as a judicial critic may easily be gathered. That in this field, as in the matter of theory, he was an innovator is plain; for he points unmistakably to more illuminating methods of criticism, to methods that deal primarily with aesthetic values. Nor is he concerned solely with fault-finding; his appreciations have their positive side as well; and with the exception of his remark on Melanippe, his judgments for the most part have lasting value. The truth is that those judgments were invariably based on the theory he had developed, each judgment being but the

---

[1] 1454b, 1. [2] 1454a, 29. [3] 1454a, 32.
[4] 1461b, 21. [5] 1454a, 31. [6] 1451b, 21.
[7] 1456a, 18, 21; see Bywater, notes, *loc. cit.* [8] 1456a, 29.

application of that theory. And this accounts largely for his reasoned estimates, for the sanity and penetration of his remarks, which concern themselves solely with the essentials of the poetic art. Nor in this connexion is his conception of the ideal critic irrelevant; for elsewhere in his writings he makes it plain that he distrusts the judgment of the expert or specialist in aesthetic matters.[1] His preference is for the collective judgment of the many, the verdict of an educated public which is based on the whole rather than on certain aspects of a literary work. And in the representative of that public, a man of educated tastes, he finds the ideal critic, the touchstone of literary values.

Such then in general are the main lines of Aristotle's theorising in his *Poetics*. It is a comprehensive treatment of poetry, its nature and art, revealing many of the first principles of literary theory and the canons of the dramatic art, and constituting, besides, a valuable study of critical method, a mine of suggestive ideas, and one of the few pieces of systematic criticism that have come down from the ancient world. In form it is primarily a philosophical treatise; but there is a sense in which it is also the first of the poetic "Arts", and yet another in which it is the earliest "Apology" for poetry. In it are also included elements of rhetoric, grammar, and judicial criticism; and these were elements which at a later date were to form separate studies. Of the defects of the work something has already been said—its unedited and mutilated form, its cryptic utterance, its ambiguities, its contradictions and omissions—and these are notoriously matters that brought confusion to later critical effort, and have taxed the scholarship of all the ages. Other defects were in some measure the outcome of Aristotle's own qualities; his scientific and logical bias, for example, which, while it enabled him to bring out the rational element of poetry, yet rendered him less capable of treating its aesthetic qualities. He does not altogether ignore the "transport" of poetry; but he is more concerned with it as reasoned utterance, with its structure and its thought, rather than with its charm and colour; and there is much in Greek poetry alone that escapes Aristotle's analysis. Then again in his philoso-

[1] *Pol.* III, 11, 1282 a, 1–21; see Butcher, *op. cit.* p. 211.

phising a lack of free speculation is perceptible; it is as if his range was prescribed by the charges he had to meet. Of tragedy as an interpretation of life he says but little. He nowhere refers to the great problems that give vitality to Greek tragedy, problems relating to man and his cosmic relations, to the workings of Fate, human destiny and the like. It would seem that he was merely careful to frame a reply to Plato's indictment; and with this he is apparently for the most part content. For the skill, on the other hand, with which he employs his psychological methods, no praise can be too high. Their working is seen from beginning to end, from his early statement about the origin and development of poetry to his later deductions regarding the nature of tragedy. And yet here too, to our modern thinking, there is something vague and imperfect; for he fails to recognise the part played by the imagination in all poetic activity. Elsewhere in his works he speaks of "phantasia" (φαντασία) as an image-forming faculty,[1] capable of reproducing images of sensible objects. But it is reproductive merely, without creative or transforming power. The idea of "imagination" is to some extent implicit in his conception of "imitation" and the fictional element in poetry; but it is nowhere explicitly treated in Aristotelian theory.

Nevertheless, in spite of shortcomings, the *Poetics* remains one of the greatest contributions to literary and critical theory, one of those rare books that have had lasting influence on the minds of men. With Aristotle came first the conception of theory as opposed to practice, of literary matter as opposed to literary form; and, after he had written, the way was prepared for a further analysis of art, free from prejudices of an ethical or political kind. Among the more important of his pronouncements is that in which poetry is defined as a concrete expression of the universal, and therefore representative of the highest truth; though equally significant is his challenge of the ethical view of poetry, his contention that the poet's function is primarily to give pleasure. So that, from now on, there was no excuse for regarding poetry as a copy of reality or for confusing aesthetic with moral standards in judging art. Then, too, there

[1] *De Anima*, III, 3, 429a, 1; see Butcher, *op. cit.* pp. 125–6.

is his theory of "imitation", which in spite of later misunder-standings has the merit of making clear those relations of nature and art which undoubtedly exist in poetry; while, following Plato, he also emphasises the supreme importance of organic unity in all artistic work. In his treatment of tragedy he introduces us systematically to the logic of art, to the technique of dramatic structure, the theory of "probability" and the rest; and there is this further to be added, that while his doctrine of "catharsis" is something more than an ingenious piece of special pleading, his remarks on *hamartia* and *peripeteia* bring to light some of the most distinctive features of tragedy in its truest form. Elsewhere he calls attention to the place of the marvellous in poetry as affording a legitimate aesthetic delight, to the need for a certain distinction of language in poetic diction; and in numerous other places does he open up new trains of thought by means of casual hints which it was left for later ages to develop and complete. That his theorising lent itself at times to later misconstruction is also, of course, true; and the uncertain position he takes up with regard to metre is an illustration of this. There is also the doctrine of the "kinds" for which he was incidentally responsible. To him it was probably nothing more than a convenient classification of the practice of poets, whereas to later ages it came to denote a system of fixed "types", with definite qualities and hard-and-fast rules, a theory which lay at the root of much of the later heresy. Then, too, it is significant that, although much of his work was concerned with formal questions, his definition of poetry was couched in terms of subject-matter, not form; and so for ages to come the essence of poetry was held to reside in the ideas conveyed, that is, in the *inventio*, an idea that was seemingly confirmed by the prevailing study of rhetoric. Nor were his methods altogether free from later misinterpretation. His *Poetics* had been written in a coldly logical manner; and this did much to encourage the false idea that the emotional effects of poetry could be normally attained by following rules of composition, by orderly arrangement, sound structure and the rest, a conception which led on naturally to the later worship of the rules.

Yet, when all is said, the *Poetics* is perhaps the most living of Aristotelian works. Written in the severest of styles, devoid of all literary grace, it forms a treasury of ideas of lasting value, the full significance of which it has taken centuries to understand. In it we see Aristotle as the first of the systematic theorists, an early exponent of the historical and psychological methods, and incidentally a pioneer in the business of sane literary judgment; so that alike in the theory and the practice of criticism the work stands at the beginning of things, developing and extending the findings of Plato. Of late the small treatise has been subjected to some amount of depreciation, a reaction doubtless from the extravagant praise of former ages. Yet in the history of criticism its importance is unquestionable and fundamental. It is neither an infallible guide nor yet an antiquated text-book, but for breadth of outlook and sanity of judgment, for sheer penetrating power into the mysteries of art, the work is unrivalled; and all modern theorising has still to reckon with the contents of its "discreet, unromantic" pages.

CHAPTER V

THE DEVELOPMENT OF RHETORICAL THEORY: ISOCRATES, ARISTOTLE, AND THEOPHRASTUS[1]

SO far we have been tracing the critical activities of Plato and Aristotle, more particularly in relation to poetry. We have noted Plato's challenging questions and Aristotle's reply to those questions; the substantial body of poetic theory, as well, that was the outcome of those discussions. And, were this all that the fourth century B.C. had to offer in the way of criticism, it would still stand out as the most fruitful and significant epoch in the whole of critical history. Yet this is by no means the whole story of the critical achievement at this date. Along with the inquiry into poetic theory there went a corresponding development in rhetorical theory; and this too was destined to play a large part in later history, owing to the light it shed on the principles of oratory and prose style. Connected with the movement were Isocrates, Aristotle, and Theophrastus; though to these must be added Anaximenes and Heraclides of Pontus, as well as a host of others such as Alcidamas, Lycophron, Polycrates, Callipus, and Pamphilus, of whose work however but little or nothing is known. And it was from the three first-mentioned that the main contribution came; each of those writers working on separate lines, and each making a characteristic addition of his own to rhetorical theory. It is true that the full details of their theorising are no longer available; the teaching of Isocrates and Theophrastus, more especially, having come down in but fragmentary form. Yet sufficient

---

[1] *Texts and Translations.* ISOCRATES: *Works*, text and trans. by G. Norlin (Loeb Cl. Lib.), 3 vols., London and New York, 1928; *The First Ten Orations*, trans. J. H. Freese (Bohn Lib.), London, 1894. ARISTOTLE: *Rhetoric*, ed. with trans. (in notes) by E. M. Cope, 3 vols., Cambridge, 1878; trans. J. E. C. Welldon, London, 1886; trans. R. C. Jebb (ed. J. E. Sandys), Cambridge, 1909; ed. with trans. by J. H. Freese (Loeb Cl. Lib.), London and New York, 1926; trans. (with commentary) by Lane Cooper, New York, 1932; Hobbes's Digest of the *Rhetoric*, ed. T. A. Moxon (Everyman's Lib.), London, 1934. *Extracts*, in Saintsbury, *Loci Critici*, pp. 22–31; in J. D. Denniston, *Greek Lit. Crit.* pp. 136–44. THEOPHRASTUS: A. Mayer, *Theophrasti περὶ Λέξεως Libri Fragmenta*, Leipzig, 1910.

has survived to enable us to form a general estimate of their performances. And all three, it might be added, were later on the accepted authorities on rhetoric at Rome, as is shown by the frequent references to their doctrines in the works of Cicero, Dionysius of Halicarnassus, Demetrius, and Quintilian.

For the causes which led to this new form of critical activity we must look to the contemporary conditions and to influences that were at work in the state. With the decline of imaginative literature in the course of the century it was inevitable, to begin with, that the earlier preoccupation with poetry should cease. In its place were substituted interests of a political kind, arising out of the turmoil into which the state was plunged; and thence arose a new oratory full of absorbing interest, in which grave national issues were debated and noble causes defended. Thus did the law-court take the place of the theatre as the centre of public life; the speeches of Demosthenes became the representative achievements in art. And as a result attention was directed anew to the task of improving public speech, fresh impetus being given to the study of oratory in general. To meet this new demand, however, but little systematic guidance had come from the preceding generation. And Plato's sweeping strictures on the earlier rhetoricians were well founded, when he censured their empirical methods, their scholastic subtleties, and their concern in general with the non-essentials of the art. He himself, it is true, did not a little to correct such abuses, in adding to his censures certain important principles of a constructive kind. Yet in practice his influence did not make for an advancement of the study. To him dialectic was "the crown of all the sciences";[1] and the study of rhetoric he regarded as a challenge to that position. Moreover, against the new art he harboured a certain prejudice; in his eyes it was nothing more than a flattery and a sham; and it is not without its significance that it forms no part of his educational scheme in his *Republic*. These, then, were the conditions which led to the attempts made by Isocrates, Aristotle, and others to improve oratory, and, incidentally, prose style. As philosophers of a more practical turn they were alive to the political

[1] *Rep.* 534.

and educational values of rhetoric, to its possibilities as well as an instrument of expression; and both teachers, it should be noted, included it in the curriculum of their schools. Different conceptions of the study were however formulated by each; though, as if conscious of its challenge to philosophy as the main instrument of education, both described the new rhetoric as a philosophy of sorts. To Isocrates, for instance, it was a system of culture which enabled men to speak and write on matters of universal import, thus preparing them for service to the state. To Aristotle, again, it was a pendant of dialectic, capable of being organised on philosophical lines. And in accordance with these views a new rhetoric was developed, which, while marking an advance on what had gone before, embodied also not a few principles of lasting value in the study of rhetoric and prose style.

First among the new teachers was Isocrates[1] (436–338 B.C.), that "old man eloquent", a contemporary of both Plato and Aristotle, whose school of rhetoric, opened about 392 B.C., led to the establishment of his fame throughout the whole Hellenic world. As a distinguished pupil of Gorgias he gave instruction in the art of speaking on political subjects; and for more than forty years he was the most famous teacher in Athens, and one of its most influential men. Among his pupils were included the historians Ephorus and Theopompus, the orators Hyperides, Isaeus, and Lycurgus, besides men like Nicocles, afterwards king of Salamis in Cyprus; and it was the popularity of his school—an undeserved popularity, according to the view traditionally assigned to Aristotle—that induced the latter to set up subsequently a school of his own. Isocrates, it was asserted, had concerned himself mainly with beauty of diction, while neglecting the essentials of the art; and Aristotle aimed at counteracting his efforts by inaugurating a study on more scientific lines. Of works written by Isocrates bearing directly on literary criticism, practically nothing has come down. He is held by some to have written a formal *Rhetoric*, of which however but few traces remain;[2] and for his ideas on the subject we have to refer mainly to his educational discourses or

[1] For an account of his life and works see Jebb, *Attic Orators*, II, 1–260.
[2] See *Isocratis Orationes*, ed. Benseler-Blass, II, 275.

essays, *Against the Sophists* (390 B.C.) and the *Antidosis* (353 B.C.);
though his political discourses *Panegyricus, Panathenaicus, Areo-
pagiticus*, and the like, have for us this further interest, that in
the absence of a formal *Rhetoric* they furnish some idea of that
conception of style which entered so largely into his oral
teaching. He wrote also three hortatory letters or letters of
advice, *To Demonicus* (393 B.C.), *To Nicocles* (374 B.C.), and
Nicocles (372 B.C.); early examples of a device which became
later a convention among Roman rhetoricians, namely, the
conveyance of instruction in epistolary form to the son of some
distinguished member of the writer's circle of friends. Moreover in the discourses *Busiris* (390 B.C.), *Helen* (370 B.C.), and
Evagoras (365 B.C.) he is seen in the light of a practical critic,
reviewing the current treatment of mythological subjects and
panegyrics, and showing how he himself would have dealt
with such things. Of all these writings, however, the greatest
interest for our present purpose lies in the two educational
discourses. In his pamphlet *Against the Sophists* he enunciates in
part his literary and educational creed by distinguishing his
position from that of the earlier sophists; in the *Antidosis*,
again, a speech professedly delivered in connexion with a law-
suit, he completes his vindication of himself and his art by
revealing the principles that had animated him throughout his
long career. And it is here that we get his main body of theory,
the ideas that underlay his teaching and practice.

On the whole it is in the new direction, the fresh impulse he
gave to the study of rhetoric, that the influence of Isocrates in
criticism is perhaps most clearly seen. It was his solution of the
problem, then exercising the minds of his contemporaries, regarding the form of higher education best suited to Athenian
needs. The sophists had advocated a study of rhetoric along
with a sort of encyclopaedic training; whereas Plato, on the
other hand, while decrying the traditional schemes of poetry
and rhetoric, had stood for an education based on the pursuit of
philosophy or abstract truth. And now Isocrates comes forward
with a scheme of his own, ostensibly a reversion to the position
of the sophists, but in reality embodying some substantial
differences. Thus the sophists had been concerned mainly with

the oratory of the law-courts. Aiming solely at persuasion they had lost themselves in a maze of tricks and devices; and whereas they had attached to mechanical methods an infallible efficacy, the themes they had handled had invariably been of a trifling kind, consisting either of barren disputations on mythological subjects or of petty details bound up with legal pleading. What Isocrates had in mind was something quite different; something more than the art of composing successful speeches or of argument for argument's sake. Rhetoric for him implied a "philosophy", a cultural study, in which fitting expression was sought for elevated themes, and the art of speaking or writing on large political topics was inculcated as a practical training for the active duties of a citizen. Hence his broader conception of the aims of rhetoric. A union of philosophy and the earlier rhetoric was in fact what he suggested; for to the acquiring of sound views on life he attached a prime importance. And, besides reforming rhetoric in the substance of its ideas, he at the same time extended its field by turning the attention primarily to declamatory or epideictic eloquence; while, mindful of the demands of art, he also innovated freely in matters of composition and style. Such then was the rhetoric which Isocrates advocated as the best training for life. It was a training that provided men with a healthy mental gymnastic, that furnished them with sound general ideas, and developed in them also the power of expression. It was in short a "philosophy" with a practical end; and rhetoric thus defined took on a new status.

With this then as his animating purpose, it was but natural that part of his criticism should be concerned with the defects of the prevailing rhetorical teaching. And in the first place he attacks the teachers of "eristic", a debased form of dialectic, which consisted of disputation for disputation's sake in the field of ethics.[1] Among such teachers were probably Antisthenes and Euclides; and their methods he ridicules as being mere imposture. Then, too, there were the rhetoricians who professed to give instruction in the art of speaking in the law-court and the Assembly. According to their claims they could make

[1] *Against the Sophists*, 2–8; *Antidosis*, 261; *Panathenaicus*, 26.

an orator of anyone, the process being merely one of acquiring certain rules; and such claims Isocrates also derides in the strongest of terms.[1] Or again, there were the earlier writers of *Arts* of rhetoric. They had confined themselves solely to oratory of a forensic kind; and their efforts were condemned by Isocrates as treating of the least worthy branch of rhetoric, and dealing with petty quarrels instead of large and elevating ideas.[2] Nor are his censures couched only in general terms. He finds occasion to condemn certain details of the earlier rhetorical procedure; and in each instance his remarks are highly significant. Thus he notes specially the mechanical conception of oratory then prevalent, in that rhetoricians regarded what after all was a creative process ($\pi o\iota\eta\tau\iota\kappa\grave{o}\nu$ $\pi\rho\hat{a}\gamma\mu a$) as nothing more than an art with hard and fast rules.[3] Such a notion, he conceded, held good in connexion with the correct use of letters, that is, the art of spelling; for there it was a question of elements that admitted of no variation. In speaking (or writing), however, there were many subtle factors to be considered, and no such fixed rules were possible. Elsewhere again, he attacks the practice of rhetoricians in choosing, as the themes of their declamatory exercises, subjects obviously futile and designed merely to air their own cleverness.[4] Thus he mentions such paradoxical themes as "that one cannot lie", or "that nothing exists", or "that the same things are both possible and impossible"; and such themes he attributes to Protagoras, Gorgias, and others. But ingenious displays of this kind, he maintained, were nothing more than an offence to men of sense; they were of no practical value, being remote from actual life. Moreover the avoidance of serious themes he regarded as in itself a confession of weakness; it was as if the speaker (or writer) refused to come into the open, fearing competition or censure. Trifling subjects, he added, were easily handled; and to descant on the virtues of "bumble-bees" or "salt"[5] called for no great genius. In short, it was only in treating of great

---

[1] *Against the Sophists*, 9 ff.   [2] *Ibid.* 19–20.
[3] *Ibid.* 12.   [4] *Helen*, 1–13.
[5] Other references to such trivial subjects occur in Plato, *Symposium*, 177 b (salt) and Aristotle, *Rhet.* ii, 24, 2 (mice); see also Jebb, *Attic Orators*, ii, 103 f.n.

issues that great utterance was possible; so that these subjects, and these alone, were necessary for true epideictic eloquence. And here, it might be noted, Isocrates was anticipating the later protests which were to be made at Rome against similar rhetorical abuses then current.[1]

Of greater importance, however, is his positive teaching which consists of statements concerning the value of eloquence in human life, some remarks on the proper methods of teaching the subject, and, thirdly, an exposition of the principles under-lying an artistic prose. Such theorising, it is true, is to be found systematically treated in no one of his works; it lies scattered throughout his numerous writings and has to be pieced together from remarks made here and there. Yet some idea of his main theories may nevertheless by this means be formed, theories which doubtless underlay his oral teaching. And in the first place there are his enthusiastic pronouncements on the value of eloquence, which are repeated more than once. The power of speech in general he describes as the source of most human blessings. It is the faculty that distinguishes men from the brute beasts, and has enabled them to live the civilised life, by assisting in the founding of cities, the establishment of laws, and the invention of arts.[2] In all human thought and action, moreover, it is the guide; it is the instrument of those who have most wisdom. By eloquence, for example, evil is confuted and goodness extolled; disputes are cleared up, advances in know-ledge made; the ignorant are instructed and wise men tested. Then, too, it is said to have a transforming power. Thus great-ness it can represent as littleness, or bestow greatness in turn on insignificant themes.[3] It can also render well-known facts more impressive, making by its treatment old things new and new things familiar. Nor is such eloquence confined to public speech; its processes are employed also by those who deliberate (βουλευόμενοι).[4] And at its best it may be described as the mark of an understanding mind, a reflexion of character, and an outward image of inward virtues of soul (ψυχῆς ἀγαθῆς καὶ πιστῆς εἴδωλον),[5]—an anticipation of "Longinus's" later dictum

---

[1] See vol. II, 145.   [2] *Nicocles*, 5–9; *Antidosis*, 254.
[3] *Panegyricus*, 8.   [4] *Nicocles*, 8.   [5] *Ibid.* 7.

that "great utterance is an echo of greatness of soul". Here then was set forth in impressive fashion a claim for the recognition of eloquence in the affairs of life. And there is this further to be said, that, since Isocrates has throughout a reading public in mind, his statement is as much concerned with a literary prose as with oratory or the prose of public speech. Nor is the force of his remarks lessened by the fact that some at least of his statements were commonplaces at the time. This was evidently true of the faculty ascribed to eloquence of "making small things great and great things small"; a claim which Plato derided in his remarks on Tisias and Gorgias.[1] Again there is the statement that civilisation had developed under the guidance of eloquence, and as a result of man's power of speech and his ability to persuade. This doctrine had not originated with Isocrates; along with other ideas it was probably derived from earlier sophists, who in their turn had drawn on yet earlier sources, adapting for rhetoric the claim which had previously been set up for poetry as the great civilising agency in primitive times.[2] One of the commonplaces of antiquity was the power of Logos, of reason or intelligence as it expresses itself in speech; and at various periods this primitive civilising function was to be claimed for poetry, rhetoric, and philosophy alike. But to Isocrates, it would seem, belongs the credit of having given currency to the doctrine in connexion with rhetoric; and by Cicero it was later on adopted as one of his basic theories.

Then, too, in Isocrates's exposition of the theory underlying his methods are some highly important details, which, practical in their nature as opposed to the theoretical principles of Aristotle, were to become an integral part of later rhetorical studies. In rhetoric, as we have seen, he held that there were no fixed rules, no infallible devices. A good style he regarded, not as a work of science, but rather as a piece of art, to the making of which there went some amount of natural ability ($\phi\acute{u}\sigma\iota\varsigma$), besides constant practice ($\acute{\epsilon}\pi\iota\mu\acute{\epsilon}\lambda\epsilon\iota a$) and a knowledge of the resources of art ($\acute{\epsilon}\pi\iota\sigma\tau\acute{\eta}\mu\eta$); and of these requirements native endowment and exercise came first, since knowledge of

---

[1] *Phaedrus*, 267a.   [2] See pp. 13, 29 *supra*.

technique by itself could do but little.[1] Furthermore, the procedure for the learner was to be the same as in gymnastics; he was to learn by imitation, by following the methods of his master. "By imitating a master", so Isocrates explains, "one writes with more grace and distinction than others."[2] And here we have what is substantially the creed of later writers on rhetoric, a statement of the need for *natura*, *exercitatio*, and *ars*, together with the process of *imitatio*, in the formation of a good style. The main ideas, it is true, were also being promulgated by Plato. But Isocrates seems to have been the first to emphasise the importance of example or imitation; and in the light of later history it is perhaps worth noting that he also recommends as models not the earliest but the most finished craftsmen.[3] Moreover he also lays stress upon industry and exercise, for he aimed at developing the learner's faculties through the learner's own efforts; and the formulation of the method as a whole is due to Isocrates.

Most important of all however are his scattered remarks on the principles underlying an artistic prose. And from the first it is clear that he has something new in mind. He refuses to be limited by the pedestrian standards of forensic oratory;[4] nor is he satisfied with the artificialities of Gorgias's poetic prose. What he conceives of is a style of oratory (or writing) which should be as artistic as that of poetry, affording as well the same degree of pleasure;[5] and such a style he describes as imaginative (ποιητικός) and diverse (ποικίλος), with thoughts dignified and original, and adorned with a number of striking figures. Or, as he defines his ideal elsewhere, it is to speak (or write) "as all men are apt to think they could if they would, but as none can do without toil and application".[6] Nor does he take a narrow view of the possibilities of such a style. His remarks, though applicable in the first instance to political discourse, would seem from the context to have a wider bearing. He notes, for instance, the existence of many branches of prose composition; as many, he states, as those of verse.[7] And the

---

[1] *Against the Sophists*, 14–15; *Antidosis*, 187–8.　　[2] *Against the Sophists*, 18.
[3] *Panegyricus*, 10.　　　　[4] *Ibid*. 11.　　　　[5] *Antidosis*, 47.
[6] *Panathenaicus*, 3 (tr. Jebb).　　[7] *Antidosis*, 45.

inference seems to be that the literary prose he advocates would serve for critics of poetry, historians, and writers of dialogue. It might even invade fields hitherto reserved for poetry, as he suggests in another place. Thus panegyrics, he notes, were usually couched in verse; but this he regards as no longer essential.[1] To praise adequately in prose, he concedes, presented some difficulties, since to poets were permitted many graces (κόσμοι) denied to writers in prose—the use of new and unusual words, of metre, rhythm, and the like. Yet the attempt, he maintains, was nevertheless worth making; it meant innovation, it is true, but without innovation, he adds, no advance was possible.

And in keeping with these aims were his more detailed comments on the art of oratory or prose-writing itself. In the first place he lays stress on the importance of subject-matter. To speak (or write) well on great themes rather than to refine on trifles is his motive throughout; and more than once he urges the pursuit of original subjects, of thoughts lofty and novel, or else a fresh treatment of matters previously handled.[2] Then, too, he is aware of the necessity for a general observance of propriety or fitness. The most skilful speaker (or writer) is said to be the man who speaks (or writes) in a fashion appropriate to both his subject and the occasion;[3] and a practical application of this principle by Isocrates himself is seen where he refrains from discoursing on Homer and other poets as being untimely and inappropriate.[4] Apart from this, propriety is shown to be of general validity; it is that which determines the speaker's (or writer's) selection of devices from among all the resources of art.[5] And as a general counsel, applicable both to conduct and art, Isocrates advises a falling-short rather than an overdoing of the effects aimed at; since "the happy mean is found in defect rather than in excess".[6] Equally significant however are those stray precepts on the technique of prose style which have come down, and which, on the evidence of Maximus

---

[1] Evagoras, 5–11.
[2] Against the Sophists, 12–13.
[3] Ibid. Also Panegyricus, 9; Helen, 11.
[4] Panathenaicus, 34.
[5] Against the Sophists, 16–17.
[6] To Nicocles, 33 (tr. Norlin). Cf. also Cicero, Orat. 22.

Planudes, a late Byzantine scholar of the thirteenth century, originally formed part of an *Art of Rhetoric* put together by Isocrates.[1] First, there are his remarks on diction. With the later Atticists he is said to have shared in a dislike for newly-coined words;[2] and his advice was to use words which were metaphorical (μεταφορᾷ), but not harshly so, or those which were most beautiful (κάλλιστα), least artificial (ἥκιστα πεποιημένα), and most familiar.[3] Then with regard to harmony and rhythm he also has something to say. To begin with, hiatus or the clash of vowels he condemns (τὰ φωνήεντα μὴ συμπίπτειν) as an interference with harmony, on account of its halting or uneven (χωλός) character.[4] Previous to this, occasional objections had been taken to this particular effect; but with Isocrates the rule becomes absolute, and it was to be generally accepted by later writers and theorists. Furthermore, he urges that it is a defect in style to begin and end with the same syllable, or to employ the same conjunctions close together, without a certain interval between them;[5] in each case the result being a defective harmony. And as for prose rhythm, on that he makes what is perhaps his most familiar statement. "Prose", he asserts,[6] "must not be merely prose, or else it will be dry; it must not be metrical, for then artifice is manifest; it must rather be compounded of all sorts of rhythms, of which the ones most commonly used should be the iambic and trochaic." Apart from this, there are two further remarks which are worthy of note. One deals with the proper arrangement of matter, and enjoins in narrative a regular and orderly sequence of incidents, an unbroken and progressive movement.[7] The other has to do with the architecture of the sentence. The periodic style is recommended, with "its separate thoughts completed and rounded off" (περιγραφόμεναι);[8] and here, without a doubt, was one of the most characteristic elements in Isocrates's teaching.

Such then in the main was Isocrates's contribution to the

---

[1] See Max. Planudes, *Scholia on Hermogenes* (Walz, *Rhet. Graec.* v, 469); Jebb, *op. cit.* II, 257 ff.; *Isocratis Orationes*, ed. Benseler-Blass, II, 275.

[2] Walz, *op. cit.* v, 498.   [3] Benseler-Blass, *loc. cit.*

[4] *Ibid.* (τέχνη, 6).   [5] *Ibid.*

[6] *Ibid.*   [7] *Ibid.*   [8] *Ibid.*

development of rhetorical theory; and not least valuable are
those fragments of his teaching which may possibly have formed
part of an *Art of Rhetoric*. Of criticism in the wider sense of the
term his works show but few traces, though there are occasional
remarks on poets and poetry, as well as references to the
critical activities and tastes of his day. Thus Homer and the
tragic poets he praises for the skill with which they had combined the delights of fiction and sound teaching in their works;
an illustration, as he puts it, of their insight into human
nature.[1] He has elsewhere a passing allusion to the blasphemies
of the poets against the gods, where he states it as his opinion
that not only the gods but their children also were free from
vice.[2] And while in general he accepts the current myths and
legends, at the same time he demands from them some amount
of verisimilitude, ruling out historical absurdities and serious
breaches of *decorum*.[3] For contemporary comedy he gives
evidence of some amount of dislike; mainly on account of its
licence of speech and of those vulgarities which attracted, to
the neglect of more serious literature.[4] Concerning rhetorical
matters, too, he has something to say. He mentions in one
place the forced appeals of an emotional kind, which were a
common feature of oratory in the law-courts;[5] and in another,
he derides the affectations of orators generally, with their stock
excuses of lack of preparation, difficulties, and the like.[6] His
fiercest censures are however reserved for the contemporary
critics; and here he speaks with considerable feeling. The
snarling critics of his day he describes as mere detractors of
other men's work, unable themselves to create or to say anything of value;[7] and he alludes with scorn to the discussions on
Homer that went on, consisting either of mere rhapsodising, or
else of the serving-up anew of opinions expressed by others.[8]

Interesting, however, as such comments may be, they are
after all but incidental to Isocrates's main purpose, which was
that of inaugurating a new mode of expression in prose,

---

[1] *To Nicocles*, 48.
[2] *Busiris*, 38–43.
[3] *Ibid.* 8, 37, 41; see Jebb, *op. cit.* pp. 99–100.
[4] *On the Peace*, 14; *To Nicocles*, 42.
[5] *Antidosis*, 321.
[6] *Panegyricus*, 13.   [7] *Antidosis*, 62.
[8] *Panathenaicus*, 18.

suitable for declamatory oratory and for the political discourses of which he was a master. And in this effort he may be claimed to have been eminently successful. That his treatment of rhetoric in general has its limitations cannot of course be denied. Throughout his discussions he would seem to have recognised but two branches of rhetoric; the declamatory, which dealt mainly with matters of national interest, and the judicial or forensic, which dealt with interests of a private kind.[1] Moreover to him is generally ascribed the invention of the fourfold division of the speech, namely, proem, narrative, proof, and epilogue.[2] And upon these and other of his doctrines Aristotle was subsequently to comment in philosophical fashion. Yet his actual achievement is by no means slight. He reformed declamatory eloquence in the substance of its ideas and its style; he pointed out new methods of teaching the subject; and thus founded a literary rhetoric which was later to challenge philosophy as an instrument of education. Nor can there be any doubt about his influence on his contemporaries and later ages. Cicero likened his school to the Trojan horse from which came forth none but heroes;[3] and on Cicero himself, and through him on modern prose-writers, the influence of his teaching may be plainly seen. Much of that influence, it is true, was exercised through his oral teaching; still more perhaps was due to the charm of his written prose. Yet something must also be ascribed to his exposition of his theories. Like Dryden, he wrote to the end with unfading energies and judgment undiminished;[4] and his place in the development of criticism has been long assured.

Turning now to the second of the great writers on rhetoric belonging to the fourth century B.C., we find in Aristotle's *Rhetoric* work of a yet more arresting kind, embodying as it does a treatment that is logical, compact, and comprehensive, as compared with the scattered though suggestive remarks characteristic of Isocrates. The treatise, it has already been said,

[1] *Antidosis*, 46–50.
[2] Lysias had however used it before him; see Jebb, *op. cit.* II, 68.
[3] *De Orat.* II, 94.
[4] *Antidosis*, 310. Cf. *Essays of Dryden*, ed. Ker, II, 249: "Thoughts come crowding in so fast upon me that my only difficulty is to choose or to reject".

was traditionally ascribed to a "feud" between Isocrates and Aristotle. During his earlier period of residence at Athens (367–347 B.C.) Aristotle is said to have viewed with scorn Isocrates's methods of teaching, and to have sneered at the bundles of the rhetorician's speeches that were hawked about by the booksellers.[1] Hence, so it is stated, his resolve to attempt an exposition on more adequate lines; and this project he completed after Isocrates's death, and during his second period of residence at Athens (335–322 B.C.).[2] Yet the "feud", if "feud" there was, does not seem to have been serious; at any rate it apparently ceased with Isocrates's death. In the *Rhetoric*, it is true, Aristotle corrects rather forcibly some of Isocrates's doctrines;[3] on the other hand, to no writer does he turn more frequently for illustrations of his teaching, whereas Demosthenes he practically ignores, probably for political reasons.

It would therefore be wrong to regard the *Rhetoric* as nothing more than the outcome of hostility felt for Isocrates; and for a proper understanding of the genesis of the work other considerations than the author's relations with that earlier teacher have to be taken into account. Previous to this, Aristotle had already written certain works on rhetoric: *Gryllus*, for instance, a dialogue named after the son of Xenophon and intended for popular reading; also the *Theodectia*, a treatise on rhetoric written for his pupil Theodectes, and concerned mainly, so it would seem, with matters of style, composition, and arrangement.[4] Both belonged probably to his earlier activities as a teacher; and now, in his latter years, when he takes up the subject anew, he approaches it from a different angle and with different objects in view. At the time he was engaged in a survey of man's intellectual world, and in formulating his scheme of sciences, theoretical, practical, and productive. And viewing rhetoric, as he had already viewed poetry, as a form of human activity, he includes it in his philosophical scheme as one of the productive sciences; and thus submits in his *Rhetoric* yet another of those acroamatic works designed for readers with

---

[1] Dion. Hal. *On Isocrates*, 18; quoted by Jebb, Trans. of Aristotle's *Rhetoric*, p. xvi.
[2] See Jebb, *op. cit.* p. xix.
[3] Cf. *Rhet.* III, xvi, 4.
[4] Cf. *Rhet.* III, ix, 9.

some knowledge of his philosophical teaching. Nor is this the only respect in which the *Rhetoric* differs from his earlier work. Whereas in the *Theodectia* he had treated only certain aspects of the study, what he now attempts is a more comprehensive treatment; and he proceeds to define rhetoric anew, and to consider the subject in all its bearings. While, however, these larger philosophical interests were mainly instrumental in determining the nature of the *Rhetoric*, there were other factors as well that had their influence; and among them were the earlier pronouncements of Plato on the subject of rhetoric. Plato's attitude to the study had been one of contempt. To him rhetoric was no true art, but merely a knack, an "artificer of persuasion"; though elsewhere he had also hinted that improvements in its practice might be effected by attaching greater importance to subject-matter, and by applying psychology to the task of expression.[1] That Aristotle was influenced by these views of Plato there can be no doubt. For one thing his whole treatment is designed to confute Plato's general denunciation of rhetoric as an art; and this is made clear by the opening statement of the work, where verbal echoes of the *Gorgias* point to his acceptance of Plato's challenge.[2] On the other hand, equally clear is Aristotle's acceptance of what was sound in Plato's theorising; and, more particularly, the suggestion that a new study of rhetoric might be based on reasoning and psychology. So that, altogether, Platonic influence played no small part in the genesis of the *Rhetoric*; here, as in the *Poetics*, Aristotle is partly concerned with replying to Plato's strictures, while at the same time he draws on that philosopher for inspiration and guidance.

Before proceeding to deal with Aristotle's contribution to rhetorical theory, something must first be said concerning the form and general character of the *Rhetoric* itself. In the first place, the work will be found to consist of three Books, of which Books I and II are wholly concerned with subject-matter (εὕρεσις), that is, with the finding of arguments and how to

[1] See pp. 58 ff. *supra*.
[2] See W. Rhys Roberts, "References to Plato in Aristotle's *Rhetoric*" (*Class. Phil.* XIX, 342–6, 1924).

confute them; though incidentally Aristotle defines anew the function of rhetoric (I, i, 1–14), specifies its three main branches (I, iii, 1–3), and adds further an analysis of human emotions and character (II, i–xviii), with a view to enabling the orator to understand the nature of the emotions he wishes to arouse, as well as the characters of those to whom he makes his appeal. At the same time there is much in these two books that has but slight bearing on our present purpose. Instruction for example is given on proofs sophistical and valid, on arguments appropriate to the various branches of oratory, and on a host of other technical details concerned rather with logic or ethics or politics. On the other hand a peculiar interest is attached to the analysis of the emotions, including as they do the emotions of pity and fear, envy and anger; and of interest, too, are the descriptions of typical characters, notable as constituting the first "character-sketches" in literary history, and destined to provide the later standards of judgment by verisimilitude or *decorum*. Then in Book III Aristotle proceeds to treat of the formal side of rhetoric. And in this connexion he discusses style ($\lambda\acute{\epsilon}\xi\iota\varsigma$) at some length (III, i–xii), and after that the arrangement ($\tau\acute{\alpha}\xi\iota\varsigma$) of subject-matter in a speech (III, xiii–xix)—the former of these discussions being in some ways the most important section of the work. Here Aristotle is treating of that side of rhetoric which had occupied the attention of earlier writers; and this section is sometimes described as a concession to earlier rhetorical teaching, a sort of afterthought or appendix to the earlier sections. That it consists of material taken over from the *Theodectia* is highly probable; yet it does not follow that Book III is not a component part of the whole. In point of fact, style to Aristotle, though less important than to most of his predecessors, is yet a significant element in his conception of rhetoric; and Book III thus forms a necessary and an integral part of the whole work.

With regard to its general treatment, the *Rhetoric* has not a few points in common with the *Poetics*. Thus it is written in the same esoteric style, suggesting a collection of lecture-notes that takes much for granted; though traces of a more consecutive style are at times apparent, as for instance in Book III, x, where the thoughts are written out in normal and unbroken form. Then, too, there is evident the same approach to the subject from the historical point of view; and this is shown mainly by Aristotle's repeated references to earlier theorists, and his desire to lay down new principles in the light of current deficiencies. For this historical treatment he had previously prepared by reviewing the historical course of the study, and by bringing together in his *Collection of Oratorical Treatises* neat summaries of the existing systems. Similar inquiries had preceded his expositions of politics and metaphysics; and the fruits of the *Collection* (now lost) are seen in the *Rhetoric*. Nor must we overlook the use made by Aristotle of psychological methods in his theorising. For here, as in the *Poetics*, his treatment of the subject is firmly based on a study of human nature; and his doctrines are therefore no arbitrary speculations, but reasoned statements, arrived at from first principles, and determined in some measure by psychological necessity.

When we turn to consider the actual theory of Aristotle, it becomes plain at once that his first object is to establish rhetoric as an art, and to present it as a coherent part of a comprehensive philosophical system. Plato, as we have seen, had refused to recognise it as an art, had moreover described dialectic as "the crown of all the sciences"; and in his opening words Aristotle challenges Plato's position. Rhetoric he describes as the counterpart (ἀντίστροφος) or sister art of dialectic;[1] both being branches of the art of probable reasoning in general. And he further claims for it the normal function of an art. Thus all men, he explains, make use of rhetoric, either by the light of nature or with a knack that comes with experience; and in view of these facts it was possible to inquire into the reasons for success or failure—a process which he describes as the characteristic business of an art. Hence his description of the function of rhetoric as being not that of persuading, but "of discovering all the available means of persuading" (τὸ ἰδεῖν τὰ ὑπάρχοντα πιθανά);[2] and here, it will be noted, he discards the earlier sophistic definition for one more in keeping with his philosophical standpoint. Moreover, with this as his definition

[1] I, i, I.　　　　[2] I, i, 14.

of rhetoric in general, he further conceives of its division into three species or kinds. According to the principle laid down elsewhere,[1] everything is defined or determined by its end (τέλος); and since the persuasion of an audience is the object of a speech, and audiences may be of three kinds—those of the law-courts, the Assembly, and occasional displays—he divides rhetoric into three kinds: the forensic addressed to the judges of the law-courts, the deliberative addressed to the Assembly, and the epideictic to audiences of show-speeches, panegyrics, and the like.[2] Previous to this, earlier classifications had been loose and somewhat vague; Isocrates and Anaximenes, for instance, had conceived of but two kinds with numerous sub-divisions. The triple division, on the other hand, was first set forth by Aristotle; and it was to commend itself to most of the later theorists by its logic and its reasonableness.

Having thus defined rhetoric, its province and its kinds, Aristotle then proceeds with his main business, which is an exposition of the art of oratory or the prose of public speech. He notes, to begin with, that the study had hitherto been conducted on lines too narrow; that forensic oratory had engaged too much of the attention, and that essential matters had been neglected for what was accidental.[3] His concern, however, was with oratory as a whole and with its governing principles; and in the importance he attaches from the outset to sound subject-matter (εὕρεσις) he reveals the first, and in some ways the most far-reaching, of his rhetorical doctrines. It is not without its significance, for instance, that he devotes to the consideration of this matter no less than two Books. His treatment is of a comprehensive and detailed kind, full of technical points; and for our present purpose perhaps no more is necessary than to note his main contentions. He begins by deprecating that oratory which relied solely on emotional appeals, and on the exciting of prejudice, pity, anger, and the like, since all such devices he describes as irrational and unconvincing.[4] The first thing necessary, he maintained, for

---

[1] *Eth. Nic.* III, x. [2] I, iii, 1–3.
[3] I. i, 3–10. [4] I, i, 3–8.

procuring conviction was soundness of argument; "our facts", he says later,[1] "should be our sole weapons"; and he emphasises throughout the need for right reasoning on every subject. Hence his analysis of the ideas of the useful, the beautiful, and the just, on which are based the several forms of eloquence; his discussions, too, of the various commonplaces useful in each type of oratory. Moreover, since persuasion implied in addition the control of minds, a knowledge of psychology also was said to be essential.[2] And he therefore shows how the orator could add to the force of his arguments by his way of presenting them; by a studied appeal to the passions of his audience, and his skill in managing those passions. Then, too, elsewhere he has some important remarks to make on methods of arrangement (τάξις), on the most effective ordering of subject-matter;[3] and here he condemns as mere pedantry all those meticulous divisions and sub-divisions of a speech prescribed by Theodorus, Licymnius, and others. The only essential parts of a speech, he declares, are statement and proof; it is necessary to state the facts and then to prove them. At the same time he is prepared to accept with some reservation the current fourfold division ascribed to Isocrates, that is, proem, narrative, proof, and epilogue. But beyond these, he argued, it was impossible to go, since further distinctions would be superfluous and never-ending. And throughout this discussion on subject-matter and its presentment Aristotle was obviously following in Plato's steps. He emphasises, as Plato had done, the need for sound thinking, the need also for applying psychology to the task of expression; and in addition he ridicules the technical ingenuities of contemporary rhetoricians, while advocating saner methods for the arrangement of subject-matter.

It is however in Book iii, in the section dealing with style, that we get what is perhaps the most interesting part of Aristotle's rhetorical doctrine, namely, his contribution to the theory of literary style in general. The subject, it should be noted, arises naturally out of what has gone before. Aristotle had already dealt with the arguments of the orator, and with

[1] iii, i, 5.   [2] ii, iff., xiiff.   [3] iii, xiii, 1–5.

certain methods of making them effective. He now discusses further means of adding to their effectiveness, means bound up with their proper presentation in words; and this leads on inevitably to an investigation of style. As he himself puts it, "it is not enough to know what we are to say, we must also say it in the right way".[1] At the same time his attitude to style as such is not without its significance. Considered as an element that adds emotional value to expression, he views it apparently with some amount of suspicion. His ideal would seem to have been a bare statement of facts, free from any sort of appeal to the feelings; "no teacher", he explains, "commends geometry by graces of style".[2] Yet he is also conscious that such an ideal could not be realised, save in a community of supermen; and it is mainly as a concession to human weakness that he allows the desirability of a heightened form of expression. It is true that he also admits, rather grudgingly it would seem, that attention to style might be in some slight degree helpful, since in all forms of exposition it might conduce to clearness. Yet even this slight admission he is inclined to retract; it is all a matter of fancy, he suggests, on the part of popular audiences (or readers).[3] And from such views as these the limitations of Aristotle's conception of style are in some measure apparent.

In spite of these uncertainties, however, what Aristotle has actually to say on the matter of style is of the highest importance. And he begins his exposition as usual with a historical comment, pointing out that it was only of late that the art of composition (λέξις) had come to be studied, and that, even so, it was generally regarded as a subject unworthy of the attention of serious minds.[4] Moreover, the first improvement in style, he notes, had been made by the poets. And since much of their reputation seemed due to their way of saying things, it was not unnatural that their ideals should in time be shared by the prose-writers, whose style in consequence took on a poetic colouring. Of these Gorgias is mentioned as the most striking example; and "to this day", adds Aristotle,[5] "writers of this poetic prose are considered by the uneducated to be the finest stylists". Against such standards as these, however, he makes

---

[1] III, i, 2.   [2] III, i, 6.   [3] *Ibid.*   [4] III, i, 5.   [5] III, i, 9.

a determined protest. He recalls the fact that in poetry itself
ideals of style had changed, and were still in process of change.
Just as the earlier writers of tragedy, he points out, had dis-
carded the trochaic tetrameter for the iambic measure in their
efforts to approach more nearly to the rhythm of ordinary
conversation, so yet more recently the tendency in tragedy had
been to avoid all words which formed no part of everyday
speech, even though they had been employed by earlier poets,
and were still in use in epic poetry. With such changing
standards in poetic style, he argued, it was useless to look to
poetry for standards of prose. Indeed, the prose of Gorgias had
embodied not a few features which were no longer recognised
as correct in poetry. The truth therefore was that this new
movement in prose was altogether ill-founded; "the style of
prose", adds Aristotle,[1] "is distinct from that of poetry"
(ἑτέρα λόγου καὶ ποιήσεως λέξις).

Turning then to the task of expounding his own views on
style, he begins by defining what he regards as the fundamental
virtues of all good writing. He mentions two, and two only,
namely, clearness first, and propriety in the second place.[2] And
Aristotle selects these in accordance with his doctrine that the
virtue of anything is determined by its special function, in the
performance of which its excellence lies.[3] Thus the function of
speech is to explain one's meaning; and this is done effectively
only when expression is both clear and in every way fitting.
With this then as the foundation of his theory, he proceeds to
indicate how such qualities might best be attained; and, to
begin with, he considers the choice of diction, the nature of that
vocabulary that conduces most to intelligibility and fitness. In
the first place he maintains that for clearness of utterance
ordinary current words are indispensable,[4] since they are
familiar and understandable by all; and in thus emphasising
the value of the vernacular as the basis of a good style Aristotle
in characteristic fashion goes to the root of the matter. At the
same time he is conscious that something more is also possible,
and that dignity and beauty might result from the use of un-

[1] III. i, 9.   [2] III. ii, I.
[3] *Eth. Nic.* II, 5 *init.*; see Cope, *The Rhetoric of Aristotle*, III, 13 n.   [4] III, ii, 2.

familiar words, which brought with them an element of pleasing surprise and novelty.[1] Yet such words, he added, should be rarely and sparingly used. In poetry they were said to form an essential feature, the poetic vocabulary being largely made up of strange words, compound words, coinages, and the like. But, in prose, things were different; there the less exalted themes did not admit of such departures from the normal idiom, which in the circumstances would be too odd to be fitting. There was, however, one other, and an important, source of power in words upon which prose-writers could draw; and that was language of a metaphorical kind. To this element, so Aristotle explains, the greatest attention should be given, seeing that prose depended for its effects on fewer resources than verse; and he himself spares no effort to reveal the true significance of metaphors in prose. Already in the *Poetics* he had referred to the subject;[2] and he repeats in the *Rhetoric* his earlier statement that the proper use of metaphor was a mark of genius and could not well be taught.[3] But here also he enters into the subject more fully, metaphors being to him obviously one of the chief sources of charm in style; and he deals at some length with their psychological value and their proper use. Thus by means of metaphors, he points out in the first place, the combined effects of familiar and unfamiliar words are obtained, with the resulting qualities of clearness, charm, and strangeness—and these in the highest degree.[4] Clearness, for instance, was the outcome of the familiarity of metaphorical language, since "all men in their ordinary speech make use of metaphors".[5] Their charm, again, arose from the intellectual pleasure given by the resemblances noted. All men, explained Aristotle,[6] take a natural pleasure in learning quickly; and since metaphors, of all words, conduce most to that end, they afford the greatest pleasure. And as for the quality of strangeness, that was due to the surprising nature of some of the resemblances discerned.[7] Then, too, Aristotle calls attention to the proper methods of employing metaphors; and in general, he states, they must be in keeping with the theme or purpose. Thus if the aim be that

---

[1] III, ii, 2.   [2] See p. 98 *supra*.   [3] III, ii, 8.   [4] *Ibid.*
[5] III, ii, 6.   [6] III, x, 2.   [7] III, xi, 5.

of enhancing beauty, the metaphor should be taken from objects exalted or beautiful, whereas, for burlesque, things of a more degraded kind would supply the metaphor needed.[1] He further points out that metaphors must not be far-fetched, or of such a nature that the affinity may not easily be seen.[2] And finally he urges that, wherever possible, words beautiful in themselves should be used for this purpose. Such beauty, he points out, may reside in either the sound or the sense ($\phi\omega\nu\dot\eta$ $\dot\eta$ $\delta\dot\upsilon\nu\alpha\mu\iota\varsigma$); hence the different effects produced by such metaphors as "rosy-fingered" and "red-fingered" when applied to "the dawn".[3] And this recognition of the aesthetic qualities of words themselves is not without its significance. Aristotle, it would seem, took the idea from Licymnius; but it was subsequently developed by Theophrastus, and led to fruitful results in later rhetorical study.

But while the proper choice of words plays a great part in the formation of style, yet more important are the effects due to words in combination ($\sigma\dot\upsilon\nu\theta\epsilon\sigma\iota\varsigma$); and this matter of "composition" constitutes the second and more lengthy section of Aristotle's disquisition on style, in which he deals with various aspects of the subject. First comes his demand for pure and idiomatic Greek ($\tau\dot o$ $\dot\epsilon\lambda\lambda\eta\nu\dot\iota\zeta\epsilon\iota\nu$), free from all solecisms, barbarisms, and the like;[4] as when he insists on such elementary points as the proper use of connective particles, or the observance of grammatical number and of genders as distinguished by Protagoras.[5] Even here, however, his main preoccupation with "clearness" is seen to be uppermost; and it is perspicuity of style, rather than purity of idiom, that he has in mind in more than one place. Thus in his practical way he urges the necessity for a suitable arrangement of clauses, the sparing use of general and abstract terms,[6] and the avoidance above all of ambiguity in expression, unless indeed it was the deliberate intention of the writer to be obscure.[7] Such, he caustically adds, is the trick of those who, having nothing to say, yet make a pretence of saying something; and among such writers he mentions the poet Empedocles, who by his circum-

[1] III, ii, 10. [2] III, ii, 12. [3] III, ii, 13. [4] III, v, 1.
[5] III, v, 2, 5, 6. [6] III, v, 3. [7] III, v, 4.

locutions is said to mystify his readers. Furthermore, there is the striking pronouncement that "in general, every written composition must be easy to read" (δεῖ εὐανάγνωστον εἶναι τὸ γεγραμμένον);[1] and to this end he condemns the undue multiplication of clauses, uncertainties of punctuation such as were seen in the works of Heraclitus, as well as a careless use of parenthetical clauses.[2]

Besides "correctness" however Aristotle demands for style a certain elevation or dignity; and he proceeds to show how this may be contrived by methods of "composition". He begins by recommending the use of metaphors and descriptive epithets, provided that too poetic a colouring does not result;[3] and among the other devices he mentions are the employment of the plural instead of the singular, and the use of connectives which would be omitted if brevity were aimed at.[4] Of greater interest is the method which he associates with the fourth-century poet Antimachus, namely, the description of an object by the qualities which it does not possess.[5] This device of description by negatives he describes as a mode of amplification that might be carried to infinity; and as such it is suggestive of subtle and sublime effects. Examples of its use, often in series, may be found in all great literature—in Homer and the Greek tragic poets, in Shakespeare, Milton, the English Bible, and elsewhere[6]—and Aristotle's comment here illustrates his penetrating insight into literary effects.

Then again he requires in "composition", as in the choice of words, an observance of propriety (τὸ πρέπον).[7] And by this he means that expression must be in keeping with the nature of the theme selected, with the emotional effects intended, and with the character of the speaker as well. In the first place he explains that it would be disastrous to treat a lofty subject in a careless way, or again trivial matters in the grand fashion. He likewise points out that compound words, unusual words, and epithets are most suitable for impassioned utterance, since

---

[1] III, v, 6. [2] III, v, 6–7. [3] III, vi, 3.
[4] III, vi, 4–6. [5] III, vi, 7.
[6] Cf. *Odys.* VI, 43; Soph. *Antig.* 1071; Eur. *Hecuba*, 669; *Hamlet*, ed.Verity, I, v, 77; *Par. Lost*, III, 373 ("Immutable, Immortal, Infinite"); Revelation, xxii, 5 ("And there shall be no night there"). [7] III, vii, 1 ff.

these are the words used by men when "enthusiastic" or inspired. And this indeed is the reason he gives why such diction is in place in poetry; for "poetry", adds Aristotle, "is an inspired thing" (ἔνθεον ἡ ποίησις).[1] Moreover he insists on the importance of adopting the fashion of utterance appropriate to the speaker's (or writer's) rank or age or sex or nationality; since an old man and a young man, he maintains, would speak (or write) in different styles, as would also a well-bred man and a rustic, a man and a woman, a Laconian and a Thessalian.[2] And here Aristotle is laying down the law of *decorum* as it concerned characterisation, a law which was to play a conspicuous part in later critical history. Nor are the reasons he advances for observing propriety in general without their significance. He makes it plain that he advocates propriety of utterance, not so much as an added source of aesthetic pleasure, but rather as a means of rendering statements more plausible, and hearers (or readers) more readily convinced of their truth;[3] and the statement is one that throws a further light on Aristotle's attitude to style.

Of all Aristotle's comments on style, however, none are more important than his remarks on what Dryden later termed "that other harmony of prose"; and among his most familiar pronouncements is that which required that "prose should have rhythm but not metre" (ῥυθμὸν δεῖ ἔχειν τὸν λόγον, μέτρον δὲ μή).[4] In this demand he had been preceded by Isocrates;[5] while yet earlier, if imperfect, witness to the doctrine had been borne by the rhythmical excesses of Gorgias and his school. Now however Aristotle expounds the theory in more reasoned and adequate terms; and his teaching forms the basis of much of the later theorising on this particular point. In the first place he explains the necessity for rhythm in prose as arising out of the very nature of things; and for this purpose he employs certain metaphysical doctrines, doubtless originated by the Pythagoreans, and subsequently adopted by Plato. According to the Pythagoreans, who traced the laws of the universe in numbers, it was number that gave definiteness to all things;

---

[1] III, vii, 11. [2] III, vii, 6. [3] III, vii, 4.
[4] III, viii, 3. [5] See p. 130 *supra*.

and Plato, applying the doctrine to music, poetry, and prose, had described rhythm as that which brought order and measure into expression as a whole.[1] Hence Aristotle's contention that composition devoid of rhythm was indefinite and illimitable; and since what is illimitable is displeasing, being beyond human grasp, some limiting principle was therefore necessary; and this he points out was supplied by rhythm in prose.[2] At the same time he explains that it must be rhythm, not metre; and that the limiting principle must not consist of the regularly recurring movements characteristic of poetry. In other words he implies (he does not actually say so) that the rhythm of prose must be ever-changing and of infinite variety; and he gives characteristic reasons for his statement.[3] In the first place he maintains that the presence of metre carries with it an air of artifice, and therefore fails to bring about conviction. And in the second place he suggests that it tends to divert the attention of the reader from the subject-matter, the main effort of the latter being unconsciously devoted to awaiting the recurrence of the cadence. Furthermore, he has something to say concerning the rhythms most suitable to prose. The hexameter, for one, he does not recommend, on the ground that it is too stately and too remote from the rhythm of ordinary conversation.[4] The iambic, on the other hand, he recognises as part of everyday speech, being the characteristic rhythm of common talk; yet this too he dismisses as lacking in majesty and in power of appeal. And as for the trochaic with its tripping measure, this he describes as reminiscent of the comic dance and therefore totally devoid of dignity and sobriety. What he specially recommends is the paeonic measure (i.e. $-\cup\cup\cup$ or $\cup\cup\cup-$), first employed by Thrasymachus. This he regards as the most fitting of all, besides being the one rhythm that could not easily be made into a regular verse, and therefore least likely to suggest artifice in prose.[5] And in this discussion Aristotle is covertly criticising Isocrates, who had commended for use the iambic and trochaic measures.[6]

From the harmony of prose consisting of its rhythmical

---

[1] Cf. Plato, *Phil.* 23 e; see also Cope, *op. cit.* III, 85.   [2] III, viii, 2.
[3] III, viii, 1.   [4] III, viii, 4.   [5] III, viii, 5.
[6] See p. 130 *supra*.

effects, Aristotle next turns to that larger harmony arising out
of sentence-form. And he states at once that style in general
may be either loose or periodic;[1] the loose style being made up
of sentences in an unbroken chain, linked together by connective
particles; the periodic style, of sentences each of which is complete in itself while also at times forming part of a larger whole.
The loose style he further describes as the ancient one, adding
that whereas formerly it had held the field, of late it had fallen
into disuse;[2] and this he accounts for by its inherent defects of
structure, its endlessness and indefiniteness, which were displeasing to readers. On the other hand the periodic style was
said to embody a more determinate form, being made up of
one or more sentences, having a beginning and an end and a
magnitude which could easily be taken in at a glance.[3] From
this it followed that such a style was both pleasing and readily
intelligible; it was free from the indefiniteness of the more
irregular form. And in addition, prose of this kind was more
easily committed to memory, since its symmetry of form had
the quality of measure or number—the same quality, in short,
which made poetry easy to remember. Aristotle's advocacy of
the periodic style is therefore clear and unmistakable; and in
this matter he is in agreement with Isocrates. Moreover he
has certain practical injunctions to give, some of which he
illustrates from passages taken from Isocrates's *Panegyricus*. Thus
he points out the necessity for each periodic sentence to be
brought to a definite conclusion and to embody in itself a
complete idea.[4] Its component clauses, he adds, should be
neither too long nor too short; for statements unduly prolonged
resulted in a breaking of the thread of the discourse, whereas
untimely brevity caused the reader to stumble.[5] Or again, he
shows how within the periodic structure facilities are given for
the employment of devices such as antithesis, parallelism of
structure (παρίσωσις) and parallelism of sound (παρομοίωσις):
figures previously introduced by Gorgias and his school.

With this then Aristotle brings to a close his exposition of
style, concluding with some discursive remarks on the methods
of giving vivacity and pungency to expression, and after that

[1] III, ix, 1.   [2] III, ix, 2.   [3] III, ix, 3.   [4] III, ix, 4.   [5] III, ix, 6.

with some comments on the styles characteristic of the three branches of rhetoric. In the first place he recommends as the chief means of giving animation and vivacity to style the use of metaphors (including similes), antithesis, and vividness of representation (ἐνέργεια);[1] though he also recognises such devices as puns, plays upon words, hyperboles, and the like. Of the liveliness of metaphors (and similes) he had already treated; and here he quotes by way of illustration the saying attributed to Pericles, that "the youth, who had perished in the war, had vanished out of the city in such sort as if the spring were taken out of the year".[2] Concerning the effects of antithesis he also has something to say. It is a device, he states, that pleases because of the light thrown on contraries by reason of the opposition;[3] and in its use he recommends brevity of expression, since by that means the contrast is made more striking and vivid.[4] And a similar effect of liveliness is attributed to ἐνέργεια, which consists of a device for bringing things vividly before one's eyes, by describing them in an active state. Of this he gives as an example Homer's "spear-point quivering with eagerness";[5] and the vivifying of inanimate objects, he suggests, adds animation to the style.

Then come finally his remarks on the styles effective in the several branches of rhetoric. Hitherto his whole treatment had been concerned with style in general; and it is not without its significance that only towards the end, and then in somewhat cursory fashion, does he enter into those distinctions upon which such stress was to be laid by later theorists. As his main principle he states that each branch of rhetoric has necessarily its fitting style;[6] and this he applies, in accordance with his definition, to the forensic, the deliberative, and the epideictic kinds. The forensic style, to begin with, he describes as the simplest and most straightforward, though admitting at the same time of exactness and finish. Since however it is employed before small audiences and before a single judge, it

---

[1] III, x, 6.
[2] III, x, 7 (tr. Jebb); see Cope, *op. cit.* I, vii, 34n. for the authenticity of this saying.
[3] III, ix, 8.   [4] III, xi, 9.   [5] III, xi, 3.   [6] III, xii, 1.

depends least on rhetorical devices and affords but little scope for emotional effects.[1] The deliberative style, on the other hand, intended for larger audiences, is said to involve methods resembling those of scene-painting (σκιαγραφία) which, though rough and unfinished in its various details, when viewed at a distance gives the necessary effects. And similar effects are aimed at in the deliberative style; it is one in which fine touches are thrown away, high finish being superfluous and even detracting from the actual results.[2] Of greatest interest however are his remarks on the epideictic style, with which he includes the style of written prose (λέξις γραφική); so that under this head he treats of writing of all kinds—philosophy, history, politics and the like. This style in general he describes as exact and finished, capable of minute and delicate touches, expressive of all the finer shades of feeling;[3] and from the other two styles it is said to differ materially, being more ornate than the forensic, less broad in its effects than the deliberative style. Concerning the written style, he adds that it is ineffective for public speaking, the speeches of literary men as a rule appearing thin and bloodless in actual delivery. On the other hand, successful speeches of the forensic or deliberative kinds, he points out, when read in private, seem lacking in workmanship; since the use of such characteristic devices as *asyndeta* and repetitions then appear foolish and trifling. Having thus discriminated on general lines between the three main styles of rhetoric, Aristotle, it is significant to note, refuses to go further in the matter of classification. His suggestion is that the principles he had laid down—"clearness" and "propriety" more particularly— would be found to cover all further differentiation of style;[4] and it was left for later writers to refine on his theorising by introducing among other terms those of "grand", "middle", and "plain".

Such then in its main outline is Aristotle's treatment of rhetoric. And as a contribution to the theory of oratory and prose style it has qualities that distinguish it from the tentative efforts of preceding writers, while it also embodies principles that were to form the basis of all later treatments. At the same

---

[1] III, xii, 5. [2] *Ibid.* [3] III, xii, 2. [4] III, xii, 6.

time in the *Rhetoric* there are further details of interest which
cannot well be passed over, *obiter dicta* with a bearing on
literary criticism in the wider sense of the term; and among
these must be mentioned Aristotle's occasional remarks on the
literary art, as well as his judicial comments on style and poetry
generally. In the first place there will be found scattered
throughout the work traces of that studio wisdom which
entered also into the *Poetics*; and in most instances they are
practical hints of a most valuable kind. Fundamental in
character, for example, is the injunction he lays down as to the
necessity for the concealment of art. "We must disguise our
art" (δεῖ λανθάνειν ποιοῦντας), says Aristotle, "and seem to
speak naturally, not artificially; the natural is persuasive, the
artificial is the reverse; for men are prejudiced against it as
against an insidious design, just as they are suspicious of
doctored wines."[1] And here stated for the first time is the
famous doctrine that was to colour so much of the ancient
critical teaching. Equally interesting however are his remarks
arising out of his insistence on "propriety", or the observance
of "the mean" in the use of artifice. All excess he condemns;
and, following Isocrates,[2] he recommends a falling-short rather
than an overdoing of the effects aimed at. Thus "too much
art", he explains, "does more harm than utter carelessness; the
latter is not good, but the other is positively bad".[3] And elsewhere he points out as a corrective for every exaggeration of
style the familiar trick of orators, namely, that of pronouncing
censure on themselves at the time of speaking. The result, as
Aristotle points out,[4] is to disarm criticism; the exaggeration is
thought to be justified, seeing that the speaker knows what he
is doing. Then, too, there are his remarks on methods of
narration and on the value of suitable introductions in all
forms of composition. It is true that he discusses these matters
mainly in connexion with epideictic compositions; but his
remarks have also a wider and a more general bearing. Thus he
describes as absurd the rule that narrative should necessarily
be rapid;[5] and his recommendation is that narrative in order to

---

[1] III, ii, 4 (tr. Jebb); see also III, xvi, 10. [2] See p. 129 *supra.*
[3] III, iii, 3 (tr. Jebb). [4] III, vii, 9. [5] III, xvi, 4.

be effective should be broken up and not continuous. "It is undesirable", he states,[1] "to relate all our facts consecutively, since this mode of exposition is apt to tax the reader's memory"; and to English readers Prospero's narrative in *The Tempest* will occur as an admirable illustration of the method advocated by Aristotle. Of like importance, however, is his insistence on the need for adequate explanation in introducing a subject. He notes that definite indication of purpose was given in their opening lines by epic poets; and he quotes as illustrations the exordia of the *Iliad*, the *Odyssey*, and Choerilus's epic on the Persian War.[2] He notes further that similar explanations had been given by dramatists such as Sophocles and Euripides; and incidentally he approves of Euripides's use of the prologue for this purpose. Hence in all these devices, he maintains, a necessary artistic end had been served. Such explanatory introductions, he points out, relieved the reader of all suspense, removed from his mind that indefiniteness which bewilders, and thus made it easy for him to follow the matter in hand.

Then again along with these practical hints will be found numerous passing references to literary theory, bearing on art in general, on tragedy and comedy. First comes his statement that "no art considers the particular" (οὐδεμία δὲ τέχνη σκοπεῖ τὸ καθ' ἔκαστον),[3] a reminder of his earlier doctrine that art deals with universals. Then, too, in the *Poetics* Aristotle had already described the pleasure which was derived from the imitative arts as being ultimately based on the love of learning; and that pleasure, he had stated, was produced, even when the subject was unpleasant, provided that the imitation was an exact one.[4] In the *Rhetoric* he now traces that pleasure, not merely to the love of learning, but to the element of wonder (τὸ θαυμάζειν) as well;[5] and it is to the latter source that he traces the delight of thrilling stories embodying tragic catastrophes or hairbreadth escapes[6]—a species of narrative neither unknown nor unpopular in modern days. Moreover, something further of his notions of tragedy may indirectly be gathered

---

[1] III, xvi, 1–2.   [2] III, xiv, 6.   [3] I, ii, 11.
[4] 1448b, 10–20.   [5] I, xi, 23.   [6] I, xi, 25.

from what he has to say concerning pity and fear—the purging of which emotions was said to be the aim of tragedy. The objects of pity, he had previously made clear, were good men, and men of like nature to the beholders of the sufferings.[1] Here however he adds the significant statements that "it is piteous that an evil should befall from a quarter whence good fortune was due";[2] and, further, that "all evils caused by Chance are piteous, provided they are sufficiently great".[3] At the same time he distinguishes between the effects of pity and fear, the former being caused by the spectacle of suffering friends, the latter by sufferings which touch the beholders yet more closely; and in the latter case, he adds, the emotion of fear drives out pity.[4] Hence his further statement that "those things inspire fear in us which, when they befall others, are piteous".[5] Apart from these, however, not without their interest are his incidental remarks on the elements of comedy. And notable in the first place is his statement that "the causes of laughter must be pleasant, whether they be people or words or deeds" (ἀνθρώπους καὶ λόγους καὶ ἔργα);[6] a statement upon which was to be based the later treatment of "the laughable" in Cicero's *De Oratore* and the *Tractatus Coislinianus*. On the humour arising from verbal artifice he has something more to say. The effects produced by jokes, puns, and the like, he describes as being due to the element of surprise, to the deception resulting from an unexpected turn given to the expression; and for success in such efforts "fitness" was indispensable, though compactness and neatness also counted for much.[7] Elsewhere he points out that all jokes are not becoming to all men, and that each man should choose his own line of pleasantry. Thus irony is described as more in keeping with an independent (ἐλευθεριώτερον) mind than buffoonery; the ironical man being said to joke for his own amusement, the buffoon for the amusement of others.[8] Or again, there is his happy description of "wit" (εὐτραπελία) as "cultured insolence" (πεπαιδευμένη ὕβρις);[9] and also his hint as to the use of good-natured ridicule, when he approves of

---

[1] Cf. II, viii, 13, 16. [2] II, viii, 10; see p. 91 *supra*. [3] II, viii, 8.
[4] II, viii, 12. [5] II, viii, 8. [6] I, xi, 29.
[7] III, xi, 6–9. [8] III, xviii, 7. [9] II, xii, 16.

Gorgias's earlier statement that "one should rout an opponent's seriousness with ridicule, and his ridicule with seriousness".[1]

Nor must the attempts at judicial criticism in the *Rhetoric* be entirely overlooked; for Aristotle here deals with some of the prevailing defects of style as seen in the panegyrics and declamations of contemporary rhetoricians and orators. Thus he points out,[2] with illustrations, the turgid effects of compound and archaic words in the prose of rhetoricians like Gorgias, Lycophron, and Alcidamas; their misuse, too, of the redundant epithet (e.g. "damp sweat", "white milk"), which, allowable in poetry, was to be sparingly used in prose; while common to rhetoricians and orators like Androtion and Democrates was a want of taste in the employment of metaphors and similes. His strictures on the misuse of metaphors are perhaps a little puzzling to modern readers, since among the expressions to which he objects are Gorgias's sentence, "Having sown disgracefully, you have reaped an evil harvest", or again Alcidamas's description of the *Odyssey* as "a fair mirror of human life".[3] Both figures are now commonplaces in modern prose; and Aristotle's description of them as "too poetical" may possibly point to certain limitations of his on the aesthetic side, or else to his desire above all for a severely simple prose. For the rest, his comments in this section are valuable as illustrations of his doctrine rather than as appreciations of literature; and judicial estimates of a more direct kind will be found in his passing references to the satirical preoccupations of the comic poets,[4] and his contemptuous judgments of the ambiguous styles of Empedocles and Heraclitus.[5] Of greatest interest, however, are his remarks on Euripides whom he censures for occasional lack of taste in his use of metaphors;[6] though on the other hand, as we have seen, he commends Euripides's prologues,[7] and points as well to the fundamental change in style effected by the same dramatist. It was necessary in tragedy, he suggests, to produce the resemblance of ordinary speech, varying in accordance with character. And this verisimilitude, he claims, is what Euripides had achieved.[8] He

[1] III, xviii, 7. [2] III, iii–iv. [3] III, iii, 4. [4] II, vi, 20.
[5] III, v, 4, 6. [6] III, ii, 10. [7] See p. 150 *supra*. [8] III, ii, 5.

had produced the necessary artistic illusion by selecting and arranging words drawn from ordinary life; and, as Aristotle states, he was the first innovator in this direction, a direction, it might be added, in which later tragedy has consistently moved.

It is however as a contribution to literary theory that the *Rhetoric* figures in critical history; and as an attempt at correcting what was defective in previous efforts and at establishing on a scientific basis the laws that govern oratory and prose style, the work ranks with the *Poetics* as one of the most valuable treatises that have come down from antiquity. Of the soundness of its treatment something has already been said; its rational and inductive methods based on first principles, and its consistent concern with the laws of human nature, being among the features that give to it enduring value. Moreover, the real substance of its teaching lies in the principles already mentioned; in the demands for sound subject-matter, for clearness and propriety both in diction and structure, for due rhythmical effects, a sane use of figures, a concealment of art; and throughout the whole work, like a constant refrain, runs the injunction for the observance of propriety or *decorum*. Yet the full significance of the work is not grasped by viewing it in isolation. It is as much a product of its time as was the *Poetics*; and its theorising, therefore, like that of the *Poetics*, is not wholly the result of free reflexion, but is affected also by contemporary influences and conditions. Thus its form, for one thing, is partly determined by the need of replying to Plato's strictures on rhetoric as an art; its doctrines, again, include the best that had been thought and said on the subject. But most influential of all were the prevailing tendencies in prose, the set in the direction of the false splendours of the Gorgianic style; and to counteract and correct these tendencies was Aristotle's chief object. In other words, the conception of style he submits is largely conditioned by the vogue of Gorgianic prose. And this is seen in the emphasis he lays throughout upon the appeal, not to the feelings, but to the understanding. Of the beauty of elevated diction, or of the colour, the music, and the suggestive quality of words he says but little; propriety of utterance, again, the use of metaphors, rhythm, and the rest he demands, not for their emotional, but their intellectual, effects; and as for the figures, so prominent in the earlier and the later teaching, they play but a small part in his actual scheme. What he does is to inculcate a style with a strong logical appeal by way of combating the current emotional standards; and with this same end in view, he ignores the grand style of Demosthenes, leaving it for later writers, Dionysius of Halicarnassus among their number, to supply his omissions on the aesthetic side. Yet despite their limitations, such principles as he advocates were probably the best basis for a future development of the study. With language established primarily as the medium for sound sense, new graces and subtler effects could safely be left for time to reveal; they were but amplifications of the subject which he had chosen to neglect. It is therefore for its foundation work that Aristotle's treatise is above all things valued. To the study of rhetoric, and incidentally of prose style, he opened up a new line of approach, calling attention to fundamental laws that were good for all time; and with him a sound theory of prose style may be said to have begun. Nor must his influence on later ages be overlooked; for the main lines of his treatment, with some modifications, were adopted by most of his successors. Thus his treatment of subject-matter (εὕρεσις), arrangement of material (τάξις), and style (λέξις) gave rise to the later divisions of *inventio, dispositio,* and *elocutio;*[1] while his classification of rhetoric into the forensic, the deliberative, and the epideictic kinds was likewise destined to persist. In addition, traces of his teaching may probably be found in the conception of style formed by the Stoics; that is, a style clear and correct, but devoid of all graces. And last but not least is his recognition of the possibilities of the written word, a service in which he had been anticipated by Isocrates. The latter had written as a rhetorician with prose style in mind. He had hoped that the *Antidosis* would prove for him a "monument more noble than statues of bronze";[2] whereas Plato had decried the use of the written word, declaring that "he, who

---

[1] See e.g. Quintilian, *Inst. Orat.* III, 3, 1.
[2] *Antidosis,* 7; cf. Hor. *Odes,* III, 30, 1.

writes, writes in water, with the aid of words unable to defend themselves or to teach the truth ".[1] And now Aristotle includes the art of writing in his treatment of rhetoric. To him it was a means of extending the range of a thinker; and under the head of epideictic rhetoric he treats of the qualities of written prose.

There yet remains to mention the third of the outstanding contributors to rhetorical theory during this century; and in Theophrastus (372–287 B.C.), Aristotle's favourite pupil and his successor as head of the Peripatetic school, we have yet another of those writers whose influence was to be great in later critical history. Of his immense output but little has come down; and practically nothing but fragments of his critical writings. To him are attributed works *On the Ridiculous, On Enthusiasm,* a *Poetics,* several rhetorical treatises including one *On Style,* besides his famous *Characters,* which alone has survived. In the *Characters* we have a series of sketches of human types designed apparently for orators, the object being by the light thus thrown on human nature to enable orators to rest their appeals on sound psychological grounds. The work has therefore much in common with that analysis of passions found in Aristotle's *Rhetoric;* and originally it may have formed part of a larger treatise on rhetoric. But whatever its origin and aim, it is a volume full of clever description, shrewd psychology and wit; and it is otherwise notable in literary history as having inspired the "character-literature" of seventeenth-century England, to which Overbury and Earle were the chief contributors. With regard to his work of a critical kind, there is less that can be definitely said. For any knowledge of his actual theorising we are wholly dependent on stray references in the work of later critics and grammarians; and an appreciation of his critical efforts is therefore a matter of some difficulty. At the same time, fragmentary and inadequate as this evidence may be, it is not without its value. It shows for instance that Theophrastus was held to be a recognised authority for centuries to come; it suggests further that his main efforts were devoted to developing and systematising the teaching of his master, Aristotle; and it also provides some slight details of his actual theories.

[1] *Phaedrus,* 276 c.

It is his lost treatise *On Style* (Περὶ Λέξεως) that in all probability best illustrates his position in the critical development, and his influence on later writers. In the first place he seems to have treated style, as Aristotle had done, as a unit; in other words, what he discussed were the principles of style in general and not the characteristics of separate individual styles, whether grand, or plain, or middle. It is true that the later doctrine of the three styles has not infrequently been associated with his name. According to Dionysius of Halicarnassus he is said to have considered Thrasymachus as representative of the "mixed or middle" style;[1] a description which suggests that conceptions of other styles—grand and plain—also formed part of his theory. Yet this is not the only, or even the most likely, interpretation to be placed on this reported opinion of Theophrastus. To him Thrasymachus may well have illustrated the virtue of the "mean", in that he avoided the two extremes of bareness and over-ornateness. And this would at least be in accordance with the doctrine of Aristotle, who held that the secret of all excellence in style lay in observing "the mean" (τὸ μέσον).[2] On the other hand, the doctrine of the three styles would more naturally arise at a later date when the styles of the various Attic orators were being discussed with a view to imitation. Some such categories as grand, middle, and plain, would then be a convenience in distinguishing the qualities of such orators as Demosthenes, Isocrates, and Lysias.[3]

Concerning the details of his theory there is this much to be said, that while evidence exists of his indebtedness to Aristotle, yet more clear are his attempts at developing Aristotelian theory. That he to some extent followed in the tracks of his master is suggested by the definition of "frigidity" (τὸ ψυχρόν) in style attributed to him by Demetrius at a later date. Thus Theophrastus is said to have defined that quality as "that which overshoots the expression appropriate to the thought";[4]

---

[1] Dion. Hal. *de Demos.* 3.

[2] *Rhet.* III, xii, 6.

[3] See G. L. Hendrickson, "The Peripatetic mean of style and the three stylistic characters" (*A.J. Phil.* xxv, 2, 1904, pp. 125 ff.) and J. F. D'Alton, *Roman Literary Theory and Criticism*, p. 72.

[4] Demetrius, *On Style*, 114 (tr. W. Rhys Roberts).

and this conception is one that is in keeping with Aristotle's treatment in his *Rhetoric*.[1] Then, too, Demetrius notes his approval of the use of paeonic rhythms in prose for purposes of elevation;[2] and here Theophrastus was evidently following Aristotle in preference to Isocrates, who had advocated the use of iambic and trochaic rhythms. Or again, there is "Longinus's" reference to the device for disarming criticism mentioned by Theophrastus, according to which excessive boldness of metaphor was said to be condoned by inserting such phrases as "as if", or "as it were", or "if one may say so".[3] This point also had previously been made by Aristotle; and here again, it is not unreasonable to suppose, Theophrastus was drawing on that authority, though the trick, as Aristotle notes, was familiar at the time.

More substantial in character perhaps are the indications of Theophrastus's efforts at developing the teaching of Aristotle. And one of his most familiar statements seems to have been his definition of verbal beauty as that "which gives pleasure to the ear or the eye or has noble associations of its own". This statement of Theophrastus is quoted by both Dionysius of Halicarnassus[4] and Demetrius;[5] and in less detailed form it had appeared in Aristotle's *Rhetoric*. But whereas Aristotle refers to the matter merely in passing, as outside his main purpose, Theophrastus, it may be surmised, gave to it greater consideration. Thus Aristotle's recognition of sound-values he extends to appeals to both the eye and the ear; and from the later quotations it would seem that to Theophrastus was largely due the conception of "the word" as not only the logical and grammatical, but the aesthetic, unit of expression as well.[6] Then, too, there are his remarks on the essential virtues of style. With Aristotle there had been two only, clearness and propriety; but with Theophrastus they were enlarged to four and consisted of clearness, correctness, ornateness, and appropriateness.[7] Furthermore, the quality of ornateness or dis-

[1] III, iii.   [2] Demetrius, *op. cit.* 41.
[3] "Longinus", *On the Sublime*, XXXII, 3.
[4] *Arrangement of Words*, 16 (W. Rhys Roberts, p. 163).
[5] *On Style*, 173.   [6] See Sikes, *op. cit.* p. 162.
[7] Cicero, *Orator*, 79.

tinction in style he is said to have ascribed to the choice of words, their proper arrangement, and the use of Figures;[1] and in this method of treatment he was followed by most of the later rhetoricians. Hence may be seen his tendency in the direction of further analysis and systematisation; while notable too is the place here given to the figures, as compared with their slight treatment in the work of Aristotle. At the same time Theophrastus was responsible for something more than this; and in one place at least evidence is forthcoming of his keen insight into artistic effects. Nowhere for instance is his delicacy of observation, his psychological grasp, more clearly apparent than in his injunction concerning the need for artistic restraint, and for imaginative co-operation on the part of the hearer (or reader). According to Demetrius he had stated that for an effective style it was necessary not to labour or exhaust any given matter. "Not all possible points", he wrote,[2] "should be punctiliously and tediously elaborated, but something should be left to the comprehension and inference of the hearer, who when he perceives what you have left unsaid becomes not only your hearer but your witness (μάρτυς), and a very friendly witness too. For he thinks himself intelligent because you have afforded him the means of showing his intelligence. It seems like a slur on your hearer to tell him everything as though he were a simpleton." Here then a subtle principle of art was enunciated by Theophrastus. And something of the same kind was present in Shakespeare's mind when in *Henry V*[3] he adjured his audience "to piece out all imperfections with (their) thoughts", and to bring into play "(their) imaginary forces". The principle, in short, is of fundamental importance, with a bearing on all good writing; and in the light of the passage quoted, it is not difficult to understand Theophrastus's influence on later writers.

Before leaving Theophrastus, however, reference must be made to those definitions of tragedy and comedy which have been attributed to him on the strength of certain passages

[1] Dion. Hal. *de Isoc.* 3.
[2] Demetrius, *On Style*, 222 (tr. W. Rhys Roberts).
[3] Act I, Chorus.

found in the writings of the fourth-century grammarians Diomedes and "Donatus." According to Diomedes, Theophrastus is said to have stated that "tragedy is an action involving (a reversal in) the fortunes of heroic characters" (τραγῳδία ἐστὶν ἡρωϊκῆς τύχης περίστασις);[1] to this was added a definition of comedy, namely, that "comedy is an episode of everyday life involving no serious dangers" (κωμῳδία ἐστὶν ἰδιωτικῶν πραγμάτων ἀκίνδυνος περιοχή)[2]—a definition that appears also in the pages of "Donatus".[3] And in the light of these statements it has been suggested that Theophrastus was responsible for those definitions of tragedy and comedy which, identical for the most part with those already mentioned, were to dominate European thought at a later date. Furthermore it has been urged[4] that these definitions are ultimately based on Aristotle's popular treatment of the subjects in his lost dialogue *On Poets*; and that this would therefore account for discrepancies existing between the definitions as they stand and Aristotle's views as represented in the *Poetics*. These theories however have not met with any general acceptance. For one thing, it is significant that the definition of tragedy alone is actually attributed to Theophrastus, and that, only in one place, by Diomedes; and for another, the definitions of comedy are ascribed by both grammarians, not to Theophrastus, but to a Greek tradition (*apud Graecos*), so that their ascription to Theophrastus rests on no secure ground. Nor again can the attempt to trace back the definitions to a work of which practically nothing is known be described as in any degree convincing. On the other hand a more probable theory would be that both definitions were modifications of Aristotelian doctrine arrived at in Hellenistic times. And with this the statements of both Diomedes and "Donatus" with regard to comedy could be reconciled; while Diomedes's reference to Theophrastus, if not mere conjecture, may yet be an attempt to associate with a traditional doctrine the authority of a great

---

[1] Keil, *Grammatici Latini*, I, 487.   [2] *Ibid.* 488.

[3] See "excerpta de comoedia" (v, 1), prefixed to Donatus, *Commentium Terenti* (ed. Wessner, vol. I, 22, and notes on p. 500).

[4] See A. P. McMahon, "On the Second Book of Aristotle's *Poetics*" and "Aristotelian Definitions of Tragedy and Comedy" (*Harv. St. in Class. Phil.* XXVIII, 1–46, XL, 97–198).

name. Of the importance of these definitions in later history, on the other hand, there can be no question;[1] but in the light of existing evidence they cannot safely be associated with the name of Theophrastus.

To Isocrates, Aristotle, and Theophrastus may thus be attributed the main advances in rhetorical study during this period; and of the remaining critical activities in this field there is less to be said, though they are by no means devoid of interest, as illustrating the nature of contemporary work. Among the earlier rhetoricians were Lycophron, Alcidamas, and Licymnius, all of whom are referred to by Aristotle in his *Rhetoric*; and whereas Licymnius wrote an *Art of Rhetoric* upon which Aristotle apparently drew, to Alcidamas is ascribed a declamation *On the Sophists*, in which he urged the value of extemporary methods of discourse, as contrasted with the elaborations of written composition commended by Isocrates. Apart from this there was the *Rhetorica ad Alexandrum* (340 B.C.), a work formerly ascribed to Aristotle but now generally accepted as the production of Anaximenes (380–320 B.C.). In it we have a treatment of the subject characteristic of the fourth century, and reflecting the traditional theory and practice of earlier rhetoricians. There rhetoric is taken to mean the art of persuasion, and traces of the earlier mechanical methods survive in its stereotyped treatment of the parts of an oration (προοίμιον, διήγησις, and the rest). It has also a section that deals with subject-matter (εὕρεσις) and style (λέξις) after the fashion of Aristotle, a feature that has been explained as due to the influence of the *Theodectia*, Aristotle's earlier treatise. Then, too, some amount of historical interest is attached to the writings of Heraclides of Pontus (*fl.* 340 B.C.), a pupil first of Plato and then of Aristotle, who wrote on rhetoric, poetry, and music, though none of his works has actually come down. To him are attributed writings on literary history, a field in which the later Peripatetics were to show considerable activity. He wrote for instance *The Age of Homer and Hesiod* and *On Archilochus and Homer*; and in critical work of this kind his contemporaries,

---

[1] For a detailed and valuable account of this matter see A. P. McMahon, *op. cit.* (*Harv. St. in Class. Phil.* XI., 108–98).

Aristoxenus of Tarentum and Chameleon, also shared. From the former came writings on tragic poets and tragic dancing, while the latter was author of works on the earlier poets, on the satyric drama, and ancient comedy. It is in the field of poetry however that the writings of Heraclides are of special significance; for in his *Poetics* (περὶ ποιητικῆς καὶ τῶν ποιητῶν) he would seem to have treated his subject on the plan of *ars* and *artifex*, and to have discussed, first, questions relating to the poetic art, then matters relating more especially to the poet. Such a procedure was probably inspired by Platonic influence, since, with Plato, "inspiration" of the poet counted for much, whereas from Aristotle this side of the poetic activity received but slight consideration. But whatever its origin, this treatment of poetry is not without its interest. It has in short been claimed to be the earliest example of the plan subsequently adopted by Neoptolemus of Parium, a fellow-countryman of Heraclides, and later on by Horace in his famous *Ars Poetica*.[1] Nor must we overlook the contribution of Zoilus (*fl.* 350 B.C.), one of the professional interpreters of Homer, whose criticism of that poet, embodied in a work probably entitled *Homeromastix* and consisting of nine books, was of a nature that made him the prototype of all the "snarling" critics that followed. He was concerned with what he regarded as incongruities of thought and language; and the result is a mass of petty quibbling on the Homeric subject-matter, together with some attacks on grammar. He objects for instance to Homer's treatment in making innocent mules and dogs the first victims of Apollo's arrows (*Il.* I, 50); he ridicules the artificial symmetry with which exactly six men were lost from each ship in the fight with the Cicones (*Od.* IX, 60); he finds a difficulty in understanding Homer when he states that "like a vapour the spirit fled *beneath* the ground" (*Il.* XXIII, 100); and he notes besides many so-called absurdities attributed to the gods and heroes.[2] As an attempt at judicial criticism the work left much to be desired. It betrayed a complete unconcern with the aims

---

[1] See K. Barwick, "Die Gliederung der rhetorischen τέχνη und die Horazische Epistula ad Pisones" (*Hermes*, LVII (1922), 54 ff.).

[2] See J. E. Sandys, *History of Classical Scholarship*, I, 109–10.

and methods of poetry, as well as a lack of that historical sense which the subject obviously required. It was in fact just that type of judicial criticism which Aristotle had successfully controverted in his *Poetics*, though without any marked effect on later practice.

These then are some of the minor achievements which, along with the works of Isocrates, Aristotle, and Theophrastus, throw light on the nature of rhetorical studies in the fourth century B.C. And altogether it was a miscellaneous output, various in its aims and methods, yet full of pregnant ideas which were to be subsequently expounded and developed. Apart from this it is perhaps worth noting that before the close of the century there were already signs of slackening in the critical activities, and of changes in the conditions which had inspired those activities. For one thing, poetry and poetic creation had now ceased to be of absorbing interest; though some amount of theorising still went on, as was shown by the pronouncements of Praxiphanes (*fl.* 300 B.C.), a pupil of Theophrastus, who declared that good subject-matter did not always make a good poem, and that the artistic element in poetry was of the first importance. Then too the time had come when, with the decay of city life and the loss of political freedom, the importance of oratory visibly decreased, and with it the study of rhetoric. The golden age of Attic oratory was over; and already in the work of Demetrius Phalereus (*d.* 283 B.C.) may be detected the first signs of the decline. With him rhetoric is already being directed to scholastic ends; and it was a tendency which was rapidly to increase, since rhetoric had become recognised as one of the instruments of education, the result being a narrowing of the study in which technicalities were to gain the upper hand. Moreover in those wider questions of art which had been the subject of inquiry by earlier philosophers there was also a waning of interest. Philosophical studies were about to take a new turn, to concern themselves primarily with the practical conduct of life; and by Zeno (*fl.* 300 B.C.) and Epicurus (*b.* 342 B.C.) were being inaugurated two important schools of thought which were to affect a scorn for rhetoric and the arts. Zeno, it is true, compared dialectic to the closed fist, rhetoric to the open palm;[1] but it was the closed fist with which later Stoics were to be mainly concerned. Moreover to Epicurus is attributed the saying that "writing was easy enough", while his disciple Metrodorus condemned poetry as a useless thing; all of which foreshadowed a cessation of those critical activities which had given distinction to fourth-century thought.

[1] Cf. e.g. Quintilian, *Inst. Orat.* II, 20, 7.

CHAPTER VI

THE NEW POETICS: NEOPTOLEMUS OF PARIUM, CALLIMACHUS, AND ARISTARCHUS

THE history of literary criticism in the two centuries that followed seems at first sight to be little more than a blank. It is not merely that nothing comparable to the performance of either Plato or Aristotle was forthcoming; or that no influential figure like Isocrates appeared. The fact is that of the learned prose-writings produced in the third and second centuries B.C. almost all have completely vanished. A list of prose-writers, together with scanty fragments of their work, is practically all that has survived; and hardly a single work of criticism is in consequence available. That the period however was concerned with critical matters, and that on no negligible scale, so much at least may be inferred from evidence of various kinds. Apart from the titles of works supplied by Diogenes Laertius, for instance, there are fragments of doctrine embedded in the later *scholia*, references and discussions in Strabo, Plutarch, and others, echoes of controversy in some of the extant contemporary poems, a summary of Homeric criticism preserved in a tenth-century manuscript at Venice, as well as notices of Hellenistic theorists, and material for the partial reconstruction of at least one *Poetics* derived from certain papyri recovered at Herculaneum. Nor are these activities without their significance in the history of criticism; for they are the result of the first impact of Greek art on the outside world. Thus they witness to fresh tendencies in the sphere of criticism; they bring to light new views on the subject of poetry; and they also help to explain something of the later developments at Rome.

As to the nature of these critical activities, their main characteristics are best understood in the light of those changed conditions in Asia and Egypt which followed the conquests of Alexander (356–323 B.C.), and which marked a revolution in Greek life and culture. By 300 B.C. Athens had ceased to be the centre of Greek intellectual life; and in the course of the next two centuries its place was taken by new centres of influence in which Hellenism was to assume a modified form. At Alexandria first, the capital of the Ptolemies, then later at Pergamum, the capital of the Attalids, Greek art and scholarship may be said to have blossomed anew; and a similar efflorescence took place in other city-states, at Antioch and Syracuse, Rhodes and Halicarnassus, Tarsus and Ephesus, everywhere in fact where Greek colonies had been established and the seeds of Greek culture sown. It was thus a new world in which Hellenistic culture developed; and it was one in which the predominant intellectual interests were those of scholarship and science, a scholarship and a science made possible by the patronage of princes, and fostered by the institution of libraries at Alexandria, Pergamum and elsewhere. Chief among the tasks was that of preserving the ancient culture, and at Alexandria more particularly a host of scholars devoted themselves to establishing and elucidating the texts of Homer and the earlier Greeks. This marked the birth of textual criticism and of philological studies generally; for now emerged the grammarian who theorised on questions of language, as well as the scholiast who applied those theories to the earlier literature. At the same time science also flourished, and the researches of scholars like Euclid, Archimedes, and Eratosthenes made of this period one of the most brilliant in all antiquity. And in history too there were notable developments; there was a new care for truth, a more extensive outlook, and with Polybius was to come a new conception of historical study. On the other hand, something was lost of the earlier range and intensity in the spheres of philosophy and rhetoric alike. No longer interested in such matters as politics or metaphysics, men sought for new creeds of rational wisdom, and their needs were met by Stoic and Epicurean thinkers. Moreover with the decline of the political importance of oratory, the study of rhetoric also underwent an eclipse. It was still a prime factor in the educational system; but divorced from life it became a mere mechanical process, a study of meaningless terms and unending rules.

Nor were there wanting developments in the sphere of literature. For a culture that had become cosmopolitan in character new artistic vehicles and themes had necessarily to be found; and in the works of the chief poets, Alexandrian for the most part, may be detected forms and experiences which differed vitally from those characteristic of the productions of earlier Greece. The drama for instance no longer held its privileged position; though Menander had kept alive the interest in comedy, and after Sositheus in the third century B.C. satyr-plays once again came into vogue.[1] The earlier lyric and the epic on the grand scale were also still cultivated; but the forms now favoured were the elegy, the idyll, the pastoral, the didactic poem, and the romantic epic, poetic types which responded to new motives and moods. In the meantime, moreover, important changes had taken place in the spirit and content of literature; for the artist, no longer interested in the state, literature ceased to be in the old sense an expression of the community, and became rather the craft of coteries, with whom "Art for Art's sake" was a guiding principle. Hence the larger issues of patriotism and religion were no longer cultivated; in their place were themes which commended themselves to scholar-poets, notably the less familiar myths of ancient tradition, which were handled with learning and considerable technical skill. Elsewhere, too, the spirit of the age was revealing itself in an increased realism, in a treatment of the individual man and the phenomena of everyday life; so that art tended to become a faithful copy of the actual instead of an idealised version of its varied details. Nor were there wanting signs of what later ages were to term "romantic" tendencies. Whereas earlier literature had been devoted to the exclusive cult of man, two new motives of imaginative art now appeared, if not for the first time, at least with a change of emphasis; and with these themes of love and external nature there appeared also new methods of treatment, new notes and effects. Emphasis for instance was laid on the original, the picturesque, and the fanciful, while a free rein was given more generally to the expression of personal feelings, which often took the form of vain longings and regrets. Interest was also found in diversity as opposed to organic unity, in a series of idylls as opposed to a sustained act

---

[1] See W. R. Paton, *Greek Anthology* (Loeb ed.), II, 707.

of creative imagination; and altogether there emerged a more varied, if also a more confused, conception of art, at any rate something quite different from that of the classical period. At the same time, it must be added, certain qualities had also been lost. Taste in general had become less sure, and the feeling for fitness, for the earlier moderation and balance, had been somewhat disturbed. There were mannerisms, excess, and some neglect of form; and this is seen in Hellenistic prose generally, and more particularly in the new style of oratory, the chief exponent of which was Hegesias of Magnesia (*c.* 250 B.C.), who, reverting to the earlier sophistic methods in spite of Aristotle and Isocrates, gave rise to an artificial style which depended for its effects on epigrams, strained metaphors, false antitheses, over-elaborate rhythms, and the like. Throughout the third and second centuries B.C. the influence of Hegesias was felt, and the effects are seen in what became known as the "Asiatic" style, which for the time being dominated prose, and which, despite its description, represented a breakdown of earlier traditions, rather than a fusion of the Asiatic and Hellenic geniuses. Moreover, by the beginning of the first century B.C., further developments became visible in yet another phase of this vicious style. Throughout the Greek world a second "Asiatic" style became popular; and magniloquent, sonorous, and bombastic in its effects, it represented a denial of all sound principles, a perversion of the teaching of the age which had preceded.

With these changes of conditions in the intellectual life of the time, it is not strange to find new departures in critical activity; new methods of approaching literature being evolved and fresh problems of interest engaging the attention. For one thing the disappearance of Aristotle's texts was not without its influence. On the death of Theophrastus (287 B.C.) the Aristotelian texts had come into the possession of a certain Neleus of Scepsis in the Troad, by whom they were concealed on account of the book-collecting zeal of the Attalids. And whether subsequently they remained in that retreat, until, restored to Athens about 100 B.C. and conveyed to Rome after 86 B.C., they became accessible to scholars in a somewhat mutilated form, or whether,

according to another account, they were procured at an earlier
date for the Library at Alexandria, in either case the result was
much the same. The actual text of Aristotle's *Poetics* played no
great part in the ancient world. No traces remain of any
ancient commentary on it; it was but rarely quoted by ancient
writers. Something of its teaching and terminology, it is true,
survives in works of compilation; its doctrine filtered through
by means of summaries. But it was Aristotle for the most part
at second-hand; and to Hellenistic theorists at any rate his
Poetics was in all probability inaccessible. At the same time
interest in poetry and poetic theory still remained; and from
now on the study of poetry became a discipline in itself, devoted
to scholastic ends, and formulated by grammarians and philo-
logians instead of philosophers as heretofore. And as a result
its treatment underwent change. What was aimed at was not
so much a consideration of some of the profounder problems of
poetry, as a practical exposition, embracing remarks on the
nature of poetry, and more especially definite indications of the
ways of writing it, with rules and classifications drawn up in
ordered fashion. Such a systematisation had to some extent
been implicit in Aristotle; though with him it had been blended
with philosophical speculation of an abstract kind. Now however the didactic and technical side becomes uppermost; and
here it is not difficult to see the influence of those earlier τέχναι
which in connexion with rhetoric had attained considerable
success. Then, too, the attitude of the new age to poetry
differed vitally from that of the preceding period in the views
held concerning the nature of the earlier literature. By
Aristotle poetry had been treated as a whole; it was regarded as
the outcome of free creative activities which had gone through
various developments and had produced certain literary forms
which culminated in the drama. Now, however, for this
dynamic view was substituted one of a more static kind. All
the poetic forms of the past, the most ancient as well as the
most recent, were alike regarded as models for the guidance of
future writers. And since with each poetic form were associated
certain formal and stylistic characteristics, hence arose the
conception of the literary *genres*, that of certain pre-established

types, inherent in the earlier literature, to which all later creations had necessarily to conform. Of the significance of this change of outlook but little need here be said. It was of fundamental importance, for its influence was felt throughout the Hellenistic and the Roman periods in antiquity; and it was also perpetuated in later ages down to the Renascence. Nor were these the only factors that influenced the study of poetry at this date. As a legacy from the past had come down more than one unfinished controversy: those relating for example to the function of poetry, or to the relative values of subject-matter and form, of natural endowment and artistic skill in poetic composition. And, in addition, Alexandrian poetry itself was not without its influence, traces of the current innovations in theme and form alike being reflected in the new theories. Altogether then it is clear that the conditions were such as rendered some modification of the earlier theorising on poetry inevitable. In fact, it is the study of poetics that will be found at this stage to constitute the main line of critical development; and however vague and inadequate the extant results may seem, the movement is nevertheless one of first-rate importance, calling here for consideration in view of its influence on the theorising of later ages.

Such then are the main factors underlying the critical development at this stage; though that there were other critical interests is also of course true. Of the work done however in the fields of literary history, philology, rhetoric, Homeric criticism and the like, something will be said later; whereas the first place in importance must undoubtedly be given to the emergence of the new poetics. Nor are we limited for our knowledge of that movement to considerations of a general kind. For definite evidence as to the nature of those studies we may turn to certain writings of the succeeding period, wherein references to Hellenistic theorists make it possible to form some idea at least of the activities in question. Thus it is we learn of the teachings of Neoptolemus of Parium, Heracleodorus, Andromenides and others, theorists of the third century B.C.; while elsewhere may be gathered something of the views put forward by Eratosthenes, Callimachus, and Simylus. And it is by piecing together such details as these that some conception of this obscure but significant phase of Hellenistic culture may be arrived at, and ideas formed of the changing methods, the prevailing questions, and the resultant theories characteristic of the age. Of outstanding importance in this connexion is what has come down of the work *On Poems* (περὶ ποιημάτων) by Philodemus of Gadara (first century B.C.). All that survive are charred fragments of papyri recovered within modern times from the ruins of Herculaneum, and consisting mainly, but not entirely, of passages of Book V of the treatise, which embody summary statements rather than literal quotations from various earlier writers. Yet the value of those fragments it would be difficult to overrate; for while they throw light in general on the theorising of the third century B.C., from them has also been attempted a reconstruction in part of the actual *Poetics* of Neoptolemus of Parium[1]—an achievement which partakes of the nature of a romance of scholarship. Neoptolemus is known to have been a grammarian-poet of Parium in Bithynia, to whom a *Poetics* (*de arte poetica*) was subsequently attributed by the scholiast Porphyrio (third century A.D.). And in virtue of these fragments not only is that claim confirmed, but indications of its plan and contents are also supplied, sufficient to give a shrewd idea of the contemporary study of poetics in general.

Nothing in the first place is more significant than the changes which took place in the methods pursued in these inquiries, and the consequent alterations in the form of the new *Poetics*. Such modifications are already visible in Neoptolemus; his *Poetics* being divided into three main sections, one dealing with *poesis* (ποίησις), in which poetry was considered as a whole and with special reference to subject-matter,[2] the second with *poema* (ποίημα) which dealt with matters of form, the various *genres* and their component parts,[3] and the third with *poeta* (ποιητής), with matters relating to the poet himself.[4] This three-fold category had developed in view of the scholastic needs of the

---

[1] See C. Jensen, "Neoptolemos und Horaz" (*Abh. Pr. Akad. d. Wiss.* 1918, no. 14), and his *Philodemos Ueber die Gedichte*, Fünftes Buch, 1923.
[2] See Jensen, *Philodemos etc.* col. 11, ll. 27–9.
[3] *Ibid.* col. 9, ll. 6–9; col. 12, ll. 26–7.
[4] *Ibid.* col. 8, ll. 33 ff.; col. 11, ll. 2 ff.

time, which called for a treatment that was practical, orderly, and schematic, and for a presentment of material that was intelligible and accessible to all. At the same time it was also based on principles generally accepted, by the Peripatetics at least, as fundamental to the study. The first of these principles was that technical training as well as natural gifts were needed for the composition of poetry; and a treatise on poetry had therefore in the first place two main sections, one dealing with technique or art (τέχνη, ars), the other with the poet himself (ποιητής, artifex). The second principle was that both subject-matter and form alike were important elements of poetry; and this led to a modification of the original scheme, by which the section embodying technique was divided into two sub-sections, one dealing with the choice and invention of argument (ποίησις), the other with matters of form and expression (ποίημα). Hence in practice the emergence of the three-fold category, which Andromenidès (according to Philodemus) was the first to introduce into the study of poetics. And of these sections the one concerned with *poema* (ποίημα) as a rule came in for the most extensive treatment, possibly because this aspect of the study lent itself best to analysis and exposition. This at least was characteristic of Neoptolemus;[1] and moreover, in accordance with Aristotelian tradition, consideration in that section was mainly devoted to dramatic poetry, and to the epic in so far as it was an earlier form leading up to the drama. Such then in all probability was the normal outline of the Hellenistic *Poetics*; and it was a scheme of treatment that, with all its defects, was destined to influence most of the later manuals of instruction, and to supply in particular the framework of those isagogic works at Rome of which Horace's *Ars Poetica* and Quintilian's *Institutio Oratoria* were the most famous examples.[2] In rhetoric, too, it was well represented; and indeed it is uncertain whether the scheme was originally evolved in connexion with rhetorical or poetic studies. That it was due to the Peripatetics however and was subsequently adopted by the Stoics would seem highly probable; and in any case the schematic treatment is one of

---

[1] Jensen, *op. cit.* col. 8, ll. 33 ff.; col. 11, ll. 2–3.
[2] See Norden, *Hermes*, XL (1905), 481–528.

considerable historical interest. It helps for instance in interpreting such a work as Horace's *Ars Poetica*; and incidentally
it also throws light on later theorising, as when Ben Jonson
(following Scaliger) discusses in his *Discoveries*[1] matters relating
to "the Poeme, the Poesy, and the Poet".

Equally interesting however are the theories associated with
this new poetics, for they too were instrumental in giving direction to many of the later discussions. And it was around certain
problems already referred to that the theorising apparently
centred, if we may judge from Philodemus's later references.
First, there was the relative importance of native gifts and
technical training in the make-up of the poet; secondly, the
question whether subject-matter or form was the essential
element in poetry; and thirdly, the closely related question as
to what constituted the real function of poetry. All three were
questions to which no decisive answer had been given in the
past; and they were now revived with not uninteresting results.
In the first place there can be no doubt that the old antithesis
between art ($\tau\acute{\epsilon}\chi\nu\eta$) and nature ($\phi\acute{\upsilon}\sigma\iota\varsigma$) in all branches of
human activity was being frequently discussed by the Stoics,
and now with special reference to literature; and as might be
expected more stress at this date was laid on the need for a
knowledge of art than on the workings of poetic genius. That
the theory of "inspiration" still held its ground is seen elsewhere from the reference to the subject made by Callimachus,
to whom Hesiod's account of his initiation by the Muses while
tending his flocks on Mount Helicon[2] became the accepted
explanation, as well as the origin, of the convention of the
singing shepherd. Moreover an extension of the theory to the
effect that such inspiration was brought about by a draught
from the holy well—whether Hippocrene or Arethusa—seems
also to date from this period; it apparently does not occur
before, whereas from now on it becomes a familiar commonplace. On the other hand yet clearer is the growing sense of the
importance of a knowledge of art and of the need for a technical
training. According to the Aristotelian tradition a knowledge
of technique as well as inspiration was held to be necessary for

[1] § 130.   [2] See p. 12 *supra*.

the poet; while the very nature of the Hellenistic *Poetics*, with its ample instruction on the poetic craft, seems to point to a widespread adoption of this view. Neoptolemus for his part identifies himself with the Peripatetic position, according to which native gifts (δύναμιν τὴν ποιητικήν) as well as technical skill (τέχνη) were necessary.[1] In one place moreover he distinguishes between the writer skilled in poetic technique (εὖ ποιῶν) and the good poet (ἀγαθὸς ποιητής) with his natural gifts,[2] thus suggesting that technical skill in itself was not enough. And in this indeterminate fashion the question was handed on for discussion by the generations that followed.

With regard to the second of these questions opinion was likewise divided; there were those who attached all value in poetry to the subject-matter alone, while others looked to the form or expression as representing the essential element. By Aristotle, it will be recalled, both views had been more or less reconciled. Though much of his work was concerned with formal details, his definition of poetry was couched in terms of subject-matter, not form; so that while stressing in a sense the importance of the ideas conveyed, he recognised also the value of the element of form. At this later date however the problem was reopened and differences of opinion found expression in new poetic theories. As before, there were those who like the Stoics approached poetry as a sort of philosophy, and who sought for ideas and truths under the veil of allegory. Thus Cleanthes regarded poetry as a more effective vehicle than any discourse for the conveyance of philosophical truths; "metre and song and rhythm", he maintained,[3] "come nearest to the truth in the contemplation of the divine". According to the definition of Ariston of Chios, again, poetry was essentially a combination of ethical wisdom and a good style—a conception that had much in common with that of Plutarch at a later date. And in such views we have what is perhaps the characteristic doctrine of this period; the earlier conception of the poet as teacher never quite died out. At the same time other conceptions of poetry also emerged; and Neoptolemus for one,

---

[1] Jensen, *op. cit.* col. 11, ll. 5 ff.   [2] *Ibid.* col. 7, ll. 18 ff.
[3] Philod. *Vol. Herc.* 1, 28, quoted by Sikes, *op. cit.* p. 170 n.

following the Peripatetics, attached value to subject-matter and
form alike,[1] though his idea of subject-matter differed somewhat from that of Aristotle. With Aristotle the "probable" or
the "universal" had formed the substance of poetic themes;
whereas to Neoptolemus the subject-matter of poetry consisted
of things actually or historically true. Such material alone, he
implied, was capable of edifying; and in one place he recommends the poet to concern himself not merely with the originality, but also with the truth (ἀλήθεια) of his themes.[2] Nor were
the changes that were taking place in contemporary poetry
without their influence on theorists; and this was seen in the
further departures being made from the philosophical position
that had been taken up by Aristotle. By Aristotle actions that
were absurd or false (ἄλογον, ψευδές) were excluded from
poetry (except from the epic), as were also empirical facts and
historical material (γενόμενον). Now however such restrictions
no longer commended themselves to either poets or theorists.
The "probable" was interpreted in a less restricted sense, and
recognition was given to the absurd and fabulous, as well as to
empirical facts, to history and legend. Hence the new Hellenistic theory, according to which the subject-matter of poetry
might consist of (1) the probable (πλάσμα), (2) the absurd or
fabulous (μῦθος), and (3) the actual or true (ἱστορία). It was
a classification which included all the themes of earlier poetic
forms, was in general accord with the far-fetched fancies and
the realism of Alexandrian poetry; and it became familiar at a
later date to Roman critics under the heads of *res ficta, fabula,*
and *fama.*[3]

In marked contrast to this was the attitude of those who, like
Heracleodorus, conceived form or style to constitute the essence
of poetry; with the result that a fresh importance was attached
to poetic "composition" (σύνθεσις) in its technical sense, that
is, the harmonious arrangement of words, a subject which
Dionysius of Halicarnassus was subsequently to make one of his
main themes. The movement in a sense was the outcome of the

---

[1] See Jensen, *op. cit.* col. 9, ll. 25–7.   [2] *Ibid.* col. 5, l. 4.
[3] Cf. *Ad Her.* I, 8, 13; Quintilian, *Inst. Orat.* II, 4, 2. See Rostagni, *op. cit.*
p. lvii.

Stoic interest in the character of speech, though the Peripatetic concern with style may have been a yet more important factor. According to the Stoic doctrine, the five excellences of style were purity of Greek ('Ελληνισμός), lucidity, conciseness, appropriateness, and freedom from colloquialisms; and the vices to be avoided were barbarisms (or violations of current or historical usage) and solecisms (or incongruous constructions).[1] The Peripatetic teaching on the other hand was probably represented by Neoptolemus, who required in the treatment of subject-matter and style alike the qualities of brevity (συντομία) and clearness (ἐνάργεια); and for the more elaborate poems such qualities as splendour, harmony, gravity.[2] Of yet greater significance however is the teaching of Andromenides, of whom otherwise but little is known, though his pronouncements on these matters would seem to have been of no uncertain kind. According to his view, "what was most becoming in poets was the careful elaboration of speech, their task being not to say what no others say, but rather to speak as no others can, and to work out for themselves a clear utterance, making use of the rhythms, the sounds, and the happy sequences (ἁρμονία) of the Muses".[3] Moreover, he explained, a care for rhythm was inborn in man, as was shown by the fact that babes were put to sleep by a meaningless song; and he added further that "the poet must take to himself beautiful words to influence his hearers, as well as clear-sounding letters chosen in accordance with their quality and quantity".[3] Nor is this the only place where stress was laid on the part played by euphony in poetry. For Andromenides in this matter was followed by the Stoic Crates of Mallos (second century B.C.), so that in all probability the doctrine formed part of the teaching of the school at Pergamum. In discussing the criticism of poetry (κρίσις ποιημάτων)—which formed the final stage of grammatical study —Crates for instance laid down the test of delight or "charm", whereas of the test of instruction as the outcome of subject-matter he has nothing to say. Moreover of the sources of this poetic delight he mentions words (ἔπη) only. To that element indeed he assigns the sovereignty, so that to him poetry was

---

[1] Diog. Laert. VII, 59.   [2] Jensen, op. cit. col. 3, ll. 12 ff.   [3] Ibid. p. 142.

essentially an art that had to do with verbal effects; and in forming poetic judgments the ear was said to be the guide, a point made by Ariston of Chios and Crates alike.[1] Hence the importance attached by these grammarians to euphonic and symphonic values in poetry, to the sound-effects of words, syllables, and letters; and here may be traced the influence of the Alexandrian poets, with their verbal elegances and chiselled felicities of phrase.

Closely bound up with these discussions was the third question already mentioned, namely, that relating to the function of poetry. And according to the views held concerning the essential element in poetry, so the conception of this function varied. By those who held subject-matter to be all-important, poetry was said to have a didactic, utilitarian aim; whereas those who regarded form as the essential element held that poetry aimed merely at giving delight. Here again was one of those unsolved problems that had come down from the past; and though Aristotle had gone some way towards reconciling the points of view, at this date the matter came up anew and formed a recognised part of the new poetics. On the one hand were the Stoics who exaggerated the function of utility, and who sought in poetry merely teaching of a practical or moral kind, as if its aim were only that of presenting abstract or hidden truths. And on the other hand were authorities like Heracleodorus and Eratosthenes who maintained that poetry aimed solely at giving pleasure, a pleasure derived from the enchantment of beautiful words which moved the mind and stirred the soul. Thus Eratosthenes categorically declared that the aim of every true poet was to "divert" his audience, not to instruct them;[2] and in him we see a champion of the hedonistic theory. That theory, it is true, was by no means new; it dated from the earliest times and was one of the grounds of Plato's attack. Now however for the first time it was explicitly stated that the exclusive aim of the poet was the giving of delight; and it is somewhat surprising to find how slowly the idea was accepted by antiquity. To the Epicureans, strangely enough, it made no appeal; and

[1] Jensen, *op. cit.* p. 159.
[2] Cf. Strabo, *Geography*, I, 2, 19; see vol. II, 170.

in the popular view the giving of pleasure remained a minor aspect of the poet's task. At the same time yet another view was current, namely, that the aim of the poet was both to teach and to delight. It was a Peripatetic compromise, based on Aristotle's recognition of the aesthetic and the intellectual values of poetry; and it is the theory that is adopted by Neoptolemus of Parium. According to that authority the aim of the perfect poet was two-fold, to charm the hearers (ψυχαγωγεῖν, τέρπειν) and to be of service by his teaching (ὠφελεῖν, χρησιμολογεῖν).[1] The delight of poetry, Neoptolemus further explains, is the outcome of words and rhythm (τέρπειν μὲν τοὺς ἀκούοντας), whereas the teaching lay in the things represented (ὠφελεῖν δὲ τοὺς ὁ[ρῶντας]).[2] Elsewhere he points out that moral teaching and scientific instruction formed no part of the poet's aim, the mere representation of truth or reality being instructive and educative.[3] And this doctrine, adopted by Horace at a later date, became subsequently the orthodox teaching at the Renascence.

Such then was the main trend in the Hellenistic study of poetics; and the general tendencies thus revealed, whether of method or doctrine, are of the highest significance in the critical development. Stamped with the unmistakable features of the Hellenistic age, they witness to the rise of a new form of poetic study which, in virtue of its didactic qualities, its mechanical divisions devised for convenience of reference, and its attempts at explaining a craft which could not wholly be explained, represented something far removed from the freer philosophical treatment of the earlier age. At the same time generalisations such as these do not exhaust the information available. Further light on the theorising that went on may be obtained from the poets themselves; and illuminating in this connexion is that famous feud between Callimachus and Apollonius of Rhodes which fluttered the learned dove-cotes at Alexandria about the middle of the third century B.C. The immediate occasion of the quarrel was the appearance of Apollonius's poem *Argonautica*

---

[1] Jensen, *op. cit.* col. 13, ll. 8ff.; see Rostagni, *op. cit.* pp. xc–xci for further details. [2] *Ibid.* fr. 2, ll. 24ff.
[3] *Ibid.* fr. 1, ll. 12ff.; fr. 2, ll. 3ff.

about the year 242 B.C. It was a long narrative poem of the traditional kind, based on Homeric methods and full of Homeric reminiscences, yet embodying also new motives and moods which made of the work a blend of both epic and romance. By the critics generally it was received with derision; and Callimachus, as head of the poetic school and one-time instructor of the new poet, undertook the task of dealing with the offender. In this way began a protracted feud, a wordy battle of epigrams which rivalled in its bitterness the truculent exchanges of later Humanists. And altogether the episode was of an unedifying kind, one which, however illuminating as to the unchanging character of the *genus irritabile*, would have little claim to figure in a survey of criticism, had it not possessed a deeper significance than at first sight seems the case. For there was more in the explosion than a passing displeasure with a youthful innovator who had attempted in his poem to unite things old and new. There was involved a challenge to contemporary authority and to that unwritten creed which, established and maintained by the school of Callimachus, governed for the time being all poetic activities. In the first place it should be noted that Apollonius's poem consisted of four books only; and in this he was following the hint thrown out by Aristotle, that epics might with advantage be reduced to the length of a tragedy or a tetralogy for the sake of greater rapidity and vivacity in the treatment.[1] What angered the critics however was not that Apollonius had attempted new things in this and other respects, but rather that he had followed in some measure the ancient ways; for this ran counter to some of their main tenets. "I hate the cyclic poem" (ἐχθαίρω τὸ ποίημα τὸ κυκλικόν),[2] declared Callimachus more than once, "the common road which everyone uses." And here in brief were the root principles of Callimachean theory; a dislike in the first place for traditional and conventional methods, for those long narratives *ab ovo* of a chronological kind, with their hackneyed themes, epithets and formulas, all of which were summed up in the "cyclic" poem; and in the second place, the indirect demand for originality and novelty in subject-matter, form and expression. Elsewhere

---

[1] *Poetics*, 1459b, 19.   [2] *Epigr.* 30; *Anth. Pal.* 11, 130.

such doctrines are repeated by Callimachus in more picturesque terms when he advises poets "not to travel along roads crowded with chariots nor to follow the tracks of others; but rather to penetrate paths hitherto untrodden, to discover fresh and pure sources and to pluck new flowers".[1] This, he held, would be enough for fame; and it obviously involved a break with tradition. Nor are these the only places where light is thrown on the prevailing literary ideas. Indications of a more positive kind for instance are given when Callimachus, boasting of the merits of his learned poems, claimed for them qualities that had been wanting in Homer, namely, delicacy and finish; thus commending careful workmanship and the lesson of artistic toil. More than all however is his insistence on the idea that the day of the long epic was over, and that epigrams, elegies and the like were the only forms to be cultivated by the new age. Thus he condemns for instance the singers "whose songs were more vast than the sea";[2] he calls for poetic compositions more brief, more concise, and less ambitious than formerly ($\check{\epsilon}\pi os$ $\tau v\tau\theta\acute{o}v$, $Mo\hat{v}\sigma a$ $\lambda\epsilon\pi\tau a\lambda\acute{\epsilon}\eta$);[3] while it was the same idea that inspired his famous dictum that "a big book is a big nuisance" ($\mu\acute{\epsilon}\gamma a$ $\beta\iota\beta\lambda\acute{\iota}ov$ $\mu\acute{\epsilon}\gamma a$ $\kappa a\kappa\acute{o}v$).[4] And his position in this matter was apparently supported by Theocritus (third century B.C.), whose Lycidas was said "to hate those birds of the Muses that cackled in vain rivalry with Homer",[5] thus defending the little songs which Theocritus himself sang as against the lengthier and inferior epics written in imitation of Homer.

Interesting in yet another sense, if indeed it belongs to this period, is the fragment preserved by Stobaeus[6] (c. 500 A.D.) and ascribed to one Simylus, a didactic poet in all probability of this Hellenistic period, though according to at least one authority he may have belonged rather to the first century B.C. That he can scarcely have been a comic poet of the same name belonging to the fourth century B.C. would seem at any rate to be suggested by certain features of the diction and the verse;

---

[1] *Fr.* 293 Schn.   [2] *Hymns*, II, 106.
[3] See *Oxyrh. Pap.* 2079, vol. XVII (1927).
[4] *Fr.* 359 Schn.   [5] *Idylls*, VII, 47–8.
[6] *Florilegium*, ed. Meineke, II, 352.

while the nature of the theorising, its concern with composition, and the neatness and artistry of expression, would also be more in keeping with the Hellenistic, than with any earlier, period. But to whatever date the fragment be assigned, and it is probably post-Aristotelian, as to its value there can be no question, as the following rendering shows:

> Nature of Art bereft will not suffice
> For any work whate'er in all the world;
> Nor Art again, devoid of Nature's aid.
> And, e'en if Art and Nature join in one,
> The poet still must find the ways and means,
> Passion and practice; happy chance and time;
> A critic skilled to seize the poet's sense.
> For, if in aught of these he haply fail,
> He cannot gain the goal of all his hopes.
> Nature, good will, and pains, and ordered grace
> Make poets wise and good, while length of years
> Will make them older men, but nothing more.[1]

Here then may be seen a new trend in literary theorising, a consideration, not so much of the nature and function of poetry, as of the qualities and conditions that go to the making of a good poet. The prescription of genius (φύσις) and a knowledge of art (τέχνη), of practice (μελέτη), happy chance (καιρὸς εὐφυής) and the helping hand of a critic (κριτής), all this was to be discussed at a subsequent date, by Horace in particular, while the fragment was later on to be quoted by Ben Jonson in his *Discoveries*. But the exposition was never to assume a happier form. Revealing as it does a fresh insight into the poetic process, it supplements Aristotle, and is also significant of the new direction that was being taken by post-Aristotelian poetics.

So far then we have been tracing the rise of a new Hellenistic poetics; and this after all must be regarded as the most important critical development at this date. At the same time, the spirit of learned curiosity that characterised the age was productive of yet further activities bearing on critical theory; and it remains to notice the work done in such fields as literary

---

[1] Sandys's trans.; see his *History of Classical Scholarship*, I, 56.

history, philology, and rhetoric, as well as certain tendencies in contemporary thought which were to affect later criticism closely in one way or another. And, in the first place, in the interest that was now betrayed in literary history and the lives of literary men appeared a new factor which was to result in the collection of material indispensable for critical advance. To some extent this care for facts formed part of the Aristotelian tradition. Aristotle had begun with his *Didascaliae*, though indeed his methods throughout had been coloured by historical considerations; and the Peripatetics had carried on this side of his work, devoting themselves assiduously to historical researches of all kinds. For the main impulse however we must turn to the Alexandrian Library with its vast collection of manuscripts and its body of skilled workers; and these facilities led at this date to a multiplication of biographical and literary studies. Foremost in the work was Callimachus (*c*. 310–240 B.C.), scholar and poet, whose monumental production, his *Lists of Illustrious Writers and their Works* (in 120 vols.), represented a mine of information on the subject. A huge *catalogue raisonné*, in which the contents of the Library were classified according to type and date, it stood for something more as well. In it were included bibliography, biography, and history; and its collection of positive facts, based on organised research, marked a new stage in the development of literary history, the starting-point in fact of those historico-critical activities which went on in Alexandria and Pergamum for centuries to come. Nor was Callimachus alone in this sort of production. From Lycophron (*fl.* 280 B.C.) came a treatise *On Comedy* which ran into eleven books; and subsequently from Eratosthenes a work of twelve volumes entitled *The Old Attic Comedy*. The latter consisted of a number of monographs dealing with the authorship, the dates, the subject-matter and language of the plays; and in view of its comprehensive treatment, its sane critical judgments of preceding works, it has been judged the masterpiece of its versatile and scholarly author.

Throughout the whole of the third century B.C., then, such studies were common; and from the Stoics came also certain inquiries of a rather different kind, a development of Zeno's essay *Concerning the Study of Poetry*. Thus from Cleanthes came the treatises *On Art* and *On the Poets*, from Chrysippus other works *On Poems* and *How one should study Poetry*; and on this work of Chrysippus, it might be added, Plutarch at a later date drew in composing his essay *How to study Poetry* (*de audiendis poetis*).[1] At the same time the main interest of the Stoics where literature was concerned lay in another direction. Their doctrine of ἀπάθεια forbade any appeal to the emotions and they therefore eschewed all beauties of expression. Dialectics, on the other hand, being an essential part of their philosophy, the study of poetry with them was inevitably linked up with the theory of language. And the same zeal for learning which had led to results in literary history was instrumental also in advancing the study of grammar and philology, particularly as ample material for such researches had by this time accumulated at the various libraries. Previous to this, grammatical studies had engaged the attention of Prodicus and the sophists, while both Plato and Aristotle had subsequently touched on some of the linguistic problems. But it was during the Hellenistic period that philological studies first assumed a systematic form; and in the *Glossae* which preserved archaic and dialect forms, in the various speculations on the origin and development of language, and in the attempts at codifying grammar and prosody are to be found the beginnings of later grammatical studies. And in this work Cleanthes and Chrysippus among the Stoics, as well as Crates of Mallos, head of the school at Pergamum, played an important part; while the contribution of Dionysius Thrax (second century B.C.) calls perhaps for special mention as possessing a peculiar interest in the history of criticism. From him came what is known as the earliest Greek *Grammar*, a work still extant, of some sixteen pages, which remained for centuries the standard work of its kind. In its pages is set forth the prevailing conception of the art of grammar (γραμματική), which, so far from being understood in the modern and narrow sense of the term, was held to be concerned with the usages of writers of both poetry and prose, and to aim at an interpretation of literature in the widest sense.

---

[1] See vol. II, 311.

The various parts of grammar were therein defined as (1) accurate reading aloud, (2) interpretation of figures of speech, (3) explanation of obsolete words and customs, (4) etymology, (5) study of grammatical forms, and (6) criticism of poetry, which was described as the highest and noblest function of all. And here it is not difficult to see a new phase of analytical criticism emerging; a conscious and systematic effort being made to open up new lines of literary study, and to interpret literature with due attention to the rules of art, the proper use of words and figures of speech. In short, from now on, the *grammatici* were to be in effect the professional *poetarum interpretes*.

Sporadic and fragmentary as undoubtedly were the results in these various fields, in rhetoric there is even less to show. No complete rhetorical treatise has in fact come down from this period; and with the decline of oratory in public life and with rhetoric mainly cultivated for academic ends, there was for the time being a cessation of those more generous studies which in the hands of Isocrates and Aristotle had produced such fruitful results. At the same time such treatment as it received, mainly from the Stoics of Pergamum, was by no means without its significance; for it was now that certain changes were made in the method of treatment, a scholastic rhetoric being inaugurated which influenced later efforts for ages to come. By the Stoics the art was cultivated as a logical study, with special attention paid to subject-matter, and to such aspects of style as lent themselves to minute analysis. In place of broad principles based on human nature, what was sought was a detailed system which could be applied mechanically, a scheme of devices with extensive divisions and sub-divisions, and a technical terminology which embraced all tropes and figures, and provided for distinctions as acute as they were numerous. That such a treatment ignored the vital points of oratory need scarcely be urged; for the graces of style eluded such an analysis. For scholastic and teaching purposes, on the other hand, the methods were well suited, since they reduced the study to clear and systematic form. In them may be detected the influence of the scientific spirit of the age; and it is on account of its historical bearing, as a phase in the critical development, that Hellenistic rhetoric is in consequence mainly of interest.

Less intimately connected with the critical activities of the time, though of considerable importance in their bearing on later inquiries, were certain developments in contemporary thought, the product once again of the prevailing scientific bias. Among the speculations which engaged the attention of scholars was the question whether language could be reduced to law and order, or whether its phenomena were the arbitrary results of mere custom and usage. Aristophanes of Byzantium, a pupil of Callimachus, was probably the first to put forward the theory of Analogy, according to which there existed in language an essential regularity which rendered it capable of being reduced to rule. It was an attempt to explain rationally the variety of grammatical forms; and the theory was maintained generally by the scholars of Alexandria, including Aristarchus and his school. As against this, there was the theory of Anomaly, which held language to be a medley of forms subject to no definite law but determined solely by custom; and of this doctrine Crates of Mallos was the main expositor, though there were other adherents, Chrysippus for instance who wrote a work *On Anomaly* in connexion with grammar. The importance of this dispute was however not confined to its immediate results, or to the fact that similar linguistic inquiries were continued later on at Rome by Varro and others. A fresh impulse, it is true, was thus given to the systematic study of grammar; but the dispute was significant in yet another and a more far-reaching sense. It formed part in reality of a wider inquiry in which the general question was raised in connexion with all the arts—with grammar and medicine and ultimately with jurisprudence, agriculture, and architecture—as to whether regularity or irregularity, law or chance, analogy or anomaly was the animating principle, the ultimate determining factor of those arts. And in all fields alike the philosophical dispute followed the same lines and assumed the same form. On the one side were the empirics who maintained that all art was the result of mere practice and experience; and on the other were the dogmatics who held that art could be reduced to rule and was the result of a knowledge of cause and effect. It was in fact an attempt to approach art from a scientific point of view and to reduce it to some sort of system and law. And its influence may be seen in the literary criticism which followed, in the frequency with which the need for a systematic art was discussed in connexion with poetry and oratory, and in the bias generally betrayed in favour of the rule.

Here then in its first stages was one of those controversies which, while witnessing to a new phase in the history of the Greek spirit, at the same time opened up problems which were to be handed on from Alexandria to Rome. And similarly influential in its bearing on later criticism was yet another development of contemporary thought, namely, that scientific conception of history which was formulated and applied by Polybius (c. 210–125 B.C.) in his monumental *History* (of forty vols.), a work which marked a revolution in historical method. In that work Polybius had dealt with the Graeco-Roman world during the period 250–150 B.C.; and in outlining the general course of events he had sought to trace the working of cause and effect. To the more general causes he attached supreme importance; and he endeavoured to show how the prevailing ideas, the manners, the customs, and the institutions of the time had exercised a determining influence on the course of history. His object was to provide a practical history for statesmen, by bringing to light those conditions and factors which led to national greatness and decline. And his influence is subsequently seen in the critical sphere, and more particularly in the attempts made to account for the decline of oratory at Rome. By Tacitus, "Longinus", Quintilian and others, such inquiries were made; and these efforts, which marked an extension of the critical activity, owed their inspiration to the work of Polybius.

There yet remains to mention one further important development in the critical activities of this period, and that is the advance made in judicial criticism, and more especially in the interpretation of Homer. The work done in this sphere was in reality the outcome of a yet larger movement which had for its object the salvaging of the great literature of the past, and to the efforts of contemporary scholars it is that we owe not merely the preservation of many of the ancient texts but also the staying of the degeneration of such texts as were available. Amongst those engaged in this task were some of the most learned of the Alexandrians, notably Zenodotus (325–234 B.C.), the first librarian of the Museum, Eratosthenes (276–194 B.C.), the most versatile of scholars, Aristophanes of Byzantium (257–189 B.C.), a pupil of Zenodotus, and Aristarchus (217–145 B.C.), who won for himself the name of the first "critic" of antiquity. And all alike were concerned mainly with the Homeric text. Beginning with Zenodotus, who produced the first recension based on various MSS., each scholar added something to the editorial process, regulating texts with on the whole a wise conservatism, and supplying explanations not only of subject-matter but also of verbal, grammatical, and historical points. In this way a beginning was made with textual criticism. And writers other than Homer came in for treatment. By Aristophanes, and Aristarchus more especially, critical texts of the earlier lyric and drama were produced, including new editions of Hesiod, Pindar, Alcaeus, and Anacreon, as well as of the earlier tragic and comic poets; and since a fairly stable text of Homer had existed before Zenodotus, it was in connexion with the latter works probably that the piece of salvaging most valuable from the historical standpoint was done.

Yet indispensable as such work was for future literary studies, the mere investigation and establishment of texts does not, strictly speaking, come under the head of literary criticism; and what is of significance for our present purpose are the comments made on the literary aspects of the several works, and more particularly the attempts made at interpreting or assisting an aesthetic appreciation of Homer. Of these, as it happens, there is ample evidence; they are signs of the beginnings of a judicial criticism based on an actual examination of texts; and during this period Homeric criticism may be said to have made an appreciable advance. Previous to this Homer had been subjected to criticism of sorts. Objections, to begin with, had been raised against his mythology; and by way of retort, allegorical meanings and a complicated symbolism had been read into his work. It was a criticism almost wholly of subject-matter, and from a religious or a philosophical standpoint, the normal tests being those of morality and reality; so that Homer's poems as works of art received little or no consideration. These, it will be remembered, were the critical methods of Aristotle's day, upon which he comments at length in his *Poetics*.[1] He himself had given signs of a more aesthetic appreciation; but the methods he discusses, the formation of judgments on an ethical or matter-of-fact basis, these were handed down to the age that followed, and are methods characteristic of Alexandrian work.

Along with these however there were signs of better things, though the allegorical interpretation of Homer remained throughout the period characteristic of the Stoic school, in accordance with the tradition set up by Zeno, whose work, *Homeric Problems*, had been full of interpretations of this kind. In addition, there were those who questioned the unity of Homer, that is, of the *Iliad* and the *Odyssey*. Hitherto both poems had been accepted as authentic; and of the arguments on which the Separatists relied but little is known, except that Aristarchus summarily dismissed them and discountenanced the heresy.[2] With Eratosthenes on the other hand a change of attitude becomes visible; not only does he reject the allegorical methods, but he is also the first after Aristotle to insist on the ideal element in Homer, on the fact that he is to be judged not by standards of literal truth, nor by historical, geographical, or scientific considerations. He therefore attacks those who wished to read Homer literally, and who held that the wanderings of Ulysses were exact descriptions of actual events. "We shall find the track of Ulysses's wanderings", he stated,[3] "when we find the cobbler who sewed up the winds in the leathern wallet"; and he further explained that Homer had occasionally departed from fact in order to make a scene more marvellous

---

[1] See pp. 107–12 *supra*.   [2] See Sikes, *op. cit.* pp. 227–8.
[3] See Strabo, *Geography*, I, 2, 15; a reference to the wallet of ox's hide given to Ulysses by Aeolus (*Od.* x, 19).

or terrible, and that his scenes had been placed in distant lands so that he might "lie" the more easily.[1] Thus did Eratosthenes advance a claim for the recognition of Homer's free handling of fact. He categorically declared that the aim of every true poet was to divert his audience, not to teach history or geography or anything else;[2] and in calling attention to the imaginative element in Homer he opened up new possibilities in the sphere of appreciative criticism.

Yet more illuminating and far-reaching was the work of Aristarchus, who wrote several treatises on Homeric questions and whose editions and commentaries on Homer marked him out as the sanest judicial critic of them all. What he aimed at was an intelligent reading of Homer; and by means of a wide erudition, marked literary taste, and a shrewd common sense that amounted to genius, he established certain broad principles of literary interpretation that cut through the earlier traditions and were destined to be of lasting and permanent value. He maintained, to begin with, that the criticism of literary matter should be based on an accurate knowledge of language, on the proper understanding, that is, of the linguistic medium employed by the poet. And whereas previous scholars in their *Glossae* had dealt with rare and archaic words, Aristarchus now pointed out the need for a further understanding of Homer's use of familiar words, and of his peculiar dialect and style, if the sense of the poet was to be rightly apprehended. Such information however could be obtained only from the poet himself, and by a careful observation of his characteristic usage. Hence another of the critical principles inculcated by Aristarchus, namely, that Homer, and indeed every poet, was best interpreted by himself; a principle rediscovered and applied only in quite modern times. It is however in his recognition of the value of the historical method in literary criticism that his greatness as a critic most surely lies. Homer he regarded as a product of an earlier stage of Greek civilisation and language; and his contention was that it was only in that particular setting that Homeric poetry could be properly understood and appreciated. From Homer himself, a faithful painter

---

[1] See Strabo, *Geography*, I, 2, 19.   [2] *Ibid.* I, 2, 3.

of an heroic age, he therefore drew his conception of the conditions of that age, its civilisation, its manners, its customs, its beliefs; and these ideas and standards he applied to the interpretation of the text. Hence his acceptance of Homer's myths and fictions in their obvious sense and in all their naïve simplicity, as belonging to the childhood of the race; and likewise his refusal to read into them symbolic meanings utterly alien to the primitive way of thinking, or to judge them by the cultural standards of the Hellenistic period. In this way a new line of approach to Homer was opened up, an attempt being made to view poetry in an historical light and in relation to the circumstances under which it was produced. And Aristarchus was the first to apply the method on any considerable scale, though Aristotle had given evidence of the same historic sense when he justified a certain passage in Homer by referring to the existence of an old custom which still survived in his own day among the barbarians.[1] Nor must the famous conjecture of Euhemerus of Messina (third century B.C.) be overlooked in this connexion. In his work, *The Sacred Inscription*, he had maintained that the Olympian gods were apotheosised men, benefactors of the race in a primitive age, who after their death had been raised to the rank of gods. It was an attempt to account for the gods by viewing them in an historical light; and the doctrine, which had a great vogue, may have been not without its influence on Aristarchus and others. But however this may be, it was by Aristarchus that the idea was first applied in the sphere of criticism. He was the first to approach literature in its proper environment, and to reveal those possibilities of the historical method which were to be realised but inadequately until quite recent times.

At the same time Aristarchus as a critic is not wholly free from the characteristic defects of his age. Despite his enlightened doctrines he is found lapsing at times into judgments in conflict with his own principles, adopting as his touchstone a false *decorum*, and applying to the Homeric story standards of the court etiquette of the Alexandria of his day. It was a procedure in which he was following the methods of his pre-

[1] See p. 109 *supra*.

decessors Zenodotus and Aristophanes of Byzantium; and it was productive of a crop of absurdities. Thus earlier censures had been passed on certain details in the Homeric narrative as being lacking in *decorum* or poetic decency. An element of the unseemly had for instance been detected in the action of the goddess Aphrodite in setting a chair for Helen, a mere mortal;[1] again, the assigning to the hero Odysseus of so menial a task as the opening of the door of the wooden horse before Troy,[2] this too was condemned as unfitting; and exception was also taken to the courtesies of Menelaus in speeding his guest Telemachus,[3] on the score that such conduct gave countenance and encouragement to mendicants. And for similar ingenuities Aristarchus too is in some measure responsible. There is for example his amazing judgment on Nausicaa's expression of a wish on first meeting with Odysseus that he should remain with her and become her husband[4]—a piece of *naïveté* which Aristarchus condemns on the ground of immodesty. Nor does his sense of fitness allow him to approve of her father's subsequent proposal to the same effect;[5] it was all too hasty to be decorous. And again, there was the conduct of the ambassadors from Agamemnon in partaking of a meal twice within the hour;[6] this was also adjudged to be indecent. Such judicial pronouncements, it must be allowed, accord but ill with Aristarchus's reputation as a critic, though they do not detract seriously from his performance as a whole or from the influence which he exercised on the following centuries. Incidentally however they are not without a certain historical interest for modern readers, since similar judgments based on *decorum* were specially characteristic of seventeenth-century criticism. In both England and France towards the end of that century the conventions of a sophisticated society became the basis of literary judgments;[7] and Rymer was not alone in his perverse and astounding methods. The phenomenon at that later date was doubtless due to the conditions of the age; but it was also one that had been anticipated by the critics of the Hellenistic period.

---

[1] *Il.* III, 423.   [2] *Od.* XI, 524.   [3] *Ibid.* XV, 82.
[4] *Ibid.* VI, 240.   [5] *Ibid.* VII, 314.   [6] *Il.* IX, 222.
[7] See Spingarn, *Critical Essays of the Seventeenth Century*, I, lxvii ff.

Such then were some of the achievements of these Alexandrian critics; a beginning had been made with textual and
the "higher" criticism, portions of the earlier literature had
been saved for posterity, and, above all, the way had been prepared for a truer appreciation of Homer. In the main it was
work of a judicial kind, upon which had been brought to bear
considerable erudition; and indeed, in the learned Alexandrian
circles, literature was freely though not always wisely discussed,
if we may judge from later references to trivial themes and
to "the laborious ingenuities" which engaged much of the
attention. Closely bound up with this judicial work, however,
are certain innovations in the same field, attempts made in
various ways to arrive at a truer understanding of the great
literature of the past; and however tentative and defective such
efforts may now seem, they nevertheless form a stage in the
development of critical activities, and more especially of that
judicial criticism which formed all too rare a feature of ancient
work. Thus, in the first place, dating from this period were the
attempts made to establish the Alexandrian canons or lists of
the best writers. Aristophanes of Byzantium, so it would seem,
first drew up these lists of poets; and similar lists were subsequently formed in connexion with oratory, by the scholars of
Pergamum possibly, or perhaps later by Didymus or Caecilius
of Calacte.[1] But whatever their origin, these official lists were
not without their importance. For one thing they did much in
the way of establishing the classics and of getting the right
authors read; and their choice of certain poets seems to have
been generally sound. Incidentally, too, they prepared the
way for a comparative criticism, for a comparison of poet with
poet, which should help to bring out the special qualities of
each; though the possibilities of such methods were not fully
realised in antiquity. As against this, by their method of
classification they helped in the recognition of the poetic
"kinds"; they encouraged also the futile practice of placing
poets in order of merit; and in the Roman period their example
led to meaningless parallelisms in which Latin writers were
mechanically pitted against earlier Greeks. Nevertheless, in the

[1] See Sandys, *History of Classical Scholarship*, I, 130-1.

centuries that followed, these canons formed a feature of most studies of poetry and rhetoric; and traces of the tradition may be found in the sixteenth- and seventeenth-century works of criticism, in the "roll-calls" of poets compiled for purposes of imitation.

There yet remains to mention one other phase of the judicial criticism associated with this period, namely, the appearance of literary judgments couched in poetic form. For it was now that Meleager (first century B.C.) conceived the notion of the famous *Anthology*, which included as one of its sections numerous declamatory epigrams drawn from earlier and contemporary poets and embodying judgments of a literary kind. Among the contributors to the collection, besides Meleager himself, were Simias of Thebes, Theocritus, Dioscorides, Callimachus, Antipater of Sidon and others; and the subjects treated were the poets, the historians, and the philosophers of Greece. Of interest, in the first place, are the appreciations of the ancient poets included in the *Garland* of Meleager; the fragrant references for instance to the "crocus maiden-hued" of Erinna, the hyacinth of Alcaeus, and the flowers of Sappho, "few, but roses".[1] Elsewhere Homer is described as "the mighty-voiced", "the spokesman of the gods", "the mouth that groweth not old";[2] or again, he is said "to make faint the glory of all other singers".[3] Pindar, on the other hand, is described as "the Pierian trumpet, the heavily smiting smith of well-outlined hymns";[4] and of significance too is the reference to Aratus with "his delicate phrases, the monument of sleepless nights".[5] Equally interesting are however the references to the earlier dramatists. Thus Aeschylus is praised for his innovations in tragedy; he is said, besides, "to have carved letters, not neatly chiselled but as if water-worn by a torrent".[6] Sophocles, again, is described as "the star of the tragic Muse", famed for "his wise-hearted beauty of diction";[7] while Aristophanes, with his "deep-voiced dramas of terrible grace", is characterised as

[1] W. R. Paton, *Greek Anthology* (Loeb ed.), I, III.

[2] *Ibid.* II, 1–6 (Antipater of Sidon).

[3] *Ibid.* III, 24 (Leonidas of Tarentum).

[4] *Ibid.* II, 34 (Antipater of Sidon).   [5] *Ibid.* III, 507 (Callimachus).

[6] *Ibid.* II, 411 (Dioscorides).   [7] *Ibid.* II, 21, 22 (Simias).

"the worthy interpreter of the spirit of Hellas, hating what deserved hate and mocking where mocking was due".[1] With these then as examples of the criticism contained in the *Anthology*, some idea may be formed of the quality of the performance. Much of its value is doubtless due to its exquisite workmanship, each epithet being devised to express what was characteristic of the spirit of each writer; and the result is a number of memorable and suggestive phrases which offer in not a few cases estimates of a valuable kind. At the same time but little is supplied in the way of reasoned appreciation; and the interest of the *Anthology* for our present purpose is of an historical, rather than an intrinsic, kind. It has preserved without a doubt many of the current opinions concerning earlier writers; and at the same time it represents the first attempt at criticism in poetic form.

Such then in the main was the Hellenistic contribution to the critical development; and altogether it is seen to be a record less of positive achievement than of changing and tentative ideas on the subject of poetry, of unfinished controversies, and of gropings for new methods and points of view. Out of the confusion however there emerge the beginnings of a new poetics which was destined to influence in method and doctrine alike the efforts of later critics. From now on the conception of poetry as an affair of system and rules was in some measure sanctioned; the main lines of a new *ars poetica* were also laid down; while certain questions were posed which were to enter largely into later treatises. Nor were the theories that were formulated without their significance; for the emergence of the idea of literary *genres* in the sense narrowly understood by later writers, the clash of views between the hedonists and the moralists, the fallacious divisions of form and subject-matter, all these were details of considerable historical interest. Then, too, it cannot be denied that some positive advances were made. In the interpretation of Homer, for instance, in the development of literary history, and in ancillary studies of a philological kind, work of a substantial character had been accomplished; while in Neoptolemus of Parium and Aristarchus

---

[1] Paton, *op. cit.* III, 186 (Antipater of Thessalonica).

had appeared two critics whose influence was to be lasting. On the other hand, there was for the time being a break with the earlier and classical tradition, as well as a general tendency to approach art from the technical and scientific standpoints; and these things left their mark on the criticism that followed. The influence of the Aristotelian tradition, it is true, was still potent in the teaching of the Peripatetics, but in a modified form. It embodied neither Aristotle's thought in its integrity, nor those analytical, psychological, and historical methods by which he had arrived at his results. And in the meantime the main interest was being diverted to details of workmanship, to the teaching of that which could not wholly be taught; and this tendency was one that was to give rise to many later errors and ambiguities. The fact was that the period as a whole witnessed to a definite challenge to the classical ideal. In one sense it represents the first clash between the Ancients and the Moderns; the first phase of that secular struggle which was to be waged intermittently down through the ages, with the Moderns, it should be noted, at this stage engaged in the attack. In yet another sense it marks the rise of authority in literary matters; the first attempt on the part of scholars to guide and control the efforts of poets. It is therefore as a link between the more considerable achievements which preceded and followed that the Hellenistic contribution is chiefly notable. Conspicuous for no great outstanding additions to either literary or critical theory, it nevertheless forms an integral part of the critical development; and a knowledge of the work done at Alexandria, Pergamum, and elsewhere during this period has this especial value, that it renders more intelligible what was to follow at Rome.

INDEX